Quasi-State Entities and International Criminal Justice

This book explores the intended and unintended impact of international criminal justice on the legitimacy of quasi-state entities (QSEs).

In order to do so, the concept of 'quasi-state entity' is introduced to distinguish actors in statehood conflicts that aspire to statehood, and fulfil statehood functions to a greater or lesser degree, including the capacity and willingness to deploy armed force, but lack the status of sovereign statehood. This work explores the ability of QSEs to create and maintain legitimacy for their actions, institutions and statehood projects in various constituencies simultaneously. It looks at how legitimacy is a prerequisite for success of QSEs and, using critical legitimacy theory, assesses the legitimating narratives of QSEs and their statehood adversaries. The book links international criminal justice to statehood projects of QSEs and their success and legitimacy. It looks at the effects of international criminal justice on the ability to create and maintain legitimacy of QSEs, an approach that leads to new insights regarding international courts and tribunals as entities competing with states over statehood functions that increasingly have to take the legal implications of their actions into consideration. Most important, a close assessment of the legitimising narratives of QSEs, counter narratives, and the messages sent by international criminal justice with which QSEs have to deal, and their ability to overcome legitimacy crises, provides insight on QSEs and the complex processes of legitimation.

This book will be of much interest to students of international criminal justice, political violence, security studies and IR.

Ernst Dijxhoorn is Teaching and Research Fellow at the Department of War Studies at King's College London. He is co-editor of *Militancy and Violence in West Africa* (with James Gow and Funmi Olonisakin, Routledge 2013).

Contemporary Security Studies

Series Editors: James Gow
and
Rachel Kerr
King's College London

This series focuses on new research across the spectrum of international peace and security, in an era where each year throws up multiple examples of conflicts that present new security challenges in the world around them.

Quasi-State Entities and International Criminal Justice

Legitimising narratives and counter narratives

Ernst Dijxhoorn

Routledge
Taylor & Francis Group

LONDON AND NEW YORK

First published 2017
by Routledge
2 Park Square, Milton Park, Abingdon, Oxon OX14 4RN

and by Routledge
711 Third Avenue, New York, NY 10017

Routledge is an imprint of the Taylor & Francis Group, an informa business

British Library Cataloguing-in-Publication Data
A catalogue record for this book is available from the British Library

Library of Congress Cataloging-in-Publication Data
Names: Dijxhoorn, Ernst, author.
Title: Quasi-state entities and international criminal justice : legitimising narratives and counter-narratives / Ernst Dijxhoorn.
Description: Abingdon, Oxon ; New York, NY : Routledge, 2017. | Series: Contemporary security studies | Based on author's thesis (doctoral – King's College London, 2014) issued under title: International criminal justice, quasi-state entities and legitimacy | Includes bibliographical references and index.
Identifiers: LCCN 2016039301| ISBN 9781138224292 (hardback : alk. paper) | ISBN 9781315402864 (ebook)
Subjects: LCSH: Non-state actors (International relations) | International criminal law.
Classification: LCC KZ6405.N66 D55 2017 | DDC 341.6/9–dc23
LC record available at https://lccn.loc.gov/2016039301

ISBN: 978-1-138-22429-2 (hbk)
ISBN: 978-1-315-40286-4 (ebk)

Typeset in Times New Roman
by Wearset Ltd, Boldon, Tyne and Wear

To Jo

Contents

Acknowledgements

During the research for this book, many encouraged, helped and advised me, however this book would never have been written without the enthusiastic support of my mentor and friend, James Gow. Both on a personal and academic level I am very much indebted to James for his help and advice. Many other people in the Department of War Studies at King's College London also deserve my gratitude, especially Rachel Kerr, Funmi Olonisakin and Guglielmo Verdirame who gave me the chance to work on various research projects over the years. The Department gave me the opportunity to teach, and it is by teaching that students educate me more than they would suspect; I hope to pass on some of my enthusiasm for war studies and international law in return. Without my family's encouragement and advice I would not have been able to finish this book. I am filled with gratitude for the unremitting support my parents, Marie-Thérèse and Edward, gave, and continue to give, me. I would like to thank my sister Floor, not in the least for always welcoming me with open arms, together with Onno, whenever I am back in Amsterdam. Over the last few years Aernout made me feel at home in The Hague and greatly encouraged my academic endeavours. I would like to thank Hannah Ferguson and Andrew Humphrys at Routledge for their support and patience. Last, but certainly not least, I am extremely fortunate to have Jo in my life, and very thankful for her unrelenting support, encouragement and advice.

Abbreviations

AFISMA	African-led International Support Mission to Mali
ANSA	armed non-state actors
AQIM	Al-Qa'ida in the Islamic Maghreb
AU	African Union
CAR	Central African Republic
CNRDR	National Committee for the Restoration of Democracy and State
CSCE	Conference on Security and Cooperation in Europe (since 1995 Organization for Security and Cooperation in Europe (OSCE))
CSP	Comprehensive Proposal for the Kosovo Status Settlement (also known as the Ahtisaari Plan)
DRC	Democratic Republic of the Congo
EBRD	European Bank for Reconstruction and Development
EC	European Community
ECOWAS	Economic Community of West African States
EPLF	Eritrean People's Liberation Front
ERA	Eritrean Relief Agency
EU	European Union
EULEX	European Union Rule of Law Mission in Kosovo
FIDH	Fédération Internationale des ligues des Droits de l'Homme (International Federation for Human Rights)
GSPC	Group for Preaching and Combat
HRW	Human Rights Watch
ICC	International Criminal Court
ICJ	International Court of Justice
ICO	International Civilian Office
ICRC	International Committee of the Red Cross
ICTR	International Criminal Tribunal for Rwanda
ICTY	International Criminal Tribunal for the former Yugoslavia
IDF	Israel Defense Forces
IHC	Islamic Health Committee
ILC	International Law Commission
IMF	International Monetary Fund
IMT	International Military Tribunal

ISF	Internal Security Forces
ISG	International Steering Group for Kosovo
KFOR	Kosovo Force
LDK	Democratic League of Kosovo
LPK	Popular Movement for Kosovo
LRA	Lord's Resistance Army
MIA	Islamic Movement of Azawad
MINUSMA	United Nations Multidimensional Integrated Stabilization Mission in Mali
MNA	National Movement for Azawad
MNJ	Mouvement des Nigériens pour la justice
MNLA	Mouvement National pour la Libération de l'Azawad (National Movement for the Liberation of Azawad)
MOJWA	Movement for Oneness and Jihad in West Africa
MPA	Azawad Popular Movement
MTNM	Northern Mali Tuareg Movement
MUP	Ministarstvo Unutrasnjih Poslova (Ministry of Internal Affairs)
NATO	North Atlantic Treaty Organization
NSA	non-state actors
NSAA	non-state armed actor
NSVE	non-state violent entity
OSCE	Organization for Security and Cooperation in Europe
OTP	Office of the Prosecutor
PLO	Palestine Liberation Organization
PSP	Progressive Socialist Party
QSE	quasi-state entity
R2P	Responsibility to Protect
SCSL	Special Court for Sierra Leone
SFRY	Socialist Federal Republic of Yugoslavia
SHAPE	Supreme Headquarters Allied Powers Europe
STL	Special Tribunal for Lebanon
UÇK	Ushtria Çlirimtare e Kosovës (Kosovo Liberation Army (KLA))
UNESCO	United Nations Educational, Scientific and Cultural Organization
UNICEF	United Nations Children's Fund
UNIFIL	United Nations Interim Force in Lebanon
UNIIIC	United Nations International Independent Investigation Commission
UNMIK	United Nations Interim Administration Mission in Kosovo
UNPROFOR	United Nations Protection Force
VJ	Vojska Jugoslavije (Yugoslav Army)
WEU	Western European Union

1 Introduction

Contemporary wars are no longer fought for decisive victory by two or more state armies meeting on the battlefield. Although states still wage war, modern armed conflicts typically also involve at least one belligerent that is not a state; these are called terrorists, insurgents or rebels, but often those fighters are members of what is conceptualised in this book as a 'quasi-state entity', an entity that aspires to statehood or fights for a statehood issue, that even controls statehood functions, but that is not a sovereign state. Moreover, modern conflicts often involve coalitions like NATO or *ad hoc* coalitions 'of the willing'; regional or supranational organisations like the EU or ECOWAS might be involved as mediators or directly by sending troops as peacekeepers; whether 'blue helmets' are deployed or not, some involvement of international organisations, such as the UN, its Security Council or its institutions, is almost inevitable in a modern conflict. Finally, in contemporary war, it might be more or less obscured *who* is waging war in the first place, like the (Russian) 'Little Green Men' taking over the Crimean peninsula or, for instance, via cyber attacks, drone strikes or other means of waging non-obvious warfare.[1] The latter means that, ironically, in an era in which information is easily shared and available to many, disinformation can be deployed as a weapon, maybe more than ever before. For all these actors – states, supranational, multinational, and QSEs – success in contemporary armed conflict depends largely on legitimacy and the ability to create and maintain it in various constituencies simultaneously. In part, war is about whose narratives prevail in an era in which the means for achieving full military victory become limited because the morality of force is defined by the legality of force; narratives pertaining to the legality of conduct represent one of the various types of narrative that impact upon the legitimacy of force and those who order it.

In March 2009, the Pre-Trial Chamber of the International Criminal Court (ICC) issued a warrant of arrest for Sudanese President Omar al-Bashir; the International Criminal Tribunal for the former Yugoslavia (ICTY) could finally start proceedings against former leader of the Bosnian Serb military, Ratko Mladić after his arrest in May 2011; and in May 2012, the Special Court for Sierra Leone (SCSL) sentenced former Liberian President Charles Taylor to 50 years imprisonment. These high-profile cases were just some of the most visible examples of international criminal prosecutions, but they illustrate that over the last two decades international criminal justice went from existing only as a memory of 'Nuremberg' and 'Tokyo', to being firmly established. Between 1946 and 1993, no international mechanisms existed to prosecute violations of international criminal law. By 2016, there are *ad hoc* tribunals, hybrid tribunals and a permanent ICC to prosecute and punish those individuals responsible for war crimes, crimes against humanity and genocide.[2]

In the twenty-first century, when the world is confronted with the most heinous atrocities, calls for the perpetrators to be 'sent to The Hague' can be widely heard. Yet, at the same time, many perpetrators of war crimes and crimes against humanity are still not prosecuted, and sometimes are able commit the worst atrocities after they have been labelled war criminals. The rise of international criminal justice evidently does not mean that all those who violate international criminal law can be brought to justice. Also, the fact that a call for justice became part of the narrative surrounding war in itself does not mean that international criminal justice has a deterrent effect. However, it illustrates how international criminal procedures have become part of the discourse around war crimes, genocide and crimes against humanity. It shows that people have certain expectations of international criminal justice, including that there should be – and will be – an effort to bring justice to bear.

The enormous progress made since the ICTY was founded in 1993–1994 gave rise to these increased expectations of international criminal justice. Yet, the same high-profile cases that illustrate the successes and symbolise the promise international criminal tribunals hold for the future, also demonstrate the performance problems and shortcomings of international criminal tribunals. Despite the high hopes for international criminal justice and the extensive research that has been done on the effects of international criminal justice, it remains difficult to gauge what the effects of prosecuting and punishing individuals for war crimes, crimes against humanity and genocide are on conduct in contemporary conflict, or the course of international peace and security. First of all, law is not an exact science and the outcomes of legal proceedings do not lend themselves to exact quantitative measuring or precise prediction. Second, some of the most visible perpetrators of crimes under international law remain beyond the reach of international criminal justice. And third, assessing the effects of international criminal justice on conduct in contemporary armed conflict is further complicated by the fact that, during the same time that international criminal justice emerged, it became clear that the way war was waged had changed and that armed conflicts typically involved one or more QSEs that operated outside the realm of the international community of states and classic international law.

That the impact of international criminal justice is hard to measure does not mean it is impossible to see the structural impact of international criminal justice on the way contemporary war is waged. In particular, some effect of international criminal justice can be detected in legitimacy crises, where the main actors in contemporary armed conflict are confronted with international criminal procedures. One assumed effect, namely deterrence, has seemingly not worked on leaders – at least in openly observable ways that mean they refrained from leading, organising or allowing the commission of atrocities. Yet this is only one possible effect. Others might occur, and James Gow has provided one example in his compelling argument that Serbian leader, Slobodan Milošević did a *volte face* in his conflict with NATO and campaign of ethnic cleansing in Kosovo in 1999 in response to his being indicted by the ICTY.[3] However, while that conclusion is linked to an empirical assessment of the outcome of that conflict, it is not linked to a broader conceptual understanding of the conditions for success (and, by contrast, failure) in contemporary armed conflict – legitimacy. It does, however, suggest that there might be value in pursuing analysis of international criminal justice on legitimacy, the essential condition for success in contemporary armed conflict.

While it might be fruitful to investigate the impact of international criminal justice on leaders of states, equally, it should be noted, as Rupert Smith (among others) does, that a chief characteristic of contemporary armed conflict is the presence of non-state actors, whether this means coalitions of states, sub-state insurgencies or transnational terrorist movements.[4] Further, legitimacy is not only the most vital quality for success in contemporary armed conflict, it is even more so for non-state actors than it is for states. Given that the formal possession of sovereign statehood provides initial capital in legitimacy struggles and that the acquiring of legitimacy and its conversion into formal international recognition of that legitimacy, its translation into sovereign statehood is the most difficult challenge facing non-state actors seeking to revise the statehood status quo.[5] There is good reason, therefore, to explore what the impact is of international criminal justice on non-state actors, and on one type of non-state actor in particular: quasi-state entities – a term that is explained below and developed in Chapter 2. Before proceeding to set out more fully the contexts that give rise to this question and the broad assumptions underpinning it, it is necessary, first, to define the key concepts on which the whole project rests and which are core assumptions in this book.

Concepts: quasi-state entities; international criminal justice; critical legitimacy

This book is about the novel concept of QSEs, international criminal justice and legitimacy. The conjunction between the three is unravelled and put back together to reveal how legitimacy is imperative for success of QSEs in contemporary armed conflict, to show the workings of legitimacy and how it is gained and maintained, and to gauge the impact of international criminal justice on legitimacy. The nature and meaning of these concepts will be explained in detail below, yet, for the sake of clarity, they will be discussed and defined briefly here. First, what is meant here by 'international criminal justice' is the system of practices and institutions that were founded internationally to hold responsible and punish individuals for violations of (international) criminal law; the system of international criminal courts and tribunals. But, in a broader sense, international criminal justice 'describes the response of the international community – and other communities to mass atrocity'.[6] International criminal proceedings before international criminal courts constitute only one of the mechanisms that aim to right moral wrongs and injustices caused by the most terrible atrocities.

In Chapter 2 of this book the term quasi-state entity (QSE) is introduced to define the main subject of this study and to describe the nature and characteristics of this type of entity. Non-state entities that are parties to contemporary conflict are usually defined by what they lack: statehood. Or, colloquially, they are called rebels, insurgents or freedom fighters, but what these actors have in common is that the goals they seek to attain all have to do with 'statehood', whether these involve changing the borders of an existing state, its ethnic make-up or system. They not only aspire to change the state, but they often carry out functions usually associated with the state. These entities develop state-like institutions; provide services usually associated with statehood; operate in a state-centred environment; and in many ways behave like states. In Chapter 2 it is argued that a more appropriate term to capture this type of actor or entity would therefore be 'quasi-state entities'.[7] While a QSE is a non-state actor, not all non-state actors are QSEs, and while a nationalist movement might be a QSE, not all QSEs are nationalist movements, and not all nationalist movements are QSEs. De facto states are QSEs, those entities striving to challenge the statehood status quo, but those that have not (yet) established a more or less functioning de facto state may also be a QSE. QSEs may be organised around nationalist goals, religion, a linguistic group, ethnicity or another common goal. QSEs might want to secede, seek autonomy, challenge the make-up of a state or the system of a state, but while this is true of all nationalist political movements the distinction setting QSEs apart is that they seek to develop and, to the extent that they possibly can, practically take forms of social organisation and action that can normally be equated with a state – the provision of public and social goods, from security to education and welfare for example; exactly the same qualities that are absent where states are weak and failing.[8] In this sense, as will be seen later, Hezbollah is a quintessential QSE as it provides state functions within a state, building support, but never seeking either to take over the state (Lebanon) directly, or to create a separate state carved from Lebanon.

Here, it is argued not only that we should call these actors QSEs when they have already accomplished de facto statehood, but also to label those entities whose aspirations revolve around statehood and that provide services usually associated with the state as QSEs, whether they are well on their way towards full statehood and run a de facto state or whether they are stuck in a stalemate, in which they retain some of the characteristics usually associated with statehood, or whether they are in the middle of a struggle for statehood, or changing a state. It is suggested here that the term embraces aspects of statehood, short of official statehood; that the objective is to achieve statehood, combined with fulfilling certain functions usually associated with statehood, such as the provision of public goods and services.

'Legitimacy', as a word and as a concept, is used in divergent ways, in different contexts and situations, and sometimes with differing definitions attached to it. However the meaning is hardly ever attached to the word explained by the people using the term, at least, not in a manner that such a critical concept merits. Indeed, obscuring the substance of the term at times might even be preferred by those who use 'legitimacy' in their discourse, but that does not mean the concept is without substance. Moreover, in contrast to its use in the political arena, for the purpose at hand, a clear definition is preferable, or even necessary. Literally, 'legitimacy' refers to the condition of being within the law, and older definitions all revolve around law or right, often upon which to base a claim to power.[9] However, as used by modern social scientists, definitions of 'legitimacy' all revolve around belief or opinion. Professional definitions are, for instance, that legitimacy 'involves the capacity of the system to engender and maintain the belief that the existing political institutions are the most appropriate ones for the society'.[10] They often build on Weberian tradition describing legitimacy as 'the degree to which institutions are valued for themselves and considered right and proper'.[11] Legitimacy is described in relation to the 'quality of "oughtness" that is perceived by the public to inhere in a political regime'.[12] The notions of legitimacy and legitimacy crisis will be discussed in detail below, but for now it suffices that when the word 'legitimacy' is used it refers to what Suchman calls 'a generalized perception or assumption that the actions of an entity are desirable, proper, appropriate within some socially constructed system of norms, values, beliefs, and definitions'.[13] Legitimacy, especially in its positive form, is hard to measure. In order to gauge how, and how far, international criminal justice influences legitimacy, to see its workings, and how and when it is lost and gained, one has to interpret the signals of legitimacy crisis. Therefore a 'critical legitimacy' approach will be used to assess those moments when the legitimacy of an entity, its actions or institutions, is challenged or withdrawn, at the same moment that it is needed most in a certain group or constituency.

International criminal justice and international relations

In order to gauge the effects of international criminal justice, merely looking at international courts, their jurisdiction and the norms of international criminal law that they apply does not suffice. The wider environment in which crimes are committed has to be considered, as well as the nature of the entities in whose name armed force is used and those crimes are committed, and how these entities operate in the international system. In what would be his last work, *Thinking the Twentieth Century*, Tony Judt remarked that, 'The problem with historical events which are intricately interwoven is that, the better to understand their constituent elements, we have to pull them apart'.[14] But, he continues, '[I]n order to see the story in its plenitude, you have to inter-weave those elements back together again'.[15] The same applies to understanding the impact of international criminal justice. The constituent elements have to be pulled apart, yet they have to be woven back together with all the elements that together form the environment in which international criminal justice develops and operates. By looking at the wider international political environment in which the actors in contemporary armed conflict have to operate, and by assessing legitimacy in various constituencies of the entities in whose name crimes under international law are committed, the impact of international criminal justice can be seen.

International criminal justice could only develop because the international political environment changed. It was not coincidental that mechanisms of international criminal justice emerged in the wake of the abrupt end of the Cold War. The labels attached to the changes in the aftermath of the collapse of the Soviet Union – a 'new world order', 'the end of history', a 'clash of civilizations' – all express an understanding that the end of the bipolar world marked the beginning of a new era in world politics.[16] Similarly, the timing of Anne-Marie Slaughter's call for a 'dual agenda', integrating the study of international relations and international law, was no coincidence either. As she described in 1993: 'International legal rules, procedures, and organizations are more visible and arguably more effective than at any time since 1945'.[17] The early 1990s witnessed profound changes in the roles of, and interactions between, states, non-state actors and supranational organisations, but the end of the Cold War also signalled changes in the ways in which war is waged and the nature of the main actors in armed conflict.[18] These transformations in the international order and the nature of armed conflict had a catalyst effect on the emergence of international criminal justice. Because these developments are intrinsically interwoven with the rise of international criminal justice, they should be studied in conjunction with each other. One of the most notable changes that became clearly visible in the 1990s is the changed position of non-state entities in the international community and their role in armed conflict.[19] Both Cold War blocs had repressed nationalist, secessionist, ethnic and religious fundamentalist sentiments and conflicts, and when that structure collapsed latent conflicts emerged and many of the movements built on these sentiments gained ground and momentum.[20] The parallel conflicts fought during the Cold War had already revealed a trend towards internal conflicts fought not for a strategic victory, to take, hold or destroy something with military means, but for the will of the people, and in the 1990s the proliferation of belligerents in armed conflict that challenged the state, and their ability to employ armed force, was fully revealed.[21] The non-state entities in these conflicts cover a wide range of organisations or entities with widely diverging goals. As stated above, they are built around ethnicity, a national goal, religion or another shared identity, and they can be labelled as rebels, insurgents, freedom fighters or secessionists. But these entities are all primarily defined by the fact that they are competing with the sovereign state over statehood functions.

Statehood conflicts in a state-centred system

While the world changed in many ways in the aftermath of the Cold War, the international community firmly remained one of, and dominated by, sovereign states; states that were not always capable of providing all the functions and services usually associated with that status, however. Where a state is weak, other non-state entities can take over some, or virtually all, statehood functions. In these conflicts over statehood, the belligerents may no longer have the structured relationship states had while fighting each other in interstate war, so many rules and paradigms of war and international relations may no longer be applicable in these conflicts.[22] However the state remains of central importance and '*as such*, a *quasi* state and structure position emerged' in these conflicts, or as the outcome of these conflicts.[23]

In these statehood conflicts, human rights violations are by no means uncommon. Sometimes they are part of the strategy of one or more parties to a conflict, or even inherent to their aims.[24] To attain their (statehood) goals, QSEs sometimes commit war crimes, crimes against humanity and even genocide in order to maintain the status quo, as do their state adversaries. Atrocities in war are nothing new, but now they are committed in a time in which, as Rupert Smith describes, force is judged by its morality and legality.[25] In the early 1990s, when the UN Security Council for the first time since its inception had the opportunity to act, satellite television networks made it possible to broadcast mass murder into the living rooms of Western audiences almost in real time. This led to what Frits Kalshoven and Liesbeth Zegveld called 'a shift from concern to condemnation' in the thinking on human rights violations.[26]

Ending impunity and the preventive effect of international tribunals

The first modern international criminal courts were established during, or in the direct aftermath of, some of the 'most heinous crimes' that 'shocked the conscience of humanity'. These were atrocities that the international community, despite the new-found agreement in the UN Security Council, had been unable or unwilling to prevent. These courts were given as one of their primary justification the aim to prevent similar atrocities in the future by ending impunity. Yet, despite the ongoing attention of scholars and numerous studies into the effects of international tribunals, it remains unclear how far, if at all, international criminal justice can be successful in attaining its goals of stopping and preventing human rights violations.[27] As with domestic criminal justice, the general preventive effect of international criminal justice is extremely hard to determine. No government will make a statement that it abandoned plans for genocide because its members were afraid of going to The Hague; no rebel leader will admit he renounced human rights violations out of fear for the (not so) long arm of international criminal justice; and no guerrilla army will acknowledge it could no longer find fighters, or shelter among the population, due to the internalisation of the norms of international criminal law among the people alongside whom it fights. Typically, no one even admits to thinking about committing human rights violations, let alone admitting that international justice deterred them. But that does not mean that the (possibility of) prosecution by international courts has no influence on either the conduct of potential offenders or the capacity for success of the organisations in whose name these crimes are committed.[28]

By holding individuals responsible, international criminal justice aims to influence the conduct of individual potential perpetrators. But it also aims to have a preventive effect on the entities in whose name crimes are committed. Although crimes under international law are neither exclusively committed within the context of armed conflict nor necessarily committed in a joint criminal enterprise, they usually are. International tribunals generally focus on those crimes that are committed in armed conflict and in the name of an organised group or entity.[29] Because of their potential impact, and justifications for international criminal justice, it is appropriate to look at the impact proceedings have, or could have, on the conduct of entities ordering political violence and armed force. International proceedings might impact on both those entities under control of the state and those that are not – QSEs – whose increasing role in armed conflict played an instrumental role in the rise of international criminal justice. International criminal justice might even have more influence on the conduct of QSEs, as opposed to that of states.

Legitimacy as success

To be successful, those entities ordering the use of armed force need to establish and maintain legitimacy for their actions and institutions.[30] They have to do so primarily within their core constituencies, but parties in conflict also need to influence the core constituencies of their opponents, and ultimately they also have to create and maintain some legitimacy in the various constituencies that together make up the international community. The effect international criminal justice can have on the capacity of entities to claim legitimacy successfully is significant. It is a function of the impact of changing discourse. To gauge how, and how far, international criminal justice influences legitimacy, one can assess critical legitimacy moments, those moments when the legitimacy of an entity, its actions or institutions, is challenged in a certain group or constituency. By analysing whether international criminal justice creates critical legitimacy moments, and by assessing the ability of state-, quasi-state and supranational entities to overcome such crises resulting from international criminal justice, one can detect the impact international criminal courts and their procedures might have on the capacity of entities to reach their aims.

Every 'system of authority' attempts to establish and cultivate belief in its legitimacy.[31] QSEs, like state entities, need the ability to create and maintain legitimacy in order to be successful in attaining their goals.[32] But, unlike states, QSEs have to engage in this constant process of legitimation while operating on the sidelines of the international system of sovereign states. They lack the formal bases of legitimacy that sovereign states can usually rely on. At the very least, QSEs lack the basis of recognition as a sovereign state among equals and, typically, they are not eligible for membership of intergovernmental organisations and other forums in which state representatives meet and consult.[33] The individual leaders and operatives of QSEs, however, are subject to international criminal justice. This book looks at how this system, which aims to influence the behaviour of all potential violators of international criminal justice whether connected to the state or not, influences the legitimacy of actors in armed conflicts. It is argued that when judgement is passed over the legality of conduct in conflict, this has an impact on the legitimacy of the aims and actions of the QSE, or state, these individuals represent, at least in some of the key constituencies involved.

The process of providing legitimisation for the use of armed force is central to contemporary armed conflict, regardless of whether the entity ordering the use of force is a state government or any other type of organisation. To be successful in contemporary warfare, the idea that superior will (when properly deployed) can defeat greater economic and military power is still central, but victory can only be achieved by superior use of all available networks and effectively deployed force to send the desired messages to the multiple constituencies relevant in the conflict.[34] More important, the multidimensional character of contemporary armed conflict makes the most judicious use and deployment of force central to successfully ensuring legitimacy for the use of armed force and for the organisation itself.[35] As international judicial attention to QSEs and their conflicts spread, it became evident that legal procedures against individuals potentially had critical impact on the legitimacy of the QSEs to which they were connected. At the same time, these procedures potentially affected the ability to create and maintain legitimacy of their opponents, although the shifting of legitimacy, and the changes in narratives aimed at creating legitimacy, might reveal the impact of international criminal justice.

Critical legitimacy

The concept of legitimacy is complicated and its existence, in a certain constituency and at a certain time, is extremely hard to gauge positively. The effects of international criminal justice are equally hard to predict and measure. However, where legitimacy and international criminal justice come together they both become more tangible. In this book, it is argued that legitimacy is a prerequisite for QSE success and where and when international criminal justice influences the capabilities of QSEs to create and maintain legitimacy in certain constituencies is explored. It can be expected that legitimacy crises will typically have a discernible effect on the conduct of QSEs and their legitimising narratives.[36] It is, therefore, likely that it is in changes, whether in actions or narratives, in crises that the influence of international criminal justice can be discerned. Consequently, by focusing on legitimacy crises that are the result of the application of international criminal law by an international tribunal, and by analysing how, or if, these crises were overcome, this book seeks to reveal the impact of international criminal justice on the capacity of QSEs to maintain and create legitimacy for their actions and institutions.

In the remainder of this book it is argued that international criminal justice can present critical challenges that affect the legitimacy of QSEs, directly or indirectly, thereby affecting their prospects of success. By assessing the influence of international criminal justice on the capacity of some of the most important actors in contemporary armed conflict – QSEs – to create and maintain legitimacy, a prerequisite for their success, it is maintained that it is possible to distinguish the systematic impact of international tribunals on the outcomes of armed conflicts. In order to do so, this book will assess three different QSEs, in three different conflicts, in relation to three different international judicial bodies. These foci of investigation have been chosen precisely because they serve to explore the effects of three different international courts or tribunals on three different conflicts: KLA and the ICTY; Lebanon's Hezbollah and the Special Tribunal for Lebanon (STL); and Mali's National Movement for the Liberation of Azawad (MNLA) and the ICC.

Framework

The aim of this book is to assess the influence of international criminal justice on the capacity of QSEs to create and maintain legitimacy. This is a process that is difficult to analyse, or even to prove its existence. However, there are ways to overcome these problems. First, the effectiveness of international criminal justice is very hard to gauge, whether it is approached from the perspective of special prevention, general prevention or retribution. Many scholars have tried to determine the effects of international criminal justice on, for instance, post-conflict state building, or whether international prosecution of war crimes, crimes against humanity and genocide is working towards the prevention of these crimes, but very few studies reached conclusive answers.[37] Some argue that no conclusions can be reached because one cannot 'prove the state of mind of a perpetrator of these crimes'.[38] If conclusions are reached at all, they are usually very cautious. Theodor Meron, for instance, concludes that: 'There is some evidence, albeit anecdotal and uncertain, that the ad hoc tribunals and the prospects for the establishment of the ICC have had some deterrent effect on violations'.[39] Second, the legitimacy of an entity, its institutions and actions, within a certain group and at a certain moment, is equally hard to determine, especially in its positive form. Legitimacy is not a constant. It is not a static concept but a constantly changing 'perception or assumption that the actions of an entity are desirable, proper, or appropriate'.[40] This quality, or phenomenon, which is the outcome of the process of legitimation in which claims of legitimacy are either accepted or rejected by a certain constituency at a certain point in time, is very hard to distinguish.[41]

In the following chapters it is argued that, although both the effects of international criminal justice and the impact on legitimisation are very hard to gauge independently, it is possible to detect both the intended and unintended effects of international criminal justice on the capacities of QSEs by researching legitimacy crises, the point where international criminal justice and legitimacy come together. Therefore, the main tool used to assess the influence of international criminal justice on the legitimacy of QSEs will be interpretation of legitimacy crises, or critical legitimacy moments. Building on Jürgen Habermas, a critical legitimacy theory shall be used here. Habermas suggests that legitimacy crises can best be discerned at 'the moment crisis management fails'.[42] This signifies a 'turning point' when there are fewer means available to overcome the crisis and adapt than there are possibilities for problem solving.[43]

Taking a 'critical legitimacy' approach to bring to light the impact of international criminal justice, the legitimating capacities of QSEs have to be described, the constituencies they need to influence distinguished, and legitimacy crises recognised. David Beetham pointed out that evidence of legitimacy has to be interpreted carefully and on occasion may prove contradictory, but that the evidence is available to be seen in the public domain and not in the 'private recesses of people's minds'.[44] This is not to say this evidence will always be easy to find. Legitimacy in its positive form is extremely difficult to distinguish: it is best seen when and where it is questioned.[45] Therefore, in order to learn something about legitimacy, its workings and how and when it is lost and gained, one has to interpret the signals of legitimacy crisis.

The focus of this book is on how legitimacy crises resulting from international criminal justice affect QSEs. When state entities opposed to QSEs face a legitimacy crisis provoked by international criminal justice, this has to be taken into account. Legitimacy is not a zero-sum game, but when one narrative loses its attractiveness in a certain group the entity offering an alternative narrative will, typically, gain legitimacy. Changing QSE narratives and actions that preempt the expected effects of international criminal justice cannot be disregarded. When an entity finds itself in a spiral of legitimacy crisis, it loses the capability simultaneously to engage in the process of legitimation in all relevant constituencies. Yet, it may be able to bolster belief in its legitimacy in one group while losing it in another. Therefore, choices for narratives aimed at one group in which legitimacy is sought, rather than at another group, could tell us something about the effect of international criminal justice. Finally, one has to keep in mind that international criminal justice is only one of a myriad of factors within and beyond the control of QSEs that could affect their legitimating capacity. The primary focus here is on legitimacy crises caused by international criminal justice, but where relevant to explanation of the workings of legitimacy, factors other than international criminal justice that impact on legitimacy will be addressed.

Legitimacy depends on narratives. These legitimising narratives are aimed at various constituencies in which legitimacy is sought and in order to be successful they have to fit existing beliefs and the experiences of any given group.[46] Due to the rise of modern mass media and the Internet, and in the increasingly interconnected world technology created, every group that can, or must be influenced is increasingly subject to the same messages.[47] The messages and actions that constitute those narratives, and their counter narratives, can usually be found in the public domain. When narratives are no longer accepted, competing narratives start to prevail, or it can be seen that the legitimacy of an entity, its actions or institutions are severely questioned in certain groups. It is in those critical moments that the indicators of legitimacy can be detected. However, in an interconnected world, the same message will be available and often reach various audiences, making it harder – and sometimes impossible – to send different legitimating messages to different audiences simultaneously.

The interpretation of messages and actions, and how far these narratives will be accepted (and are successful in creating and maintaining legitimacy), will differ among different groups and at different times. The different impact that narratives have on different groups are, at least, the result of the fact that pre-existing ideas, beliefs and experiences of various constituencies differ. Yet, it is hard to put one's finger on exactly *why* a claim to legitimacy is accepted. At most, one can hope to be able to determine *whether* claims are accepted, although it is easier to see when they are not, or are no longer, accepted. It is important to consider the pre-existing ideas and experiences of a particular constituency in order to place legitimating narratives in perspective or, rather, place the same narrative in different perspectives. One should look at the aim of narratives, what the entity seeking legitimacy expected would be the outcome of their actions and statements. This should lead to understanding of the effect that the narratives provided by QSEs, their antagonists and various relevant third parties have on different constituencies, and also, ultimately, by looking at the use and impact of international criminal justice narratives provided by international tribunals and others, and the critical legitimacy challenges that result from them, to understanding the impact of these procedures on the outcomes of conflicts.

The book

This book will assess the empirical evidence of behavioural change and the changing capabilities of one type of actor, QSEs, under the influence of one factor, international criminal justice, in order to make visible the impact of international criminal justice on QSEs. Consequently, the aim is not to try to gauge the *effectiveness* of international mechanisms to prosecute war crimes per se. The primary aim here is not to assess how far international criminal tribunals can be justified in terms of their stated aims, whether the purpose of their establishment was retribution, general prevention or special prevention. This book will discuss some of the contingent effects of international criminal justice and international judicial intervention, especially the justifications of the use of armed force. It will focus on the consequences of proceedings, on empirical evidence of the effects of international criminal justice, in particular, on the legitimating capabilities of QSEs. However, assessing the effect of international criminal justice on QSEs might be able to tell us something about the wider implications of international criminal justice and its potential to reach its aims and justifications. Close assessment of both international criminal justice and QSEs is relevant to understanding contemporary conflict. Changes in the field of international criminal justice and the role of QSEs in the international system give rise both to philosophical questions and to practical issues regarding the nexus of law and politics. Changing notions of sovereignty, nations and statehood will, therefore, be discussed. This will show that, despite the long history of international criminal law, conflicts over statehood and the involvement of entities that are best described as 'quasi-state entities', developments were heavily influenced by the changing political reality after the end of the Cold War, and that these developments are interconnected. Studying international law and international relations together is as relevant today as it was in 1993 when Anne-Marie Slaughter proclaimed that the 'two disciplines that study the laws of state behaviour [should] seek to learn from one another'.[48] When Slaughter called for international law and international politics to be studied together, she referred to what we would now call 'classical' international law – the law that governs the relationships, rights and responsibilities of states.[49] It was only a month after the publication of her '*Dual Agenda*' that the ICTY was established, marking the beginning of the reincarnation of international criminal justice.[50] Yet, her main arguments hold equal validity with regard to international criminal law. For instance, Slaughter's observation that 'political scientists must revise their models to take account of legal variables' if 'international legal rules provide incentives or constraints capable of producing outcomes significantly different from those that a pure power theory would predict',[51] or that 'the postulates developed by political scientists concerning patterns and regularities in state behavior must afford a foundation and framework for legal efforts to regulate that behavior'.[52] Although the norms of international criminal law, like those of classic international law, came into being through the consensus of sovereign states, the 'incentives or constraints' international criminal law provide seek not only to regulate the behaviour of states, but of all potential subjects of international criminal law.[53] The lessons of political science regarding patterns and the behaviour of political actors can, and should, be used to analyse the impact of international criminal justice on various actors, state and non-state actors alike.

The idea that international criminal prosecutions can have an effect on the legitimacy of actors in war, as such, has been noted in passing. For instance, Otto Triffterer has pointed to the examples of Bosnian Serb leaders Radovan Karadžić and Ratko Mladić to illustrate that the ICTY 'indictments and international warrants of arrest [for Karadžić and Mladić] resulted in a loss of political and military power' and that 'by thus abolishing a condition for committing the crimes mentioned in their indictments, these cases have a strong preventive effect on the two indicted persons'.[54] Triffterer noted that individuals were limited in their ability to act in any official capacity as they could not travel abroad without fear of arrest 'and that entrusting such individuals with official functions can endanger the international reputation of their state'.[55] Priscilla Hayner argued that the SCSL's indictment of Liberian President Charles Taylor in 2003 'de-legitimised Taylor, both domestically and internationally'.[56] Hayner links the indictment to the removal of any last support for him from international partners and describes that 'once it was evident that he could not rely on international support, and especially that the United States had publicly turned against him, it became clear that he would have to leave the presidency'. She adds that it 'affected the morale of his own troops, which was already low because the soldiers had not been paid in months'.[57] However, she neither suggests how legitimacy can be detected, nor how it had impacted on the state institutions Taylor represented.

The chapters

In Chapter 2, the notion of a QSE will be explored. The concept of QSEs will be introduced and the chapter will expound on why it is advantageous to name this type of actor by the defining characteristics they have in common: their pursuit of 'a piece of the statehood cake', the ability of QSEs to exercise some of the functions usually associated with statehood, and the willingness to deploy or threaten with armed force to reach their objectives.[58] The chapter will explain how the concept of a QSE, despite the overlap with nationalist movements, de facto states and rebels or insurgents, is a distinct and useful concept. It will provide background on how this type of actor, QSEs, became key in contemporary conflict and describe the paradigm shift after the end of the Cold War. This chapter aims to assess the behaviour of QSEs in a world that, although changed, remains dominated by, and centred on, sovereign states. It will consider different forms of QSE and how these evolved in various statehood clashes. Furthermore, the chapter seeks to explain the notion of legitimacy as a factor for QSE success. To understand why it is useful to assess the influence of international criminal justice on legitimacy, one has to realise that legitimacy is a highly complex concept used in many different ways. Definitional problems regarding legitimacy will be discussed in a review of literature on the concept. This part of the chapter aims to demonstrate why the capacity to create and maintain legitimacy is imperative for any entity claiming authority, in this case, QSEs. The problems of identifying legitimacy will be discussed in this section, as well as where, when, how and why legitimacy is gained, or lost. The concept of legitimacy crisis, as described by Jürgen Habermas, will be examined. His theory of critical legitimacy moments is used both to identify the existence of legitimacy and to explain its complex workings. The final part of this chapter will show how the notion of the Trinity[3](+), as introduced by James Gow, can be used to illustrate the various constituencies that have to be influenced.[59] Moreover, it will deal with the problem of providing narratives that have to influence the different relevant constituencies simultaneously.

Before 1993, war criminals had almost nothing to fear from international law. By 2013 there were *ad hoc* tribunals, hybrid tribunals and the permanent ICC prosecuting crimes under international law, and the international STL prosecuting crimes under domestic law in an international setting. Chapter 3 of this book will first describe these developments in international criminal justice, as well as the history of international criminal justice and the international political environment that made these changes possible. It will then give a short oversight of the establishment of the ICTY, the ICC and the STL. Although primarily assessing the effect of international criminal justice rather than how far it succeeds in reaching its aims, the final part of this chapter will analyse the aims of international criminal justice. It will illustrate how international courts are justified and give an overview of research measuring the effectiveness of international legal mechanisms for prosecuting war crimes, as well as the problems such research encountered.

The chapters on international criminal justice, QSEs and legitimacy provide a foundation for assessing the influence of international criminal justice on the legitimating capacities of QSEs, providing a framework in which to detect changes in legitimacy and the influence on legitimacy in different constituencies. Critical legitimacy theory will be used to assess the impact of the ICTY, the ICC and the STL on the capacity to create and maintain that legitimacy in various domestic and international constituencies of the KLA in Kosovo, the National Movement for the Liberation of Azawad (MNLA) in Mali, and Hezbollah in Lebanon respectively.

Chapter 4 will assess the impact of procedures at the ICTY on the legitimacy of QSEs in Kosovo and the Kosovo statehood project. In order to do so, the first part will describe the history of the ICTY, its jurisdiction and its functioning since its establishment. The chapter will continue to sketch the history of Kosovo, pivotal to understanding the ethnic tensions between Kosovo's Albanian population and Serbs and the rise of the KLA. The third part will analyse the Kosovo War, both the KLA's fight against the Yugoslav Army and the NATO bombing of the Federal Republic of Yugoslavia in 1999. It will examine the impact of the indictment of Slobodan Milošević by the ICTY for crimes against humanity in May 1999, during the height of the conflict, on the legitimacy of the KLA. The chapter will conclude with an analysis of how, despite its somewhat accidental character, this indictment became the tribunal's most significant activity regarding Kosovo, and indirectly transformed the course of the Kosovo project and the prospects of the KLA and Kosovo's ambition of a new state in international society.

The impact of the STL on the legitimating capacity of Hezbollah will be assessed in Chapter 5. The first part of the chapter will consider the establishment of the STL, its limited functions and jurisdiction and the operation of the tribunal during the first years of its existence. The second part of the chapter will provide background to demonstrate Hezbollah's success in overcoming legitimacy crises. Since its inception in the 1980s as a radical Shia militia based on Islamic doctrine, Hezbollah made the transition to a social organisation and a political party participating in elections. Before the establishment of the STL, Hezbollah repeatedly found itself in a position where it had to negotiate a crisis to re-legitimise itself as a whole, and particularly its military apparatus. The chapter will discuss the assassination of Rafik Hariri, an event that not only gave rise to the establishment of the STL, but that impacted heavily on all aspects of Lebanese politics since, and on the subsequent balance of power in the region. Finally, it will assess the impact of the indictment of four (and eventually five) Hezbollah members on the legitimacy of the organisation in various constituencies. However, the efforts of Hezbollah and other pro-Syrian factions in Lebanon to delegitimise the Court and the investigation, most notably through the so-called 'false witnesses' affair, will also be discussed. Moreover, the final part of the chapter will look at the use of the leaks by the tribunal and by the UN investigation into the counter narratives of Hezbollah.

Chapter 6 will assess the influence of the ICC on the legitimating capacities of the MNLA in Mali. It will start by discussing the Rome Statute and the ICC that it created, as well as the jurisdiction of the Court. This section will also assess its image as an 'African Court' and the acceptance of self-referrals by states. Part 2 of this chapter will provide background on the MNLA as a QSE fighting the government of Mali for an independent Tuareg homeland. The organisation briefly took control of Northern Mali in 2012 and declared an independent Azawad state, only to be overrun soon after by the very Islamist militants to whom it had allied itself at the beginning of the conflict. By August 2016, no member of the MNLA had been indicted with war crimes, however the Malian government self-referred the situation in Northern Mali to the ICC in July 2012 in an attempt to delegitimise the QSEs that took control over large parts of its territory. In 2015 a case was opened against Ahmad al-Mahdi, a member of rival QSE Ansar Dine, for the war crime of attacking religious and historical buildings in Timbuktu, and he is due to stand trial in late 2016. Yet, the crimes committed in Northern Mali, especially by the factions that took control of the major cities from the MNLA, and the investigation opened by the ICC provided a narrative that fitted with pre-existing ideas in many international constituencies and reinforced existing ideas about the Northern Mali QSEs.

This book aims to build on, and further develop, existing research on critical legitimacy and international criminal justice. To do so, it introduces the concept of the QSE which helps in that defining these groups according to their goals and aspirations and the functions they provide, and acknowledging them as parties in conflicts over 'statehood' and 'statehood functions', will enhance understanding of these entities. Furthermore, a link between international criminal justice and QSEs is made by looking at the de facto effects of international criminal justice, instead of its effectiveness – an approach that leads to new insights regarding international courts and tribunals. Although international criminal justice is a relatively recent factor, entities competing with states over statehood functions increasingly have to take the legal implications of their actions into consideration. Moreover, both their members and individuals connected to their state antagonists increasingly have to face the legal consequences of their actions. Most important, a close assessment of the legitimising narratives of QSEs, counter narratives and the messages sent by international criminal justice with which QSEs have to deal, and their ability to overcome legitimacy crises, provides insight on complex processes of legitimation.

Notes

1 Libicki, M.C. 2012. 'The Specter of Non-obvious Warfare', *Strategic Studies Quarterly*, 2012, pp. 88–101.
2 *Ad hoc* tribunals are established to prosecute crimes committed in a specific territory, during a specific conflict, or during a specific time, for instance the International Criminal Tribunals for the Former Yugoslavia and Rwanda. Hybrid tribunals are also established on an *ad hoc* basis, but combine international and domestic approaches towards prosecution, such as the SCSL and the Extraordinary Chambers in the Courts of Cambodia, for instance. The ICC is a permanent international criminal court and is established to prosecute individuals for acts of genocide, crimes against humanity and war crimes committed after it came into being on 1 July 2002.
3 J. Gow, *The Serbian Project and its Adversaries: A Strategy of War Crimes*, London: Hurst and Co., 2003, pp. 295–297.
4 R. Smith, *The Utility of Force: The Art of War in the Modern World*, London: Penguin Books, 2005.
5 Legitimacy, legitimacy as success and the challenges QSEs face when attempting to change the statehood status quo are developed later, both in this introductory chapter and in subsequent chapters.
6 G. Boas, 'What's in a Word: The Nature and Meaning of International Criminal Justice', in: G. Boas, W.A. Schabas and M.P. Scharf (eds), *International Criminal Justice: Legitimacy and Coherence*, Cheltenham: Edward Elgar, 2012, pp. 1–24, p. 1.
7 For a more detailed explanation of the term 'quasi-state entity' and how this concept differs from existing concepts, see Chapter 2, this book.
8 See: Robert I. Rotberg (ed.), *When States Fail*, Princeton: Princeton University Press, 2003, pp. 2–3, 237–243. I. William Zartman (ed.), *Collapsed States: The Disintegration and Restoration of Legitimate Authority*, Boulder: Lynne Rienner, 1995, p. 106.
9 J.H. Schaar, 'Legitimacy in the Modern State', in: W. Connolly (ed.), *Legitimacy and the State*, Oxford: Basil Blackwell, 1984, p. 108.
10 S.M. Lipset, *Political Man*, Garden City, NY: Doubleday, 1960, p. 77.
11 R. Bierstedt, 'Legitimacy', in: J. Gould and W. L Kolb (eds), *Dictionary of the Social Sciences*. New York: The Free Press, 1964, p. 386.
12 R.M. Merelman, 'Learning and Legitimacy', *The American Political Science Review*, vol. 60, no. 3, 1966, pp. 548–561, p. 548.
13 M.C. Suchman, 'Managing Legitimacy: Strategic and Institutional Approaches', *Academy of Management Review*, vol. 20, no. 3, 1995, pp. 571–610, p. 574.
14 T. Judt with T. Snyder, *Thinking the Twentieth Century*, London: William Heinemann, 2012, p. 43.
15 Ibid.
16 Among others, Mikhail Gorbachev and George H.W. Bush professed a 'new world order'. M. Gorbachev, Speech at the 43rd UN General Assembly Session, 7 December 1988. G.H.W. Bush, 'Address Before a Joint Session of the Congress on the Persian Gulf Crisis and the Federal Budget Deficit', 11 September 1990. Francis Fukuyama and Samuel P. Huntington coined 'The end of history' and a 'clash of civilizations', respectively. F. Fukuyama, 'The End of History?' *The National Interest*, Summer 1989, pp. 3–18. F. Fukuyama, *The End of History and the Last Man*, New York: Free Press, 1992. S.P. Huntington, 'The Clash of Civilizations?' *Foreign Affairs*, Summer 1993, pp. 22–49. S.P. Huntington, *The Clash of Civilizations and the Remaking of World Order*, New York: Simon and Schuster, 1996.
17 A.M. Slaughter Burley, 'International Law and International Relations Theory: A Dual Agenda', *American Journal of International Law*, vol. 87, no. 2, 1993, pp. 205–239, at p. 205.
18 The early 1990s revealed the full extent of the changes in contemporary warfare became evident. See R. Smith, *The Utility of Force: The Art of War in the Modern*

World, London: Penguin Books, 2005. T.X. Hammes, *The Sling and the Stone: On War in the 21st Century*, Minneapolis: Zenith Press, 2006.

19 M. van Creveld, 'Through the Glass Darkly: Some Reflections on the Future of War', *Naval War College Review*, Autumn 2000, pp. 25–44, at pp. 39–40. Smith, *The Utility of Force*, p. 269, 301–305.

20 D.L. Cingranelli and D.L. Richards, 'Respect for Human Rights after the End of the Cold War', *Journal of Peace Research*, vol. 36, no. 5, 1999, pp. 511–534 at p. 511. Smith, *The Utility of Force*, p. 267.

21 Smith, *The Utility of Force*, p. 267, 271.

22 J. Gow, *Defending the West*. Cambridge: Polity, 2005, p. 31.

23 Ibid.

24 For instance, when changing the ethnic make-up of a territory is the goal in itself, as it was for the leaders of the Republika Srpska in Bosnia, or the Hutu leaders in Rwanda, committing human rights violations and genocide becomes a goal rather than a means to win a war.

25 Smith, *The Utility of Force*, p. 268.

26 M. Michalski and J. Gow, *War, Image and Legitimacy: Viewing Contemporary Conflict*, Abington: Routledge, 2007, p. 118. F. Kalshoven and L. Zegveld, *Constraints on the Waging of War*, Geneva: ICRC, 2001, p. 185.

27 See Chapter 3. J. Gow, M. Michalski and R. Kerr, 'Space Capsule Justice: The ICTY and Bosnia – Image, Distance and Disconnection', *Slavonic and East European Review*, vol. 91, no. 4, 2013, pp. 818–846.

28 Hannah Arendt, in her account of the Eichmann trial, notes that Dostoyevsky wrote in his diaries that in Siberia, 'among murderers, rapists and burglars, he never met a single man who would admit that he had done wrong'. In international criminal justice the acts committed are often hard to deny, but few admit that their actions constituted a crime. H. Arendt, *Eichmann in Jerusalem: A Report on the Banality of Evil*, New York: Penguin, 1963, p. 52.

29 A notable exception is the Special Tribunal for Lebanon; although the STL has jurisdiction over a crime that was deemed a threat to international peace and security by the Security Council, the murder of Rafik Hariri and connected cases were not committed in, nor amounted to, an armed conflict. Although no judgement has yet been rendered (at the time of writing), we can assume that the acts that are subject to STL procedures were committed in a joint criminal enterprise, and it is likely that the individuals responsible for the crimes acted on the orders of either a state or a QSE.

30 See Chapter 2 for more on 'legitimacy as success'.

31 M. Weber, *The Theory of Social and Economic Organization*, New York: Free Press, 1947, p. 325.

32 J. Gow, *Legitimacy and the Military: The Yugoslav Crisis*, London: Pinter Publishers, 1992, pp. 20–22.

33 The PLO is in part a notable exception as it has some access to these forums; for instance, it has held a permanent observer seat in the United Nations General Assembly since 1974. UN General Assembly Resolution 3237 of 22 November 1974.

34 Hammes, *The Sling and the Stone*, p. 208.

35 Ibid., p. 2. E. Dijxhoorn, 'Hezbollah as a Model for Success in Contemporary Armed Conflict', MA Dissertation, August 2009.

36 For more on legitimating narratives, see Chapter 2, this book.

37 I. Tallgren, 'The Sensibility and Sense of International Criminal Law', *European Journal of International Law*, vol. 13, no. 3, 2002, pp. 561–595, p. 569.

38 D.J. Scheffer, 'Should the United States join the International Criminal Court?' *U.C. Davis Journal of International Law and Policy*, vol. 9, 2002, pp. 45–52, p. 51.

39 T. Meron, *War Crimes Law Comes of Age*, Oxford: Clarendon Press, 1998, p. 463.

40 Suchman, 'Managing Legitimacy', p. 574.

41 Michalski and Gow, *War, Image and Legitimacy*, p. 203.

42 J. Habermas, *Legitimation Crisis*. London: Heinemann, 1973, p. 69.
43 Ibid.
44 D. Beetham, *The Legitimation of Power*, Basingstoke: Macmillan, 1991, p. 13.
45 Gow, *Legitimacy and the Military*, p. 20.
46 L. Freedman, 'Networks, Culture and Narratives', *Adelphi Papers*, vol. 45, no. 379, 2006, pp. 11–26.
47 Michalski and Gow, *War, Image and Legitimacy*, p. 197.
48 Slaughter, 'International Law and International Relations Theory: A Dual Agenda', p. 205.
49 Ibid., pp. 205–206. A.M. Slaughter, 'International Law in a World of Liberal States', *European Journal of International Law*, vol. 6, no. 1, 1995, pp. 503–538, at p. 503.
50 Slaughter's 'International law and International Relations Theory: A Dual Agenda' was first published in April 1993. On 25 May 1993 the UN Security Council passed Resolution 827, by which it established the International Tribunal for the Prosecution of Persons Responsible for Serious Violations of International Humanitarian Law Committed in the Territory of the Former Yugoslavia since 1991, more commonly referred to as the International Criminal Tribunal for the former Yugoslavia (ICTY).
51 Slaughter, 'International Law and International Relations Theory: A Dual Agenda', p. 205 and p. 214.
52 Ibid., pp. 205–206.
53 Ibid., p. 214.
54 O. Triffterer, 'The Preventive and the Repressive Function of the International Criminal Court', in: M. Politi and G. Nessi (eds), *The Rome Statute of the International Criminal Court: A Challenge to Impunity*, Farnham: Ashgate Publishing, 2001, pp. 137–175, p. 161, quoted in: J.F. Alexander, 'The International Criminal Court and the Prevention of Atrocities: Predicting the Court's Impact', *Villanova Law Review*, vol. 54, no. 1, 2009, pp. 1–56, pp. 23–24.
55 Ibid.
56 P. Hayner, 'Negotiating Peace in Liberia: Preserving the Possibility for Justice', *HD Report*, (Geneva: Henry Dunant Centre for Humanitarian Dialogue/The International Center for Transitional Justice), November 2007, pp. 1–31, p. 9.
57 Ibid.
58 J. Gow, 'Viable Political Communities', unpublished paper.
59 J. Gow, *War and War Crimes: The Military, Legitimacy and Success in Armed Conflict*. London: Hurst and Co, 2013, pp. 23–43.

Bibliography

Alexander, J.F. (2009) 'The International Criminal Court and the Prevention of Atrocities: Predicting the Court's Impact'. *Villanova Law Review*, 54(1), p. 23.

Arendt, H. (1963) *Eichmann in Jerusalem: A Report on the Banality of Evil*. New York: Penguin.

Beetham, D. (1991) *The Legitimation of Power*, 5th edn. Basingstoke: Palgrave Macmillan.

Bierstedt, R. (1964) 'Legitimacy', in Gould, J.R. and Kolb, W.L. (eds), *Dictionary of the Social Sciences*. New York: The Free Press, p. 386.

Boas, G. (2012) 'What's in a Word: The Nature and Meaning of International Criminal Justice'. In: Boas, G., Schabas, W.A., and Scharf, M.P. (eds), *International Criminal Justice: Legitimacy and Coherence*. Cheltenham: Edward Elgar, pp. 1–24.

Bush, G.H.W. (1990) *Address before a Joint Session of the Congress on the Persian Gulf Crisis and the Federal Budget Deficit*.

Cingranelli, D.L. and Richards, D.L. (1999) 'Respect for Human Rights after the End of the Cold War'. *Journal of Peace Research*, 36(5), pp. 511–534.

van Creveld, M. (2000) 'Through the Glass Darkly: Some Reflections on the Future of War'. *Naval War College Review*, (Autumn), pp. 25–44.

Dijxhoorn, E.E.A. (2009) *Hezbollah as a Model for Success in Contemporary Armed Conflict*. MA Dissertation thesis.

Dunning, T. (2008) '"Mind Forged Manacles": Hamas, Hezbollah and Orientalist Discourse'. Brisbane: Refereed paper delivered at Australian Political Studies Association Conference.

Fitzgerald Report (2005) *Report of the International Independent Investigation Commission established pursuant to Security Council Resolution 1595, 20 October 2005*. S/2005/662.

Freedman, L. (2006) 'Networks, Culture and Narratives'. *The Adelphi Papers*, 45(379), pp. 11–26. doi: 10.1080/05679320600661640.

Fukuyama, F. (1989) 'The End of History?'. *The National Interest*, pp. 3–18.

Fukuyama, F. (1992) *The End of History and the Last Man*. New York: Free Press.

Gorbachev, M. (1988) *Address at the 43rd U.N. General Assembly Session*, 7 December.

Gow, J. (1992) *Legitimacy and the Military: The Yugoslav Crisis*. London: Pinter.

Gow, J. (2003) *The Serbian Project and Its Adversaries: A Strategy of War Crimes*. London: Hurst.

Gow, J. (2005) *Defending the West*. Cambridge: Polity Press.

Gow, J. (2013) *War and War Crimes: The Military, Legitimacy and Success in Armed Conflict*. London: Hurst and Co.

Gow, J. (no date) *Viable Political Communities*. Unpublished paper.

Gow, J., Michalski, M. and Kerr, R. (2013) 'Space Capsule Justice: The ICTY and Bosnia—Image, Distance and Disconnection'. *The Slavonic and East European Review*, 91(4), pp. 818–846, doi: 10.5699/slaveasteurorev2.91.4.0818.

Habermas, J. (1973) *Legitimation Crisis*. London: Heinemann.

Hammes, T.X. (2006) *The Sling and the Stone: On War in the 21st century*. Minneapolis: Zenith Press.

Hayner, P. (2007) *Negotiating Peace in Liberia: Preserving the Possibility for Justice*. Geneva: Henry Dunant Centre for Humanitarian Dialogue/The International Center for Transitional Justice.

Huntington, S.P. (1993) 'The Clash of Civilizations?'. *Foreign Affairs*, 72(3), pp. 22–49. doi: 10.2307/20045621.

Huntington, S.P. (1996) *The Clash of Civilizations: And the Remaking of World Order*. New York: Simon and Schuster.

International Criminal Court. (2011) *Elements of Crimes*. International Criminal Court.

Jordash, W. and Parker, T. (2010) 'Trials in Absentia at the Special Tribunal for Lebanon: Incompatibility with International Human Rights Law'. *Journal of International Criminal Justice*, 8(2), pp. 487–509, doi: 10.1093/jicj/mqq020.

Judt, T. and Snyner, T. (2012) *Thinking the Twentieth Century*. London: Heinemann.

Kalshoven, F. and Zegveld, L. (2001) *Constraints on the Waging of War: An Introduction to International Humanitarian Law*, 3rd edn. Geneva: ICRC.

Libicki, M.C. (2012) 'The Specter of Non-Obvious Warfare'. *Strategic Studies Quarterly*, Fall, pp. 88–101.

Lipset, S.M. (1963) *Political Man*. London: Heinemann.

Merelman, R.M. (1996) 'Learning and Legitimacy'. *The American Political Science Review*, 60(3), pp. 548–561.

Meron, T. (1998) *War Crimes Law Comes of Age*. Oxford: Clarendon Press.

Michalski, M. and Gow, J. (2007) *War, Image and Legitimacy: Viewing Contemporary Conflict*. London: Routledge.

Pape, R.A.A. (2005) *Dying to Win: The Strategic Logic of Suicide Terrorism*. New York: Random House Publishing Group.

Press Release, 'ICC – Prosecutor Receives Referral of the Situation in the Democratic Republic of Congo' [2004] ICC ICC-OTP-20040419-50.

'Report of the Fact-finding Mission to Lebanon'. (2005) United Nations Security Council Report of the Fact-finding Mission to Lebanon inquiring into the causes, circumstances and consequences of the assassination of former Prime Minister Rafik Hariri. S/2005/203.

Rotberg, R.I. (2004) *When States Fail: Causes and Consequences*. Princeton, NJ, United States: Princeton University Press.

Schaar, J.H. (1984) 'Legitimacy in the Modern State'. In: Connolly, W. (ed.), *Legitimacy and the State*. Oxford: Basil Blackwell.

Scheffer, D.J. (2002) 'Should the United States Join the International Criminal Court?' *U.C. Davis Journal of International Law and Policy*, 9, pp. 45–52.

Slaughter, A. (1995) 'International Law in a World of Liberal States'. *European Journal of International Law*, 6(1), pp. 503–538, doi: 10.1093/ejil/6.1.503.

Slaughter Burley, A.-M. (1993) 'International law and International Relations Theory: A Dual Agenda'. *American Journal of International Law*, 87(2), pp. 205–239. doi: 10.2307/2203817.

Smith, R. (2005) *The Utility of Force: The Art of War in the Modern World*. London: Penguin.

Special Tribunal for Lebanon Seventh Annual Report (2015–2016) (2016).

STL (2013a) Press Release, 2 July 2013, 'STL Appoints Investigator to Probe Unauthorised Disclosures'.

STL (2013b) Press Release, 22 January 2013, 'STL Condemns Media Reports on Alleged Witness Identities'.

STL (no date) *About the STL*. Available at: www.stl-tsl.org/en/about-the-stl/creation-of-the-stl (Accessed: 18 August 2016).

Suchman, M.C. (1995) 'Managing Legitimacy: Strategic and Institutional Approaches', *Academy of Management Review*, 20(3), pp. 571–610, doi: 10.2307/258788.

Tallgren, I. (2002) 'The Sensibility and Sense of International Criminal Law'. *European Journal of International Law*, 13(3), pp. 561–595. doi: 10.1093/ejil/13.3.561.

The Lebanese Constitution 1926, c. 23 May 1926.

The Prosecutor v. Hassan Habib Merhi [2013] STL Public Redacted Indictment STL-13-04.

The Prosecutor v. Salim Jamil Ayyash, Mustafa Amine Badreddine, Hussein Hassan Oneissi and Assad Hassan Sabra [2012] STL Decision to Hold Trial in Absentia STL-ll-OI/I/TC FO112/201202011RI09799-RI09846nEN/pvk.

The Prosecutor v. Salim Jamil Ayyash, Mustafa Amine Badreddine, Hussein Hassan Oneissi, and Assad Hassan Sabra [2013] STL Public Redacted Amended Indictment STL-II-OIIPTIPTJ, F08601 AOIIPRV/201305281R 143331-R I 43372/EN/nc.

Triffterer, O. (2001) 'The Preventive and the Repressive Function of the International Criminal Court'. In: Politi, M. and Nessi, G. (eds), *The Rome Statute of the International Criminal Court: A Challenge To Impunity*. Farnham: Ashgate Publishing, pp. 137–175.

United Nations General Assembly (1974) *UN General Assembly Resolution 3237*.

Vloeberghs, W. (2012) 'The Making of a Martyr: Forging Rafik Hariri's Symbolic Legacy'. In: Knudsen, A. and Kerr, M. (eds), *Lebanon After the Cedar Revolution*. London: Hurst and Co., pp. 163–184.

Weber, M. (1964) *The Theory of Social and Economic Organization*. New York: Free Press.

Wright, R. (2006) 'Inside the Mind of Hezbollah'. *Washington Post*, 16 July, p. B01.

Zartman, I.W. (ed.) (1995) *Collapsed States: The Disintegration and Restoration of Legitimate Authority*. Boulder: Lynne Rienner.

2 Legitimacy as success for quasi-state entities

While interstate war became an anomaly, contemporary armed conflicts still revolve around issues of statehood – they are about whether an existing state is the right political form, whether its character should be adjusted, whether a new state should be created or whether the state system as we know it should be brought down (as is the mission of al-Qa'ida and ISIL). These statehood conflicts are generally characterised by the involvement of at least one belligerent, that aims to alter the borders or change the system of a state, and another belligerent, usually a state, that fights to prevent that from happening, aiming to maintain the status quo. Typically, they are about the 'redistribution of territory, populations and resources within, or across, the boundaries of existing states'.[1] Yet, while the role of states in contemporary armed conflict has changed, the international community remains firmly a society of, and is dominated by, sovereign states. The perks of sovereign statehood – the right to territorial integrity and non-interference – remain the leading principles in that international community.[2] Statehood remains the thing to aspire to for ethnic, national or religious minorities within an existing state and these tensions often lead to armed conflicts between those groups aspiring to statehood, or a share of it, and those preventing them from attaining those aspirations. These non-state entities cover a wide range of organisations, or entities, with widely diverging goals. They are built around ethnicity, a national goal, religion or another shared identity. They go by different names, but whether called freedom fighters, insurgents, terrorists or secessionists, these entities are all primarily defined by the fact that they are competing with the sovereign state over statehood functions. They are what can be conceptualised as QSEs.

Quasi-state entities

For QSEs, as for any other actor in contemporary armed conflict, legitimacy is the key to success. Success in conflicts between different groups within a territory depends on legitimacy more than anything else. The present chapter will first introduce the concept of QSEs. It will argue that in an international system that revolves around sovereign statehood, those fighting for a new state, or an alteration of an existing state, are better defined by the core of their existence than by what they lack. The first part of the chapter will discuss the meaning of sovereignty and statehood, the (legal) position of QSEs in the post-Cold War international order and the role of these entities in contemporary armed conflict. The second part of the chapter will deal with legitimacy and will first look at legitimacy as an overused, often misunderstood, and complicated, but nevertheless essential, concept to understand power relations. Next, legitimacy as a prerequisite for success in contemporary conflict will be discussed. The workings of legitimacy in a contemporary, interconnected world will be assessed, and the final part of this chapter will propose an approach by which legitimacy crises, or critical legitimacy moments will be analysed to detect the existence or absence of legitimacy.

The redefinition of 'a threat to international peace and security'

When, in 1992, the UN Security Council heads of state and government widened the definition of what could constitute a threat to 'international peace and security', it had several legal and political consequences.[3] Expanding the mandate of the Security Council created the possibility of ordering Chapter VII measures to restore international peace and security when the threat to, or breach of, international peace and security is caused, not by 'war and military conflicts amongst States', but by 'instability in the economic, social, humanitarian and ecological fields'.[4] This expanded possibility of ordering Chapter VII measures, in turn, created the possibility of ordering coercive measures, including armed force, to restore peace in internal conflicts. It turned out that this reinterpretation of a 'threat to international peace and security' also paved the way for the Security Council to establish international criminal tribunals under Chapter VII, as indeed it did for the former Yugoslavia, Rwanda and, later, Lebanon.

What, at first glance, may have seemed a minor and logical reinterpretation of the Charter had major consequences. In the eyes of some commentators, the Council even 'adopted a strikingly intrusive interpretation of the UN Charter' and its members 'endorsed a radical expansion in the scope of collective intervention just as a series of ethnic and civil wars erupted across the globe'.[5] Yet this redefinition was neither a sudden move of the Council nor an isolated decision, and the sudden rise in ethnic and civil wars was not the only cause; it was the result of ongoing changes of the meaning attributed to sovereignty. The 1992 statement reflected a trend towards a changing understanding of what sovereignty entails. By expressing that, in principle, they would not be averse to intervention in internal conflicts, the heads of state and government of the Security Council acknowledged the trend towards a different understanding of state sovereignty.[6] This trend had started earlier than 1992 but, similar and parallel to the increasing role of various types of non-state actors in contemporary conflict, including QSEs, and the rise of international criminal justice, this trend had been accelerated and made more visible by the ending of the Cold War. Although the notion of equal state sovereignty has been the leading principle governing the international community since the Peace of Westphalia in 1648, and remains the principle that provides the structure (customary) international law is built on, its meaning has proved malleable over time. Or, more accurately, the interpretation of sovereignty and the practical consequences attached to the principle have changed.[7]

Redefining or reinterpreting sovereignty

Jens Bartelson insists that 'the very term sovereignty, the concept of sovereignty and the reality of sovereignty are historically open, contingent and unstable'.[8] These changes can clearly be seen in scholarship over time. Hugo Grotius only included as sovereign an entity that 'is called Supreme, whose Acts are not subject to another's Power', and excluded the 'Nations, who are brought under the Power of another People, as were the *Roman Provinces*; for those Nations are no longer a State'.[9] In 1905, Lassa Oppenheim defined sovereignty as the 'supreme authority, an authority which is independent of any other earthly authority' over 'all persons and things within its territory, sovereignty is territorial supremacy'.[10] So internal sovereignty, or domestic sovereignty, requires public authorities to have effective control over the territory claimed by the state.[11] The external aspects of sovereignty, described by Stephen Krasner as international legal sovereignty and Westphalian sovereignty, do not necessarily involve effective control, but mutual recognition between sovereign states and the exclusion of external actors.[12] The principle of state sovereignty and the sovereign equality that stems from it is the principle that defines the international order, both politically and legally. Bartelson describes sovereignty as the 'relational interface' between law and politics: 'that which both separates these domains *and* binds them together'.[13] As Benedict Kingsbury points out, sovereignty 'represents one of the defining ideas of 20th century international relations', and it is therefore no wonder that sovereignty, by means of the axiomatic first principle of the UN Charter – '[t]he Organization is based on the principle of the sovereign equality of all its Members' – is firmly embedded in the architecture of the UN system.[14]

It was shortly after the most blatant and appalling abuse of sovereign powers the world had ever witnessed, during World War II, that sovereignty had been codified in the UN Charter, although Article 2(7) of the Charter further emphasises the principle of sovereignty by stating that: 'Nothing contained in the present Charter shall authorize the United Nations to intervene in matters which are essentially within the domestic jurisdiction of any state.' The Charter also limited the implications of sovereignty by including the exception that: 'this principle shall not prejudice the application of enforcement measures under Chapter VII'.[15] For the next four decades however, the implications of sovereignty did not change significantly. States enjoyed internal and external sovereignty, and when these principles were broken it was rarely based on a claim that this was justified by Chapter VII of the Charter, and never by a claim that violations of humanitarian law limited sovereignty. Yet, thinking about sovereignty did change; Mark Mazower noticed that 'new and much more conditional attitudes toward sovereignty' already became evident through the human rights revolution of the 1970s.[16] This was what David Lake describes as an intellectual shift in thinking about sovereignty that took place in the decades before the end of the Cold War.[17] These critiques of the classical view of sovereignty were either influenced by the increasing interdependence of states or by the inequality between states in terms of economic or military power as a result of the 'functioning of the capitalist world economy'.[18] Either way, the legal implications of sovereignty largely remained the same, although the Cold War blocs could be seen as creating a hierarchical society in practice. Again, it was the end of the Cold War that had a catalyst effect. Part of the 'veil of sovereignty' was already pierced by Nuremberg, the UN Charter, and the 'human rights revolution', but it was the radical change in the early 1990s that really changed thinking about sovereignty.[19]

Limits to the absoluteness of sovereignty

After the 1992 broadening of what could constitute a threat to 'peace and security', the idea that intervention in the domestic affairs of a state could be justified or, in extreme circumstances, could even be a moral obligation of the international community, took further hold. The increased number of internal conflicts – and what had become known as 'failed states' – called for a more active UN. Moreover, although the UN peacekeeping missions in Rwanda, Somalia and Bosnia showed the limitations of UN-led humanitarian intervention, it also meant that the idea of intervening in the internal matters of a state in certain extreme circumstances became more widely accepted. When, in 1999, NATO started air strikes against the Federal Republic of Yugoslavia – citing humanitarian reasons and with the aim of bringing to a halt ethnic cleansing in Kosovo – without an explicit UN Security Council resolution, it was clear that, at least in the Western world, the view was that the defence of humanity overrode the sanctity of state sovereignty.[20] Furthermore, it became clear that even the authority of the UN could be overridden unless it would embrace these new norms.[21]

In 1999, UN Secretary-General Kofi Annan wrote in an op-ed piece in *The Economist* that:

> State sovereignty, in its most basic sense, is being redefined – not least by the forces of globalisation and international cooperation. States are now widely understood to be instruments at the service of their peoples, and not vice versa. At the same time individual sovereignty – by which I mean the fundamental freedom of each individual, enshrined in the charter of the UN and subsequent international treaties – has been enhanced by a renewed and spreading consciousness of individual rights. When we read the charter today, we are more than ever conscious that its aim is to protect individual human beings, not to protect those who abuse them.[22]

The ideas that sovereignty no longer entailed rights for the state alone, but also a responsibility towards its people, and that the rights of a state to non-interference could be forfeited by not meeting that responsibility, were expressed in the 2005 World Summit Outcome. Although the Responsibility to Protect (R2P), as agreed upon by the General Assembly, was a watered-down version of earlier proposals, it stated that every state 'has the responsibility to protect its populations from genocide, war crimes, ethnic cleansing and crimes against humanity'.[23] It also declared that if 'national authorities are manifestly failing to protect their populations from genocide, war crimes, ethnic cleansing and crimes against humanity' the international community, through the United Nations, has the responsibility to protect populations.[24] First and foremost, this would involve diplomatic, humanitarian and other peaceful means, but should these measures prove inadequate, the Security Council would use collective action under Chapter VII.[25]

What had changed was not that the sovereign lost supremacy in a certain territory, but that something changed in the thinking about what the absoluteness of sovereignty meant.[26] The idea took hold that the state had become limited in its conduct towards its people by humanitarian law. An invisible line of a 'threat to peace and security' as a result of humanitarian disaster could now be crossed, leading to humanitarian intervention.[27] The territoriality of sovereignty remained the same; the geographic location of 'persons and things' still defines under whose rule they fall, disregarding other connecting factors such as kinship, tribes, religion and nations. Many states remained the supreme authority over different nations, ethnicities and tribes within their territorial boundaries, groups that sometimes felt no connection to that state or felt that they had a stronger connection to groups in other states. International law and the international community still protected the authority of the state, but now there were limits to how it could exercise that authority.

Sovereignty as membership

The international system remained, and remains, defined by sovereign states that recognise each other as such, and it is still the system of sovereign states upon which international relations, treaties and international law are built.[28] The principles of territorial integrity and non-interference remain the fundaments of the international community and are fiercely protected by its members. Moreover, sovereignty is status, as Abram and Antonia Chayes explain: sovereignty is 'the vindication of the state's existence in the international system' and it has been redefined to mean 'membership' of the group of entities that together make up the substance of international life.[29]

Sovereignty is a status, and membership, that many actors or entities in contemporary conflicts do not possess. Yet it is significant because these actors often aspire to this status, and start to act like states; they become QSEs.

Declarative statehood, as defined by the Montevideo Convention of 1933, is usually considered to have become part of customary international law. According to this, the attributes of statehood under international law are that 'The state as a person of international law should possess [...] a) a permanent population; b) a defined territory; c) government; and d) capacity to enter into relations with the other states'.[30] The latter means that therefore 'the political existence of the state is independent of recognition by the other states'.[31] However, according to Weber, 'a state is a human community that (successfully) claims the monopoly of the legitimate use of physical force within a given territory'.[32] Yet, statehood also goes beyond merely exercising power over a certain territory, it also includes providing services to the population of that territory and the ability to fulfil governance functions. A state has to deliver positive political goods to its inhabitants.[33] If the state is unable to fulfil the functions required of a state, or if another entity is more successful in providing these functions, the state will lose legitimacy and will eventually collapse.[34] Although successfully claiming a monopoly on violence might be the most important state function, other functions such as providing security and justice, the ability to collect taxes and a functioning bureaucracy, are also responsibilities of a successful state. All these, and many more, are functions that can be, and often are, taken over by QSEs.

While the power struggle between the two 'superpowers' caused violations of human rights, hindered the spread of democracy and prolonged many conflicts by the external sponsorship of civil wars and support for authoritarian regimes, it also contained many domestic conflicts, ethnic tensions and nationalist and fundamentalist conflicts.[35] The collapse of the structure that the two superpowers provided by policing their respective blocs led to an increase in conflicts fuelled by ethnicity, nationalism and fundamentalism, conflicts that are fought predominantly internally within the borders of a sovereign state.[36] By definition, these internal conflicts involve entities that are armed and not formally integrated into institutions such as police or the regular military of a state – although they may be informally or formally supported, armed or financed by a state actor – and are willing and able to employ armed force, or threaten with armed force, to pursue their objectives.[37] These conflicts often revolve around the fact that many states remain the supreme authority over multiple groups that feel a nationalist, ethnic, tribal, religious or linguistic connection to each other, but feel no such connection to the state. It is the sovereign state that is both the accepted legal entity in the international community and also the only form of entity with real political standing in that community.[38] Even when sovereignty is little more than an empty shell because the state lacks effective authority to enjoy the perks of statehood in parts, or all, of its territory, the international system strongly favours the state. Neither the changes in the interpretation of sovereignty nor the transforming role of non-state actors in these internal conflicts alter the central role of states in the international community. On the contrary, these conflicts are not among states, but about statehood. They are about control of existing states and how they should be run.[39] As James Gow noted, 'statehood remained central to armed conflict'.[40] These post-Cold War clashes, usually involving one or more non-state parties, are about the absence of central enforcing authority, or about 'the redistribution of territory, populations and resources within, or across, the boundaries of existing states'.[41] These conflicts are defined by the fact that there is an entity that aims to alter the character of the state, the contours, or the status of borders of the state, and an entity, usually a state, that fights to prevent that from happening and maintain the status quo.[42]

Labelling state and non-state entities

A plethora of labels can be attached to the non-state entities that are party to these statehood conflicts: insurgents, rebels, terrorists, resistance fighters, dissident armies, guerrillas, warlords or de facto governments. They diverge in size, means and level of sophistication and central coordination; they use different tactics for different aims; an organisation can transform from one type into another; and more than one label can be applicable to one entity. While some of these labels imply a value judgement, others focus on a certain characteristic. But what these categorisations do not acknowledge is that what these entities that are challenging the status quo of a state have in common is that they fight for statehood objectives.

Although some 'strong states' have to deal with entities that want to secede, often these entities fighting for statehood exist by the grace of a 'weak state'. For entities that aspire to statehood, weakened state institutions make it easier to operate state functions parallel to, or instead of, the official state. Decolonisation and the end of the Cold War left numerous states that were unable to exercise authority, provide security and fulfil other state functions in their territory. They were recognised as states by the international community; they have external sovereignty but are not able to fully exercise internal sovereignty. Depending on the level of decline of the power of the state and the reach of state institutions, these states are generally referred to as 'weak states' or 'failed states'.[43]

On the other hand, there are entities that de facto function as a state and provide services usually provided by the state (and the perks, like a monopoly of violence, justice and taxes), but are not recognised as such. These rebels, resistance fighters, insurgents or warlords are usually defined by the fact that they are not formally attached to the state; that they are armed; and that they use violence or threaten with violence in pursuance of their objectives. They are sometimes described as non-state armed actors, armed non-state actors, or violent non-state actors, but what these entities have in common is not only what they lack, sometimes only in name – sovereign statehood – but also that they all operate in a state-centred system and 'they all want a piece of the statehood cake'.[44] They are armed and they use, or threaten to use, violence in order to alter the system or the boundaries of a state. They challenge the state and they compete with the state over statehood functions. In a state-centred system, statehood is the highest prize and, in the end, all these entities want to exercise at least some of the functions usually connected with statehood.

When states prove incapable of providing all of the services usually provided by the state, when a state is weak, during an internal conflict or when a status quo is reached in which the de facto new state lacks full statehood, other entities take over some, or virtually all, of the functions usually associated with the sovereign state. Although the moniker 'de facto state' covers the type of body that is a state in all but the juridical sense under international law, it does not cover all the entities that aspire to statehood, use force or the threat of force to reach their aims, provide statehood functions, threaten the status quo of the existing recognised state, but have not reached the status of 'de facto state'. Yet these entities, whether they are called rebels, freedom fighters or secessionists, either already exercise state functions without the external recognition of statehood, or they aspire to change the borders of a state, or the make-up, or system of a state, in such a way that they can exercise that power. Hence, it is more accurate to call them quasi-state entities or QSEs.

Andrew Clapham points out that those organisations seeking to take over state power from incumbent regimes usually also act like states in important respects.[45] First, he notices that:

> [I]nsurgent movements frequently meet many if not all of the criteria which are normally used to distinguish states. Militarily effective movements meet the most basic criterion for statehood, which is physical control over territory and population.[46]

Moreover, QSEs are international actors in the sense that they conduct international transactions. They do not necessarily operate in legal international markets – as can be seen in drug and weapon trafficking in Mali, for instance, in several 'narco-states', or the 'blood diamond' trade in West Africa[47] – but they also take part in 'international economic activities, which have normally been regarded as the realm of states'.[48] QSEs establish relationships with aid organisations, for instance, to secure medicines or food relief for the population of the areas they have under their control. They deal with NGOs or they establish their own aid organisations as, for instance, the Eritrean People's Liberation Front (EPLF) did with the Eritrean Relief Agency (ERA), or Hezbollah in the areas of Lebanon that are predominantly populated by Shia.[49] Relations with diplomats and governments from other states are fairly common for these entities with statehood aspirations, regardless of whether they have established a de facto state, or have de facto control over a territory or not. Following the old proverb, 'the enemy of my enemy is my friend', Clapham notes that 'Insurgent movements have almost always benefited from the support provided by the international opponents of the states against which they were fighting, whether in the context of Cold War, post colonial or simply regional rivalries'.[50] But however overt these 'diplomatic' relations and the support for QSEs sometimes may be, they are always limited by the protection against external intervention that states enjoy.

The nomenclature of quasi-state entities

The notion of quasi-states, in itself, rather than QSEs, is not new. However, as Pål Kolstø commented, the 'study of quasi-states has been marred by an unfortunate terminological confusion'.[51] Kolstø describes two of the attributed meanings of 'quasi-state': first, 'recognized states that fail to develop the necessary state structures to function as fully fledged, "real" states';[52] and second, 'regions that secede from another state, gain de facto control over the territory they lay claim to, but fail to achieve international recognition'.[53] Robert Jackson uses 'Quasi-States' to describe the former type of state in his 1990 study, as mentioned above. He pointed out that ex-colonial states possess the same external rights as all other sovereign states – what he calls 'juridical statehood' – yet many of them, even years after they gained independence, are far from complete.[54] They lack the 'institutional features of sovereign states', or what Jackson calls 'empirical statehood', meaning that they do not enjoy the advantages that usually come with statehood.[55] The international community enfranchises these states by recognition of their independence, and often they provide other forms of (financial) support but, as internal institutions are limited, their existence remains mainly juridical.[56] However, at least under international law, and according to the international community, they are states and not 'quasi', 'almost' or 'as if' states. As Kolstø rightly points out, the often-used term 'failed states' describes these ineffectual states more accurately, and although some prefer 'weak states' or 'shadow states' to describe states that lack internal sovereignty, they indeed are usually referred to as failed states.[57]

The term 'quasi-state' has also been used to describe those states that lack external sovereignty while exercising internal sovereignty, although others prefer 'de facto state', 'unrecognized state', 'para-state' or 'pseudo-state' to describe what comes down to the same phenomenon.[58] Kolstø, for instance, used the term 'unrecognised quasi-state' but attached three criteria to qualify quasi-statehood: the leadership must: (1) be in control of (most of) the territory it lays claim to; (2) to have sought, but not achieved, international recognition as an independent state; and (3) to 'have persisted in this state of non-recognition for more than two years'.[59] The last criterion, especially, seems arbitrary. Why would a quasi-state emerge after two years of unrecognised control over a territory, and not after four, or one?[60] Nevertheless, Denise Natali uses this concept of quasi-statehood to describe the Kurdistan region in Iraq, and Michael Rywkin to describe separatist regions in the former Soviet Republics.[61] Based on high levels of autonomy, recognition, external patronage and internal sovereignty, they define these regions as quasi-states.[62] By that logic, the entities fighting for that accomplishment only become QSEs by attaining most of their goals, falling short only by lacking international recognition. Natali calls Kurdistan a 'quasi-State', based on the accomplishments of an entity, or entities, that created a Kurdish government, engaged in civil society building and strengthened autonomy, but what is considered is the existing state capabilities, not the entities fighting for the change in status quo.[63] Charles King uses 'quasi-state' for a situation that occurs when:

> after one camp has secured a partial or complete victory in the military contest, the basic networks, relationships, and informal channels that arose during the course of the violence can replicate themselves in new, state-like institutions in the former conflict zones.[64]

He describes that 'belligerents are often able to craft a sophisticated array of formal institutions that function as effective quasi states'. King's interpretation also suggests that these statehood qualities only arise after the conflict,[65] but entities already built these institutions during a conflict. They are QSEs during the conflict and well before they ensure victory, are defeated or the conflict is stalemated.

Here, it is suggested to call these actors QSEs not only because they accomplish de facto statehood, but also because their aspirations revolve around statehood, and they provide services usually associated with the state. These entities are QSEs whether they are well on their way towards full statehood and run a de facto state, like the government of Kosovo, whether they are stuck in a stalemate in which they retain some of the characteristics usually associated with statehood, like the Palestine Liberation Organization (PLO), in the middle of a struggle for statehood, or changing a state, like the Syrian Free Army, for instance. Of course, the scope of QSEs differs widely. There are examples such as Nagorno-Karabakh and South Ossetia that meet the Montevideo Convention criteria on statehood, aside from recognition as sovereign by other sovereigns. But there are also organisations such as Hezbollah which has come to have a stake in Lebanon, operates state institutions and provides services to a part of the population usually associated with the state. The South Sudanese SPLA/SPLM transformed from a QSE to the core of a new state, while the Taliban in Afghanistan went in the opposite direction and, from running the state, turned into a QSE controlling state functions in parts of the country under its control, including taxation, justice and education, while fighting state institutions.

Defining 'quasi-state entity'

A QSE is, by definition, a non-state actor, but not all non-state actors are QSEs. In the same vein, a nationalist movement might be a QSE, but not all QSEs are by definition nationalist movements, and certainly not all nationalist movements are QSEs. While a de facto state is a QSE, something falling short of a de facto state may also be a QSE. Many QSEs are organised around nationalist goals. For instance, the KLA and the MNLA are discussed below and both are organisations that fought to secede from a state. However, not all QSEs are nationalist movements; Hezbollah for instance, also discussed below, is a QSE that exercises many state functions successfully and transformed the state by doing so, but it has no aspirations to secede any part of Lebanon from the whole and defines itself as a Lebanese organisation first and foremost, even when its behaviour at times suggests it is a Shia organisation in the first place.[66] On the other hand, many nationalist movements do not behave in any way as a state. Some behave like a political party, more or less abiding by the rules of the state of which it is a part, such as the Scottish National Party, for instance. Others may be able to employ, or threaten the use of, armed force or terrorist attacks, but are unable to exercise functions and provide services that are usually associated with statehood, for example covert nationalist-terrorist movements in the Basque Country and Northern Ireland.[67]

A wider definition of quasi-statehood has been used by a number of authors, but usually in passing, or without an explanation of what is meant by the concept. In the process of 'locating Hezbollah's place within Lebanon's state and society', Brian Early correctly describes the organisation as 'both a societal organization and a quasi-state entity', however he does so without giving meaning to the concept of quasi-state.[68] The same applies, for instance, to Joan Fitzpatrick, who floats the idea that al-Qa'ida can be seen as a quasi-state, but does not elaborate on that definition any further.[69] Clapham, on the other hand, does describe why they have state-like qualities.[70] His observations are primarily based on the factual functions of these actors in that they exercise functions usually used to distinguish statehood.[71] Although a successful QSE might at some point run a de facto state, it is not defined as a QSE only when it attains *all* the characteristics of a state but falls short of full statehood. It is suggested here that the term embraces aspects of statehood, short of official statehood, that the objective of achieving statehood, combined with fulfilling certain functions usually associated with statehood, is the defining characteristic of a QSE.

Critical legitimacy

For QSEs, the key to success is legitimacy. As every 'system of authority' attempts to establish and to cultivate the belief in its legitimacy, the same holds true for state entities, but for QSEs the ability to create and maintain legitimacy is often even more crucial.[72] As Inis Claude put it:

> the lovers of naked power are far less typical than those who aspire to clothe themselves in the mantle of legitimate authority; emperors may be nude, but they do not like to be so, to think themselves so, or to be so regarded.[73]

Legitimacy for their actions and institutions is not only desired by states and QSEs; it is needed. This is especially the case in conflicts between different groups within a territory; in the internal conflicts in which QSEs fight for a 'piece of the statehood cake', legitimacy is a prerequisite for success.

In contemporary conflict, Rupert Smith maintains that the morality of force is defined by the legality of it. Because of this limitation, some of the ways and means for achieving full military victory became unacceptable. He notes that contemporary warfare is fought 'amongst the people', not for decisive military victory, but for the more malleable objective of capturing the will of the people and their leaders, and to influence their beliefs.[74] To be successful in contemporary conflict, all available networks have to be used to send messages, and the narratives transmitted have to be accepted by the multiple constituencies relevant to the conflict.[75] In contemporary armed conflict the process of legitimising the objectives of an organisation and the use of force – and the entity that is ordering the use of armed force and its institutions – become central, whether that entity is a state government, a QSE or some other type of organisation, e.g. NATO. More important, the multidimensionality of contemporary armed conflict means that it is important how that force can be best utilised and deployed to be successful in ensuring legitimacy for the use of armed force and the entity ordering armed force.

In statehood conflicts, QSEs may depend on and try to influence the beliefs of the same people that the state tries to influence. States need to create and maintain legitimacy for their actions and institutions in order to be effective, and QSEs challenging government authority and competing with the state over power and statehood functions need to create and maintain legitimacy in order to challenge the state effectively. To be successful in attaining their objectives, both need the ability to create and maintain legitimacy, not only for their institutions, but also for their actions, even if their causes and goals are deemed legitimate in themselves. However, in contrast to states, QSEs have to engage in this process while not being part of the international community of states, often without an official status within that community or even within their own territory.

Discerning where, when and how far claims of legitimacy of a certain entity are accepted is complex. It is further complicated by the lack of a single and universally accepted definition of legitimacy, the reality that legitimacy is continuously changing, hard to gauge (especially in its positive form) and has to be claimed, accepted (and analysed) in various constituencies simultaneously. The fact that legitimacy is a concept used in divergent ways and in different situations, often without an accompanying explanation of what is meant by it, further confuses the already inherently difficult task of deciding what is legitimate and what is not.[76]

Definitions of legitimacy

The main discrepancy between different meanings of legitimacy is the difference between normative and descriptive definitions. A mainly normative understanding of legitimacy tries to identify a set of standards that morally justify the authority of an entity to rule over, or take decisions for, another group, and to identify those conditions under which the institutions and actions should be regarded as legitimate.[77] It is about why an entity *ought* to be obeyed.[78] Conversely, a descriptive approach to legitimacy looks why an entity *is* obeyed, without passing judgement on the moral bases of either the claims of legitimacy made by the ruler, or the reasons of the ruled, to accept those claims.[79] Most scholars define legitimacy either as a normative concept or choose a descriptive approach. However, both Rodney Barker and David Beetham argue that the two approaches are not opposed to each other, but rather serve different purposes.[80] In many cases, it might be useful to look at legitimacy from a normative perspective, to set a benchmark of norms that determine when an entity, its actions and institutions ought to be obeyed. But, in trying to understand how legitimacy works, how it is gained and why and when it is lost in order to determine the influence of international criminal justice on QSEs, applying one's own moral convictions is not very useful. In order to be able to say something about the chances of an entity succeeding in its statehood, or state-altering aspirations, one has to consider why, and how far, its authority is obeyed and also at the capacity to create and maintain such a state. Therefore, using a mostly descriptive approach to legitimacy is more suitable.

Max Weber, the starting point for virtually every descriptive theory of legitimacy, successfully avoids a normative judgement when he defines legitimacy rather narrowly as 'the willingness to comply with rules'.[81] Weber describes three pure types of legitimising authority: First, legal or rational grounds, resting on a belief in the legality of enacted rules and the right of those elevated to authority under such rules to issue commands; second, traditional grounds, resting on an established belief in the sanctity of immemorial traditions and legitimacy of the status of those exercising authority under them; and third, charismatic grounds, resting on devotion to the specific and exceptional sanctity, heroism or exemplary character of an individual person, and of the normative patterns, or order revealed or ordained by him.[82] Although Weber realises that pure types are rarely found in reality, he argues that these types are met when asking for obedience.[83]

In so narrowly defining legitimacy as 'willingness to comply with rules' and by describing three types on which claims of legitimacy are based, both Gow and Beetham note that the Weberian typology is ruler-centric in that it looks at the claims made, not at the reasons why they are accepted.[84] Like Jürgen Habermas, they point out the limits of the usefulness of Weber's purely descriptive concept as it neglects people's second-order beliefs about legitimacy.[85] So, while a purely normative approach is of limited use in understanding actual processes of legitimation, neither is a purely descriptive approach.[86] Legitimacy is more than just the acceptance of claims, because 'legitimacy and acquiescence, and legitimacy and consensus, are not the same'.[87] When an entity has legitimacy, it has not only the capacity to run certain institutions, make decisions and have orders executed, but also its norms, rules and principles are socially endorsed.[88] This means that 'legitimacy is a social concept in the deepest sense – it describes a phenomenon that is inherently social'.[89]

In line with these shortcomings of a purely descriptive approach, Marc Suchman takes the reasons why claims are accepted into account when he defines legitimacy as:

> [T]he generalized perception or assumption that the actions of an entity are desirable, proper, or appropriate within some socially constructed system of norms, values, beliefs, and definitions.[90]

This definition makes clear that, even when looking at legitimacy from a descriptive perspective, the claims of legitimacy are judged normatively at the receiving end, and his definition stresses that legitimacy is inextricably dependent upon social perception and recognition.[91] Suchman considers that claims of legitimacy have to fit in with the pre-existing ideas in a certain society. Beetham further specifies the notion that claims to legitimacy should be 'appropriate within some socially constructed system of norms, values, beliefs and definitions'. He describes that power relationship is 'justified' in terms of the beliefs of the people at the receiving end of the relationship.[92] Suchman goes on to explain that legitimacy is 'socially constructed in that it reflects congruence between behaviours of the legitimated entity and the shared (or assumedly shared) beliefs of some social group'.[93] However, even when claims of legitimacy for an entity's actions and institutions fit within the existing ideas that prevail within a certain constituency, this 'perception or assumption that the actions of an entity are desirable, proper, or appropriate' is not a stable condition. Legitimacy is neither a static concept that an entity possesses, nor a quality that the institutions or actions of an entity (even if regarded as legitimate) have automatically. Entities that claim legitimacy have to engage in a continual process of legitimisation of their actions and institutions.

The multidimensionality of legitimacy

Besides the reality that legitimacy constantly changes, Richard Merelman warns that 'it is a mistake to believe that the levels of legitimacy [for an entity] are equally distributed throughout a society'.[94] Moreover, at least when assessing the legitimacy of entities that are involved in conflicts over statehood, the definitions discussed are 'incomplete in that they fail to take sufficient account of the various constituencies with an interest'.[95] The congruence between the behaviour of the legitimacy-seeking entity and the shared beliefs of one social group is not enough.[96] This makes the constantly changing process of legitimation even more intricate, and even harder to detect and analyse. Decisions have to be gauged against the perspectives of multiple groups, not only within the entity's own societies, but also in that of allies and opponents, and the global audience.[97]

The notion of multiple constituencies in contemporary armed conflict can be related to the 'Clausewitzian trinity' of blind instinct, probabilities and chance, and reason – characteristics that Carl von Clausewitz subsequently maps onto the people, the general and his army, and the government.[98] This 'secondary Clausewitzian trinity' of the people, military and government is still relevant, but Gow argues that in modern armed conflict there is a multidimensional trinity at work.[99] This more complex trinity – which Gow named the 'Multidimensional Trinity Cubed-Plus' or 'Trinity^3(+)' – illustrates the problem of multiple constituencies.[100] In order to be effective in attaining its goals, an entity first needs to influence its home front, comprising the trinity of political leaders, armed forces and the people. Second, each aspect of the opponent's trinity needs to be influenced, as well as all of them at the same time. Third, there are multiple global audiences that have to be influenced, 'all being subject to the same information and images, all affecting the environment in which a strategic campaign is going to be conducted'.[101] Consequently, instead of fighting a battle of wills, or hearts and minds, contemporary armed conflict is defined by 'conducting simultaneously multiple battles for multiple wills' by sending out messages to gain legitimacy.[102]

Critical legitimacy moments

The ability of an entity to engage successfully in the constant process of legiti-mating its actions and institutions in different constituencies simultaneously is extremely hard to gauge. This is not only because the outcome depends on many variables, both within and outside the control of the legitimacy-seeking entity, but also because 'that which is not in question is legitimate'.[103] Legitimacy in its positive form is hard to see. Mainly because people who are satisfied do not take to the streets *en masse* to shout 'we are satisfied' and wave signs saying 'it's all good', the signs of legitimacy are hard to discern.[104] As it is so problematic to assert or affirm legitimacy positively, it is easier to be noticed in periods when it becomes apparent that legitimacy has broken down. It is, therefore, easier to pin-point its absence in the presence of a legitimacy crisis than to identify its pres-ence.[105] A lack of legitimacy – in a certain constituency, of a certain entity or action, at a certain point in time – is easier to identify than measuring the exist-ence of it. On the basis of such observations, Habermas noted that legitimacy is best noticed in its absence, when critically challenged. He describes the moment that a crisis of legitimation emerges as follows:

> If governmental crisis management fails, it lags behind programmatic demands *that it has placed on itself.* The penalty for this failure is with-drawal of legitimation. Thus the scope for actions contracts precisely at those moments in which it needs to be drastically expanded.[106]

For Habermas, crises are 'turning points' that 'arise when the structure of a social system allows fewer possibilities for problem-solving than are necessary to the continued existence of the system'.[107] That turning point can be seen, even when legitimacy crises are to be overcome, as the change can be seen in chang-ing narratives and actions, as an entity must adapt by effectively managing the critical situation. It is by looking at those critical moments where legitimacy is withdrawn, when it is needed most, that one can see the workings of, and the influences on, legitimacy. By analysing the capacities to overcome crises, one can gauge the existence of legitimacy.

Complementing the notion of legitimacy crises as a point where legitimacy becomes visible, Gow argued that, in dissecting the concept of legitimacy crisis, the elements that constitute legitimacy could be detected.[108] These elements are legitimating ideology (bases), performance and environmental support. First, the legal, political and normative bases of legitimacy comprise rules, norms, laws and statements (both explicit and implicit) and beliefs of the actor (and others), about what it is and should be doing.[109] Second, performance is the level at which an entity or activity is effective. Strong performance can strengthen legiti-macy when the bases are weak, but the opposite is also true, when performance is weak and an entity ineffective, this will weaken strong bases of legitimacy.[110] Third, support will bolster legitimacy where legitimacy claims are accepted, as a degree of social and communal support exists and can be sustained, both in

terms of bases and performance of the entity and its actions, as well as in relation to various other entities, bodies, groups or organisations in society and in
the international community.[111]

Legitimacy as a compound concept

Understanding legitimacy as a compound concept of these elements provides the
possibility of considering the components individually, although only together
can they be understood to constitute legitimacy.[112] It also further illustrates critical legitimacy moments; not only is legitimacy needed most when it is withdrawn, but when performance is low, legitimacy is weakened, and a negative
spiral of legitimacy becomes harder to turn around. As Weber observed, 'if he
wants to be a prophet, he must perform miracles; if he wants to be a war lord, he
must perform heroic deeds'.[113] If they fail, even strong bases of legitimacy will
be weakened. In this context, international criminal justice can bring critical
challenges to the legitimacy of actors. These can affect both sides in a conflict
and, as much as they can lose legitimacy for one side, they can boost the other.

For a state, the mere fact that it is involved in a statehood conflict is an indication that its legitimacy, or at least that of some of its institutions or actions in
certain constituencies, is questioned. Yet, the actions it can take to re-strengthen
that legitimacy at the same time is limited. This is especially the case when a
state reaches a point where it uses violence to enforce decisions. It is, then, likely
to end up in a spiral of legitimacy crises which may very well spread among
constituencies. Arendt points out that loss of power becomes a temptation to
substitute violence for power, but that the use of violence is a sign of weakness
rather than power.[114] In the same vein, David Easton suggests that 'where acceptance of outputs as binding must depend upon force, the social costs are high'.[115]
If they can continue to operate at all, 'illegitimate political regimes operate far
less efficiently than legitimate regimes'.[116]

As its aims are often contrary to that of the state, the QSE vying for power
with the state can gain legitimacy where the state loses it. Legitimacy is not a
zero-sum game in the sense that when one entity loses it its opponents automatically gain it. Yet, when a regime loses legitimacy, it influences the legitimacy of
other groups in society, especially its enemies and any entity filling the authority
vacuum. For the QSEs on the other side of the statehood conflict, the ability to
create and maintain legitimacy is a prerequisite for success. They need to influence their legitimacy primarily within their core constituency, but they also need
to do so in other relevant constituencies and ultimately in the international community. If, for instance, a QSE seeks full statehood, it ultimately needs to be
recognised by other states and will need legitimacy in the international community. Often, providing a narrative that will appeal to all different constituencies will prove impossible, forcing a QSE to make choices. The organisational
sophistication of a QSE, the statehood functions it aspires to and the services it
already provides, and its legitimacy in various constituencies among other
things, will dictate which constituency is prioritised.

Gauging legitimacy

A misleading research strategy for determining legitimacy would be to ask people whether they believe something is legitimate. According to Beetham, this might encounter the problem of expecting ordinary people to understand what legitimacy is.[117] Although ordinary people probably understand very well what legitimacy entails – surely they understand when it is absent, and they take to the barricades – it would be practically impossible to take a poll to determine what a representative group in every relevant constituency thinks at any given time about the legitimacy of the relevant entities, their institutions and actions. Even if such a poll were feasible, it would still be impossible to know *why* the claims of legitimacy are accepted or rejected.[118]

To gauge legitimacy, and both how and how far international criminal justice influences the capacity to create and maintain legitimacy – and thereby the conduct of QSEs – one can scrutinise the decisions they make under the pressure of international criminal justice. In the same vein, one can consider the components that together constitute legitimacy and how far they are influenced, in a certain constituency, at a certain time, by international criminal procedures. But, most important, one can assess critical legitimacy moments. By analysing whether international criminal justice creates critical legitimacy moments in certain constituencies, and by assessing the ability of QSEs to overcome any crises that are the result of international criminal justice, one can detect the influence these procedures have on QSEs.

Legitimating narratives in an interconnected world

Success in this continuing process of legitimation and in overcoming legitimacy crises depends heavily on the legitimating entity's ability to provide a compelling narrative that fits in with pre-existing ideas and values in a certain society.[119] As Nye repeatedly pointed out: 'In the information age, success is not merely the result of whose army wins, but also whose story wins'.[120] This may be a simplification, but it is true that success largely depends on legitimacy, and that the ability to create and maintain legitimacy in turn depends on narratives, or whose story is accepted. These legitimising narratives have to be aimed at various constituencies in which legitimacy is sought and has to fit in with the existing believes and experiences of those groups in order to be successful.[121]

International criminal justice is one of the most significant factors to impact on the process of legitimisation and on the narratives used to that end. Legitimacy is not created in courts in The Hague, or in the UN Headquarters in New York for that matter. However, the narratives used in these arenas, the stories accepted in international courts and the narratives of events created by them, and then broadcast, transmitted and received – however they are actually interpreted – carry considerable weight. In particular, they become authoritative narratives in many Western constituencies in the international community. To be effective these narratives have to be public, and as Beetham already pointed out, to see the evidence of legitimacy, the best strategy would not be to attempt to look into 'private recesses of people's minds', but at the public domain.[122] The possibilities offered by modern mass communication changed this process profoundly.

In general, developments in new information and communications technology (ICT) led to interconnectivity among individuals, institutions and communities, and this growth in connectivity provided the opportunity to bypass traditional authorities, both private and public.[123] The speed of communication and transmittance of data meant that decision making was accelerated, and the extraordinary growth in information available to an unprecedented number of people created an openness of information that crowded out secrecy, ending the traditional monopoly of information by states and corporations.[124] The Internet not only made one-to-one communication (e.g. e-mail) faster, more easily available and less costly, it also democratised one-to-many communication (e.g. YouTube). The act of broadcasting or publishing to a large audience is now available to every person with access to a computer connected to the Internet. Typical of the Internet age is many-to-many communication (e.g. blogs, wiki's and Facebook) with people both creating input for and receiving information from the Internet. Although these communication networks by now cover the entire world, one should note that there is still a so-called 'global digital divide'. Large parts of the population of developing countries are disadvantaged due to their limited access to ICT.[125] Furthermore, in countries with totalitarian regimes where the population has reasonable access to the Internet, such as China, censorship blocks certain sites that are perceived as threatening. Although these blockades are easy to circumvent by using servers abroad it does impair the free flow of information.

The Arab Spring showed the importance of Facebook, Twitter and YouTube etc. in organising groups that are not necessarily geographically close, but are connected by ideas, to rally around a common idea and rally against regimes. Besides facilitating the expression of dissatisfaction, Facebook, Twitter, YouTube and other internet-based platforms spread the (visual) evidence of the ineffectiveness of, and the atrocities committed by, these regimes.[126] In Egypt, for instance, Facebook not only provided the protesters with a means to create sufficient environmental support to strengthen its basis of legitimacy but, together with YouTube, simultaneously showed the atrocities of the Mubarak regime in a way that eroded his legitimacy, which was covered in real time on Twitter.[127] Social media was not only used to organise protest, but also to show the atrocities and brutality of the regime. YouTube is even better at spreading the images of atrocities and injustices around the world almost instantly, and was used widely across the Arab Spring. As an Egyptian activist tweeted during the anti-Mubarak protests, 'we use Facebook to schedule the protests, Twitter to coordinate, and YouTube to tell the world'.[128] Al Jazeera, even before the Arab Spring, had shown that CNN might have lost most of its relevance, but also that satellite networks are still very influential, not in the least because they further spread any content produced and work as both a traditional news network and an amplifier of mass-to-mass communications.

The rise of Daesh (Islamic State/ISIS/ISIL) demonstrated the connection between environmental support and success. The strategic communications war Daesh is waging with their sleek media strategy was aimed at conveying a narrative of success.[129] At the same time the delegitimising narratives, especially those of counter-Islamic State information operations by Western governments, turned out to be inadequate and unable to send a synchronised message.[130] The counter narrative did not fit with the pre-existing ideas of young Muslims in these countries and the means of distribution meant that these messages did not reach their intended audiences as effectively as the messages of Daesh did. Ayman al-Zawahiri, now leader of al-Qa'ida, already wrote in 2005 to the then head of the organisation in Iraq, Abu Musab al-Zarqawi, that: 'We are in a battle, and more than half of this battle is taking place in the battlefield of the media [...] we are in a media battle for the hearts and minds of our Umma.'[131] Al-Zawahiri also expressed his concern that televised beheadings of hostages and attacks on Shiites could lose the 'media battle'.[132] Yet he was wrong as far as the successors of al-Zarqawi in Iraq were concerned. The ultraviolence of Daesh messages meant that messages went viral, often aided by the attention of traditional media, yet the negative messages were combined with images of camaraderie and that young people who feel disenfranchised have a sense of agency, however negative their impact might seem to the outside world. The caliphate has a consistent story coupled with a sophisticated ability to deliver it; with centrally administered outlets, it seemingly never goes off message, 'always transmitting the same carefully constructed ideas of the triumphant, defiant caliphate and the promise of community'.[133]

While Daesh aimed its narratives very clearly at producing an effect in a limited constituency, its messages had an opposite effect in many other constituencies appalled by the actions shown in its videos. What it also shows is that in the increasingly interconnected world technology has brought us, all different groups that have to be influenced are increasingly subject to the same messages.[134] The messages and actions that make those narratives, and their counter narratives, can usually be found in the public domain. When narratives are no longer accepted, competing narratives start to prevail, or it can be seen that the legitimacy of an entity, its actions or institutions are questioned in certain groups. It is in those moments that one can detect the indicators for legitimacy crises.

Strategic narratives

Narratives are not PR, or they could be, but they are not per se. A narrative is an account of a series of events.[135] It is how a story is told, which events are selected, how they are presented and connected to other events or myths, or placed in a historical or cultural context. Narratives not only structure our perception of the world around us, but at the same time influence that perception. Although it may be hard to imagine that a campaign of ethnic cleansing can be perceived in any other way than as a despicable crime, there is often a group that does so. To justify these acts, a group places the same events in a different narrative, usually one of victimhood or (existential) threat, belonging or ownership, and often based on history, myths or other pre-existing ideas. The availability of moving image narratives has a more acute impact on the perceptions of people than other means of conveying a narrative.[136] The availability of images, the technology to capture them and who is able to share and spread these images has been growing steadily over the last century and surging in the last 20 years. That is not to say that limiting or selecting the images and changing statements to make these images fit better with the pre-existing ideas, sentiments and beliefs of a certain group can no longer make a change in the perception of an action, or policy, in that group. Even in places where the public has access to all kinds of information about war, and images of its consequences that are freely available on the Internet, the images that reach them are often filtered. In the United States for instance, the audience that Fox News attracts will be exposed to different images and information accompanying those images than those watching CNBC. Members of the 'Christians United for Israel' Facebook group are exposed to different cartoons, photos and moving images than subscribers to the 'Free Palestine' group.[137] What both narratives have in common is that they fit in with the pre-existing ideas of most of their members. The members of the 'Pro-Assad' and those of the 'Syrian Revolution' Facebook groups both see YouTube clips of very similar war crimes and humanitarian disaster, but accompanied by very different narratives, and often do want to see or hear the opposing narrative.[138] In short, people tend not to listen to what they do not want to hear, and do not watch what they do not want to see.[139] However, in an interconnected world, the same message will be available and often reach various audiences, making it harder and sometimes impossible, to send different legitimating messages to different audiences simultaneously.

A legitimating narrative needs an audience to be effective. Indicators of critical legitimacy moments are therefore available in the public domain. The main indicators of legitimacy crisis are broadcast via the same channels used to convey the public narratives of those claiming or maintaining legitimacy: newspapers, radio and television broadcasts. Internet made mass-to-mass communication possible, but is self-selecting. In a way, it is very easy to send messages fitting in with the pre-existing beliefs of groups that do not share a geographical location but are formed around a common interest. However, these narratives often need an amplifier to spread the message effectively. Whether it is a retweet by people with many followers on Twitter or a YouTube clip that is picked up by a 'classic' news network, they need some form of amplification. Moreover, many of those 'internet' narratives lack credibility, especially among those groups opposing the message sent, at least until confirmed by a credible journalistic source.

Implied and explicit messages that influence the success of parties seeking legitimacy are sent in every possible way by statements, but also with actions, not only by the actors that are seeking legitimacy, but also those of other actors; international organisations like the ICC and the UN, or even NGOs, will influence their legitimacy in different constituencies. Moreover, the international community is highly susceptible to normative judgements made by international organisations and especially courts. When charged with crimes against humanity, it becomes almost impossible to regain legitimacy in the international community.

Notes

1 J. Gow, *Defending the West*, Cambridge: Polity, 2005, p. 31.
2 The affirmations about the 'uniqueness' of Kosovo should be seen in this light, and they only confirm the continued relevance of sovereignty.
3 For more on the 1992 Declaration, see Chapter 3, this book.
4 Note by the President of the Security Council at the conclusion of the 3046th meeting of the Security Council, held at the level of Heads of State and Government on 31 January 1992, S/25300, p. 3.
5 M. Doyle and N. Sambanis, *Making War and Building Peace*, Princeton: Princeton University Press, 2006, p. 1.
6 Note by the President of the Security Council, 31 January 1992, S/25300, p. 3.
7 Falk suggests that sovereignty is such a troublesome concept that it should be left to politicians and should be discarded by academic analysis. However, the impact the implications of sovereignty have on the functioning of the international community through the principle of non-intervention, the limitations of the right to self-determination and international law, are such that we cannot discard its meaning in its entirety. R. Falk, 'Sovereignty', in: J. Krieger (ed.), *The Oxford Companion to Politics of the World*, Oxford: Oxford University Press, 1993, pp. 851–853. Quoted in: J. Mayall, 'Sovereignty, Nationalism, and Self-determination', *Political Studies*, XLVII, 1999, pp. 474–502, at p. 474.
8 J. Bartelson, *A Genealogy of Sovereignty*, Cambridge: Cambridge University Press, 1995, p. 1.
9 H. Grotius, *The Rights of War and Peace*, edited and with an Introduction by R. Tuck, from the edition by J. Barbeyrac, Indianapolis: Liberty Fund, 2005, vol. I, Chapter 3, § VII. (Original title: De *iure belli ac pacis*, first published 1625) [original capitals and italics].
10 L.F.L. Oppenheim, *International Law*, vol. 1, 1905, at p. 101, quoted in B. Kingsbury, 'Sovereignty and Inequality', *European Journal of International Law*, vol. 9, no. 4, 1998, pp. 599–625, at p. 599.
11 S.D. Krasner, *Sovereignty: Organized Hypocrisy*, Princeton: Princeton University Press, 1999, p. 4.
12 Ibid., p. 3–4.
13 J. Bartelson, 'The Concept of Sovereignty Revisited', *The European Journal of International Law*, vol. 17, no. 7, 2006, pp. 463–474, p. 469 [original italics].
14 Kingsbury, 'Sovereignty and Inequality', p. 603. Charter of the United Nations, Article 2(1).
15 Charter of the United Nations, Article 2(7).
16 M. Mazower, *Governing the World: The History of an Idea*, New York: The Penguin Press, 2012, p. 379.
17 D.A. Lake, 'The New Sovereignty in International Relations', *International Studies Review*, vol. 5, 2003, pp. 303–323, at pp. 305–308.
18 Ibid., pp. 305–308.
19 This was not the first 'revolution in sovereignty'; see J. Mayall, *Nationalism and International Society*, Cambridge: Cambridge University Press, 1990, pp. 36–37. Lake, 'The New Sovereignty in International Relations'.
20 Mazower, *Governing the World*, p. 387.

21 Ibid.
22 Kofi Annan, 'Two Concepts of Sovereignty', *The Economist*, 16 September 1999. Mazower, *Governing the World*, p. 378.
23 *2005 World Summit Outcome*, Resolution adopted by the UN General Assembly, 24 October 2005, (A/60/L.1) § 138.
24 Ibid., § 139.
25 Ibid.
26 D. Philpott, 'Sovereignty', Edward N. Zalta (ed.), The Stanford Encyclopedia of Philosophy (Summer 2010 Edition).
27 Humanitarian intervention was, indeed, ordered by the Security Council in: Northern Iraq, Rwanda, Somalia, the former Yugoslavia (Bosnia), Haiti, Liberia and Sierra Leone. In Kosovo, NATO intervened without an explicit Security Council order, but based on humanitarian grounds.
28 C. Schreuer, 'The Waning of the Sovereign State: Towards a New Paradigm for International Law?' *European Journal of International Law*, no. 4, 1993, pp. 447–471, p. 447.
29 A. Chayes and A. Chayes, *The New Sovereignty: Compliance with International Regulatory Agreements*, Cambridge MA: Harvard University Press, 1995, p. 27. A.M. Slaughter, 'The Real New World Order', *Foreign Affairs*, vol. 76, no. 5, 1997, pp. 183–197, p. 195.
30 Montevideo Convention on the Rights and Duties of States, signed at the International Conference of American States in Montevideo, Uruguay on 26 December 1933, entry into force 26 December 1934. Article 1.
31 Ibid., Article 3.
32 M. Weber, 'Politics as a Vocation', originally a speech at Munich University, 1918, published in 1919 by Duncker and Humblodt, Munich 'Politik als Beruf', Gesammelte Politische Schriften (Muenchen, 1921), pp. 396–450. From H.H. Gerth and C. Wright Mills (translated and edited), from *Max Weber: Essays in Sociology*, pp. 77–128, New York: Oxford University Press, 1946.
33 R.I. Rotberg, *State Failure and State Weakness in a Time of Terror*, Washington DC, Brookings Institution Press, 2003, p. 1.
34 Ibid.
35 D.L. Cingranelli and D.L. Richards, 'Respect for Human Rights after the End of the Cold War', *Journal of Peace Research*, vol. 36, no. 5, 1999, pp. 511–534, at p. 511.
36 Cingranelli and Richards, 'Respect for Human Rights after the End of the Cold War', p. 511. Smith, *The Utility of Force*, p. 267.
37 U. Schneckener, 'Fragile Statehood, Armed Non-State Actors and Security Governance', in: A. Bryden and M. Caparini (eds), *Private Actors and Security Governance*, Geneva: DCAF, 2006, p. 25.
38 In 1949, the International Court of Justice (ICJ) in the Reparations for Injuries case ruled that international legal personality could exist beyond states and the United Nations possessed such personality. (*Reparation for injuries suffered in the service of the United Nations*, Advisory Opinion: ICJ Reports 1949, p. 179.) Other organisations that are usually presumed to have international legal personality are the International Committee of the Red Cross and the Sovereign Military Hospitaller Order of Saint John of Jerusalem of Rhodes and of Malta (R. Portmann, *Legal Personality in International Law*, Cambridge: Cambridge University Press, 2010, pp. 110–118).
39 Gow, *Defending the West*, p. 31.
40 Ibid.
41 Ibid.
42 J. Gow, 'Viable Political Communities', unpublished paper.
43 Jackson calls these states with only external sovereignty that 'often appear to be juridical more than empirical entities', 'quasi-states'. Here, these entities will be referred to as 'failed states', as it is argued that it is more appropriate to use the term

'quasi-state entity' for those entities that aspire to statehood. R.H. Jackson, *Quasi-states: Sovereignty, International Relations and the Third World*, Cambridge: Cambridge University Press, 1990.

44 Gow, 'Viable Political Communities'.

45 C. Clapham, 'Degrees of Statehood', *Review of International Studies*, vol. 24, no. 2, 1998, pp. 143–157, p. 150.

46 Ibid.

47 Ibid., p. 151.

48 Clapham, 'Degrees of Statehood', p. 151. Clapham gives the example of the National Patriotic Front of Liberia that 'entered into concession agreements with major international companies, for the export of iron ore, rubber and tropical timber, royalties on which were paid to the NPFL'.

49 Ibid.

50 Ibid., pp. 152–153. Sometimes support is provided overtly, as in Angola and Vietnam, or in the Ogaden War and in Nicaragua, as well as during the Soviet invasion of Afghanistan. Yet, despite tacit approval, or acceptance, or even full military support, Clapham also notices that the 'conventions of juridical statehood continued to impose certain limits on external intervention'.

51 P. Kolstø, 'The Sustainability and Future of Unrecognized Quasi-States', *Journal of Peace Research*, vol. 43, no. 6, 2006, pp. 723–740, p. 723.

52 Kolstø, 'The Sustainability and Future of Unrecognized Quasi-States', p. 723.

53 Ibid.

54 Jackson, *Quasi-states*, p. 21.

55 Ibid.

56 Ibid.

57 Kolstø, 'The Sustainability and Future of Unrecognized Quasi-States', p. 725.

58 See: S. Pegg, *International Society and the De Facto State*, Aldershot: Ashgate, 1998. D. Lynch, 'Separatist States and Post-Soviet Conflicts', *International Affairs*, vol. 78, no. 4, 2002, pp. 831–848. C. King, 'The Benefits of Ethnic War: Understanding Eurasia's Unrecognized States', *World Politics*, vol. 53, July 2001, pp. 524–552. V. Kolossov and J. O'Loughlin, 'Pseudo-States as Harbingers of a New Geopolitics: The Example of the Transdniestr Moldovan Republic (TMR)', in: David Newman (ed.), *Boundaries, Territory and Post-modernity*, London: Frank Cass, 2001, pp. 151–176, in: Kolstø, 'The Sustainability and Future of Unrecognized Quasi-States', p. 725.

59 Kolstø, 'The Sustainability and Future of Unrecognized Quasi-States', pp. 725–726.

60 Even Kolstø himself does not apply this last criterion consistently, as he claims that the South Ossetian quasi-state came into being on 29 May 1992 when its parliament adopted a declaration of independence. (P. Kolstø and H. Blakkisrud, 'Living with Non-recognition: State- and Nation-building in South Caucasian Quasi-states', *Europe-Asia Studies*, vol. 60, no. 3, 2008, pp. 483–509, p. 488.)

61 D. Natali, *Kurdish Quasi-State: Development and Dependency in Post-Gulf War Iraq*, Syracuse NY: Syracuse University Press, 2010, p. xxix. M. Rywkin, 'The Phenomenon of Quasi-states', *Diogenes*, vol. 53, no. 210, 2006, pp. 23–28.

62 Natali, *Kurdish Quasi-State*, p. 29.

63 Ibid.

64 Charles King, (2001), 'The Benefits of Ethnic War: Understanding Eurasia's Unrecognized States', *World Politics*, vol. 53, no. 4, 2001, pp. 524–552, p. 528.

65 Ibid.

66 For more on Hezbollah see Chapter 5, this book.

67 Although, in limited forms, the latter took on some roles, such as administering its own form of justice that could, in extremis, be argued as taking state functions in the manner of a QSE, but this only operated within the organisation and its immediate supporters.

68 B.R. Early, 'Larger than a Party, yet Smaller than a State: Locating Hezbollah's Place within Lebanon's State and Society', *World Affairs*, vol. 168, no. 3, 2006, pp. 115–128, p. 115.
69 J. Fitzpatrick, 'Jurisdiction of Military Commissions and the Ambiguous War on Terrorism', *American Journal of International Law*, vol. 96, no. 2, 2002, pp. 345–354, p. 346, 348.
70 C. Clapham, 'Degrees of Statehood', *Review of International Studies*, vol. 24, no. 2, 1998, pp. 143–157, p. 150.
71 Ibid.
72 M. Weber, *The Theory of Social and Economic Organization*, translated by A.M. Henderson and T. Parsons, New York: Free Press, 1947, p. 325.
73 I.L. Claude Jr, 'Collective Legitimisation as a Political Function of the United Nations', *International Organization*, vol. 20, no. 3, 1966, pp. 367–379, p. 368.
74 Smith, *The Utility of Force*, pp. 269–271, 278–279.
75 Colonel T.X. Hammes, *The Sling and the Stone: On War in the 21st Century*, St Paul, MN: Zenith Press, 2006, p. 208.
76 C.K. Ansell, 'Legitimacy: Political', in: Smelser, Neil J. and Baltes, Paul B. (eds), *International Encyclopedia of the Social and Behavioral Sciences*, Amsterdam: Elsevier, 2001, pp. 8704–8706, p. 8704. D. Beetham, *The Legitimation of Power*, Basingstoke: Macmillan, 1991, pp. 3–4.
77 Ansell, 'Legitimacy: Political', p. 8704.
78 Beetham, *The Legitimation of Power*, p. 5. Ansell, 'Legitimacy: Political', p. 8704.
79 Ansell, 'Legitimacy: Political', p. 8704.
80 Beetham, *The Legitimation of Power*, p. 5. R. Barker, *Political Legitimacy and the State*, Oxford: Clarendon Press, 1990.
81 Weber, *The Theory of Social and Economic Organization*, p. 328. J. Gow, *Legitimacy and the Military: The Yugoslav Crisis*, London: Pinter Publishers, 1992, p. 16.
82 Weber, *The Theory of Social and Economic Organization*, p. 328.
83 M. Weber, 'Politics as a Vocation', p. 2.
84 Beetham, *The Legitimation of Power*, pp. 10–11. Gow, *Legitimacy and the Military*, p. 16.
85 F. Peter, 'Political Legitimacy', in: E.N. Zalta (ed.), *The Stanford Encyclopedia of Philosophy* (Summer 2010 Edition). See also J. Habermas, *Legitimation Crisis*, London: Heinemann, 1976. Beetham, *The Legitimation of Power*.
86 F. Peter, 'Political Legitimacy'.
87 J.H. Schaar, 'Legitimacy in the Modern State', in *Legitimacy and the State*, W. Connolly (ed.), Oxford: Basil Blackwell, 1984, p. 109.
88 C. Reus-Smit, 'International Crises of Legitimacy', *International Politics*, vol. 44, no. 1, 2007, pp. 157–174, p. 159.
89 Ibid., p. 159.
90 M.C. Suchman, 'Managing Legitimacy: Strategic and Institutional Approaches', *Academy of Management Review*, vol. 20, no. 3, 1995, p. 574. Lipset offers a similar definition: 'Legitimacy involves the capacity of the system to engender and maintain the belief that the existing political institutions are the most appropriate ones for the society'. S.M. Lipset, *Political Man: The Social Bases of Politics*, London: Heinemann, 1960, (2nd edn. 1983) p. 64.
91 Reus-Smit, 'International Crises of Legitimacy', p. 159.
92 Beetham, *The Legitimation of Power*, p. 11.
93 Suchman, 'Managing Legitimacy', p. 574.
94 R.M. Merelman, 'Learning and Legitimacy', *The American Political Science Review*, vol. 60, no. 3, 1966, pp. 548–561, p. 552.
95 Gow, *Legitimacy and the Military*, p. 16.
96 Ibid., p. 20.

97 M. Michalski and J. Gow, *War, Image and Legitimacy*, Abingdon: Routledge, 2007, p. 201.
98 Ibid. C. Von Clausewitz, *On War* (Original Title: *Vom Kriege*, 1832, translation by J.J. Graham), London: Wordsworth, 1997, p. 24.
99 Michalski and Gow, *War, Image and Legitimacy*, p. 201.
100 Ibid.
101 Ibid., pp. 201–202.
102 Ibid., p. 201.
103 Gow, *Legitimacy and the Military*, p. 20.
104 Mohammed K. Alyahya (@7yhy) https://twitter.com/7yhy/status/344546058438848513 (accessed 23 June 2013).
105 Gow, *Legitimacy and the Military*, p. 20.
106 Habermas, *Legitimation Crisis*, p. 69.
107 Ibid., p. 2.
108 Gow, *Legitimacy and the Military*, p. 20.
109 Ibid.
110 Ibid.
111 Ibid.
112 Ibid.
113 M. Weber, *From Max Weber: Essays in Sociology*, translated, edited and with an Introduction by H.H. Gerth and C. Wright Mills, Oxford: Oxford University Press, 1946, p. 249.
114 H. Arendt, *On Violence*, New York: Harcourt, Brace and World Inc., 1969, pp. 54–56.
115 D. Easton, *A Systems Analysis of Political Life*, New York: Wiley, 1965, p. 286.
116 Merelman, 'Learning and Legitimacy', p. 549.
117 Beetham, *The Legitimation of Power*, p. 13.
118 For more about 'the difficulty of inferring value beliefs', see: Michalski and Gow, *War, Image and Legitimacy*, p. 203. J.G. Merquior, *Rousseau and Weber: Two Studies in the Theory of Legitimacy*, London: Routledge, 1980, p. 5.
119 For more on strategic narratives, see: L. Freedman, 'Networks, Culture and Narratives', *Adelphi Papers*, vol. 45, no. 379, 2006, pp. 11–26, at pp. 14–15.
120 J.S. Nye Jr, 'Smart power and the "war on terror"', *Asia-Pacific Review*, vol. 15, no. 1, 2008, pp. 1–8, at p. 5.
121 Freedman, 'Networks, Culture and Narratives', pp. 14–15.
122 Beetham, *The Legitimation of Power*, p. 13.
123 E.H. Potter (ed.), *Cyber-Diplomacy: Managing Foreign Policy in the Twenty-First Century*, Montreal and Kingston: McGill-Queen's University Press, 2002, p. 5.
124 Ibid.
125 A. Ishaq, 'On the Global Digital Divide', *Finance and Development: A quarterly magazine of the IMF*, vol. 38, no. 3, 2001, p. 2.
126 See: P.N Howard, A. Duffy, D. Freelon, M. Hussain, W. Mari, and M. Mazaid, *Opening Closed Regimes: What Was the Role of Social Media During the Arab Spring?* Seattle: PIPTI, 2011. And: J.A. Vargas, 'Spring Awakening: How an Egyptian Revolution Began on Facebook', *New York Times*, 17 February 2012.
127 E. Stepanova, 'The Role of Information Communication Technologies in the "Arab Spring"', *Ponars Eurasia Policy Memo*, No. 159, May 2011.
128 H.H. Khondker, 'Role of the New Media in the Arab Spring', *Globalizations*, vol. 8, no. 5, 2011, pp. 675–679, p. 677.
129 Cottee, S. (2015) 'Why It's So Hard to Stop ISIS Propaganda', *The Atlantic*. Available at: www.theatlantic.com/international/archive/2015/03/why-its-so-hard-to-stop-isis-propaganda/386216/ (Accessed: 15 August 2016).
130 van Ginkel, B. (2015) 'Responding to Cyber Jihad: Towards an Effective Counter Narrative', *International Centre for Terrorism and Counter-Terrorism Studies Research Paper*, p. 15.

131 Lynch, M. (2006) 'Al-Qaeda's Media Strategies', *The National Interest*, 83, pp. 50–56, p. 50.
132 Released by the Director of National Intelligence (2005) *Letter from al-zawahiri to al-zarqawi*. Available at: https://fas.org/irp/news/2005/10/letter_in_english.pdf (Accessed: 15 August 2016).
133 Winter, C. and Bach-Lombardo, J. (2016) 'Why ISIS Propaganda Works', *The Atlantic*. Available at: www.theatlantic.com/international/archive/2016/02/isis-propaganda-war/462702/ (Accessed: 15 August 2016).
134 Michalski and Gow, *War, Image and Legitimacy*, p. 197.
135 Oxford English Dictionary (online).
136 Michalski and Gow, *War, Image and Legitimacy*, p. 5.
137 https://www.facebook.com/ChristiansUnitedforIsrael?fref=ts. https://www.facebook.com/freedompage (Accessed: 15 June 2013).
138 https://www.facebook.com/ProAssad. https://www.facebook.com/Syrian.Revolution (Accessed: 15 June 2013).
139 Michalski and Gow, *War, Image and Legitimacy*, p. 197.

Bibliography

2005 World Summit Outcome, Resolution adopted by the UN General Assembly, (A/60/L.1) § 138 (2005).
Annan, K. (1999) 'Two Concepts of Sovereignty'. *The Economist*, 16 September.
Ansell, C.K. (2001) 'Legitimacy'. In: Smelser, N.J. and Baltes, P.B. (eds), *International Encyclopedia of the Social & Behavioral Sciences*. Amsterdam: Elsevier, pp. 8704–8706.
Arendt, H. (1969) *On Violence*. New York: Harcourt, Brace, Jovanovich.
Barker, R. (1990) *Political Legitimacy and the State*. Oxford: Clarendon Press.
Bartelson, J. (1995) *A Genealogy of Sovereignty*. Cambridge: Cambridge University Press.
Bartelson, J. (2006) 'The Concept of Sovereignty Revisited'. *European Journal of International Law*, 17(2), pp. 463–474. doi: 10.1093/ejil/chl006.
Beetham, D. (1991) *The Legitimation of Power*, 5th edn. Basingstoke: Palgrave Macmillan.
Chayes, A. and Chayes, A. (1995) *The New Sovereignty: Compliance with International Regulatory Agreements*. Cambridge MA: Harvard University Press.
Chulov, M., Shaheen, K. and Beaumont, P. (2016) *Thousands Gather for Funeral of Hezbollah's Mustafa Badreddine*. Available at: https://www.theguardian.com/world/2016/may/13/thousands-gather-for-funeral-of-hezbollahs-mustafa-badreddine (Accessed: 17 August 2016).
Cingranelli, D.L. and Richards, D.L. (1999) 'Respect for Human Rights after the End of the Cold War'. *Journal of Peace Research*, 36(5), pp. 511–534.
Clapham, C. (1998) 'Degrees of Statehood'. *Review of International Studies*, 24(2), pp. 143–157, doi: 10.1017/s0260210598001430.
Claude Jr, I.L. (1966) 'Collective Legitimisation as a Political Function of the United Nations'. *International Organization*, 20(3), pp. 367–379.
Cottee, S. (2015) *Why It's So Hard to Stop ISIS Propaganda*. Available at: www.theatlantic.com/international/archive/2015/03/why-its-so-hard-to-stop-isis-propaganda/386216/ (Accessed: 15 August 2016).
Doyle, M.W. (2006) *Making War and Building Peace*. Edited by Nicholas Sambanis. Princeton: Princeton University Press.
Early, B. (2006) '"Larger Than a Party, Yet Smaller Than a State": Locating Hezbollah's Place within Lebanon's State and Society'. *World Affairs*, 168(3), pp. 115–128. doi: 10.3200/wafs.168.3.115-128.

Easton, D. (1965) *A Systems Analysis of Political Life*. New York: Wiley.

Falk, R. (1993) 'Sovereignty'. In: Krieger, J. (ed.), *The Oxford Companion to Politics of the World*. Oxford: Oxford University Press, pp. 851–853.

Fitzpatrick, J. (2002) 'Jurisdiction of Military Commissions and the Ambiguous War on Terrorism'. *American Journal of International Law*, 96(2), p. 345. doi: 10.2307/2693929.

Freedman, L. (2006) 'Networks, Culture and Narratives'. *The Adelphi Papers*, 45(379), pp. 11–26, doi: 10.1080/05679320600661640.

van Ginkel, B. (2015) 'Responding to Cyber Jihad: Towards an Effective Counter Narrative'. *Terrorism and Counter-Terrorism Studies*, doi: 10.19165/2015.1.02.

Gow, J. (1992) *Legitimacy and the Military: The Yugoslav Crisis*. London: Pinter.

Gow, J. (2005) *Defending the West*. Cambridge: Polity Press.

Gow, J. (no date) *Viable Political Communities*. Unpublished paper.

Habermas, J. (1973) *Legitimation Crisis*. London: Heinemann.

Hammes, T.X. (2006) *The Sling and the Stone: On War in the 21st Century*. Minneapolis: Zenith Press.

Howard, P.N., Duffy, A., Freelon, D., Hussain, M.M., Mari, W. and Mazaid, M. (2011) 'Opening Closed Regimes: What Was the Role of Social Media during the Arab spring?' *SSRN Electronic Journal*, doi: 10.2139/ssrn.2595096.

Ishaq, A. (2001) 'On the Global Digital Divide'. *Finance & Development: A quarterly magazine of the IMF*, 38(3).

Jackson, R.H. (1990) *Quasi-states: Sovereignty, International Relations, and the Third World*. Cambridge, United Kingdom: Cambridge University Press.

Khondker, H.H. (2011) 'Role of the New Media in the Arab Spring'. *Globalizations*, 8(5), pp. 675–679. doi: 10.1080/14747731.2011.621287.

King, C. (2001a) 'The Benefits of Ethnic War: Understanding Eurasia's Unrecognized States'. *World Politics*, 53(04), pp. 524–552, doi: 10.1353/wp. 2001.0017.

Kingsbury, B. (1998) 'Sovereignty and Inequality'. *European Journal of International Law*, 9(4), pp. 599–625, doi: 10.1093/ejil/9.4.599.

Kolossov, V. and O'Loughlin, J. (1999) 'Pseudo-States as Harbingers of a New Geopolitics: The Example of the Transdniestr Moldovan Republic (TMR)'. In: Newman, D. (ed.), *Boundaries, Territory and Post-modernity*. London: Frank Cass, pp. 151–176.

Kolstø, P. (2006) 'The Sustainability and Future of Unrecognized Quasi-States'. *Journal of Peace Research*, 43(6), pp. 723–740, doi: 10.1177/0022343306068102.

Kolstø, P. and Blakkisrud, H. (2008) 'Living With Non-Recognition: State- and Nation-building in South Caucasian Quasi-states'. *Europe-Asia Studies*, 60(3), pp. 483–509, doi: 10.1080/09668130801948158.

Krasner, S.D. (1994) *Sovereignty: Organized Hypocrisy*. Princeton, NJ, United States: Princeton University Press.

Lake, D.A. (2003) 'The New Sovereignty in International Relations'. *International Studies Review*, 5(3), pp. 303–323, doi: 10.1046/j.1079-1760.2003.00503001.x.

Lipset, S.M. (1963) *Political Man*. London: Heinemann.

Lynch, D. (2002) 'Separatist States and Post-Soviet Conflicts'. *International Affairs*, 78(4), pp. 831–848, doi: 10.1111/1468-2346.00282.

Lynch, M. (2006) 'Al-Qaeda's Media Strategies'. *The National Interest*, 83, pp. 50–56.

Mayall, J. (1990) *Nationalism and International Society*. Cambridge: Cambridge University Press.

Mayall, J. (1999) 'Sovereignty, Nationalism, and Self-Determination'. *Political Studies*, 47(3), pp. 474–502, doi: 10.1111/1467-9248.00213.

Mazower, M. (2012) *Governing the World: The History of an Idea*. New York: Penguin Books.

Merelman, R.M. (1966) 'Learning and Legitimacy'. *American Political Science Review*, 60(03), pp. 548–561, doi: 10.2307/1952970.

Merquior, J.G. (1980) *Rousseau and Weber: Two Studies in the Theory of Legitimacy*. London: Routledge.

Michalski, M. and Gow, J. (2007) *War, Image and Legitimacy: Viewing Contemporary Conflict*. London: Routledge.

Montevideo Convention. (1933) Montevideo Convention on the Rights and Duties of States, signed at the International Conference of American States in Montevideo, Uruguay on 26 December 1933, entry into force 26 December 1934.

Natali, D. (2010) *The Kurdish Quasi-state: Development and Dependency in Post-Gulf War Iraq (Modern Intellectual and Political History of the Middle East)*. New York, NY, United States: Syracuse University Press.

Nye, J.S. (2008) 'Smart Power and the "War on Terror"'. *Asia-Pacific Review*, 15(1), pp. 1–8, doi: 10.1080/13439000802134092.

Oppenheim, L., Oppenheim, L. and Sir Arthur Watts KCMG QC. (1992) *Oppenheim's International Law: Part 1*. Edited by Sir Robert Jennings QC. Harlow, England: Longman.

Pegg, S. (1998) *International Society and the De Facto State*. Aldershot: Ashgate Publishing.

Peter, F. (2016) *Political Legitimacy*. Available at: http://plato.stanford.edu/entries/legitimacy/ (Accessed: 17 August 2016).

Philpott, D. (2016) *Sovereignty*. Available at: http://plato.stanford.edu/entries/sovereignty/ (Accessed: 17 August 2016).

Portmann, R. (2010) *Legal Personality in International Law*. Cambridge: Cambridge University Press.

Potter, E.H. (2002) *Cyber-Diplomacy: Managing Foreign Policy in the Twenty-First Century*. Canada: McGill-Queen's University Press.

President of the Security Council. (1992) Note by the President of the Security Council at the conclusion of the 3046th meeting of the Security Council, held at the level of Heads of State and Government. S/25300. 31 January.

Prosecutor vs Ibrahim Al Amin and Akhbar Beirut S.A.L [2016] Contempt Judge STL Judgement 06/T/CJ/F0262/PRV/20160715/R007725-R007795/EN/af.

Released by the Director of National Intelligence (2005) *Letter from al-zawahiri to al-zarqawi*. Available at: https://fas.org/irp/news/2005/10/letter_in_english.pdf (Accessed: 15 August 2016).

Reparation for injuries suffered in the service of the United Nations [1949] ICJ Advisory Opinion.

Reus-Smit, C. (2007) 'International Crises of Legitimacy'. *International Politics*, 44(2/3), pp. 157–174. doi: 10.1057/palgrave.ip.8800182.

Rotberg, R.I. (2003) *State Failure and State Weakness in a Time of Terror*. Cambridge, MA: World Peace Foundation.

Rywkin, M. (2006) 'The Phenomenon of Quasi-states'. *Diogenes*, 53(2), pp. 23–28, doi: 10.1177/0392192106065969.

Schaar, J.H. (1984) *Legitimacy in the Modern State*. Edited by W. Connolly. Oxford: Basil Blackwell.

Schneckener, U. (2006) 'Fragile Statehood, Armed Non-State Actors and Security Governance'. In: Bryden, A. and Caparini, M. (eds), *Private Actors and Security Governance*. Geneva: DCAF.

Schreuer, C. (1993) 'The Waning of the Sovereign State: Towards a New Paradigm for International Law?' *European Journal of International Law*, (4), pp. 447–471.

Slaughter, A.-M. (1997) 'The Real New World Order'. *Foreign Affairs*, 76(5), p. 183, doi: 10.2307/20048208.

Stepanova, E. (2011) 'The Role of Information Communication Technologies in the "Arab Spring"', *Ponars Eurasia Policy Memo*, (159).

Suchman, M.C. (1995) 'Managing Legitimacy: Strategic and Institutional Approaches'. *Academy of Management Review*, 20(3), pp. 571–610. doi: 10.2307/258788.

United Nations (1945) *Charter of the United Nations, 1 UNTS XVI*.

Vargas, J.A. (2012) 'Spring Awakening: How an Egyptian Revolution Began on Facebook'. *New York Times*, 17 February.

Von Clausewitz, C. (1997) *On War*. Translated by J.J. Graham. London: Wordsworth.

Weber, M. (1918) 'Politics as a Vocation' [speech at Munich University], Munich, Duncker and Humblodt.

'Politik als Beruf', Gesammelte Politische Schriften (Muenchen, 1921), pp. 396–450. From H.H. Gerth and C. Wright Mills (translated and edited), *From Max Weber: Essays in Sociology*, pp. 77–128, New York: Oxford University Press, 1946.

Weber, M. (1946) *From Max Weber: Essays in Sociology*. Edited by H.H. Gerth and C. Wright Mills. Oxford: Oxford University Press.

Weber, M. (1964) *The Theory of Social and Economic Organization*. New York: Free Press.

Winter, C. and Bach-Lombardo, J. (2016) *Why ISIS Propaganda Works*. Available at: www.theatlantic.com/international/archive/2016/02/isis-propaganda-war/462702/ (Accessed: 15 August 2016).

3 International criminal justice

The present incarnation of international criminal justice could only come to life when existing elements met new circumstances in the early 1990s. Combined, these elements and circumstances created a hospitable environment for international mechanisms to prosecute individuals for violations of international law to develop. A pre-existing body of international criminal law – including the Geneva Conventions, the UN Charter (including its Chapter VII system) and a precedent in the form of the Nuremberg and Tokyo trials – was a precondition for the establishment of international criminal courts and tribunals.[1] The end of the Cold War also revealed that interstate wars no longer were the most imminent threat to peace and security. Conflicts within states, or about statehood, with at least one of the belligerents being a QSE dominate contemporary armed conflict and pose the gravest threat to international peace and security. Yet, it was the unprecedented level of agreement among the permanent members of the UN Security Council, during a time in which human rights were grossly violated in a number of conflicts, that created the environment in which international criminal justice could emerge. Not least, this was because the international community proved unable, or unwilling, to prevent those violations while satellite television networks made the images of the atrocities committed almost instantly available to audiences around the world.

Important processes were set in motion in those first years of the 1990s. The Security Council established the ICTY and the International Criminal Tribunal for Rwanda (ICTR) in 1993 and 1994 respectively. Arising from this, the foundation was laid for the Rome Statute of the ICC, leading to its signing in 1998 and entry into force in 2002. The justification for these international mechanisms to prosecute war crimes, crimes against humanity and genocide primarily depended on forward-looking considerations. International tribunals were established with the following objectives: to 'contribute to ensuring that such violations are halted and effectively redressed'; or to 'contribute to the restoration and maintenance of peace'.[2] Or, in the case of the ICC, one of the stated purposes is 'to contribute to the prevention of such crimes'.[3] The first part of this chapter deals with the history of international criminal justice and the circumstances under which modern mechanisms to prosecute crimes under international law could be established. The second part assesses the purposes that have been attributed to these mechanisms of international criminal justice. Moreover, it will look at the various ways the effects of international criminal prosecutions have been assessed.

The history of international criminal justice

The first and main prerequisite for international criminal justice is the existence of a body of international criminal law.[4] *Nullum crimen, nulla poena, sine praevia lege poenali*, the principle that no crime can exist, and no punishment is lawful without a previous penal law, prevents prosecution based on *ex post facto* norms.[5] However, by the 1990s, an extensive body of international criminal law existed. In fact, it had a history that predated international criminal justice by centuries.[6] Almost every civilisation has put constraints both on the reasons to go to war and on the means and methods of warfare that are deemed acceptable. Both *jus ad bellum*, the law regarding the legality of waging war, and *jus in bello*, the law concerning the legal limits to conduct in war, have a long tradition in customary and codified international law and have been subject to the attention of scholars since the fifth century BC.[7] Aristotle already studied what constitutes a just war. His work inspired Augustine of Hippo in the fourth century, on whose work Thomas Aquinas further built when he defined conditions under which war could be just, in the thirteenth century. In Europe, rules of chivalry developed in the medieval period, and between the fourteenth and eighteenth centuries jurists like Francisco de Vitoria, Alberico Gentili and Samuel Pufendorf further expounded upon *jus in bello* and *jus ad bellum*.[8] In the early seventeenth century, Hugo de Groot (Grotius), the Dutch jurist, Remonstrant theologian, scholar and diplomat, noticed 'a licentiousness in regard to war, which even barbarous nations ought to be ashamed of'.[9] Grotius was deeply convinced of the existence of a law common to all nations concerning both the declaration of and conduct in war, but at the same time Grotius noticed little reverence for the laws of war, and it was those violations that incited him to write his treatise *De Jure Belli ac Pacis, On the Law of War and Peace*, first published in 1625.[10]

While norms of customary international law, and later codifications of laws of war, continued to develop, they remained equally disregarded as they were before 1625. Although the legal norms on conduct in war existed, there were no mechanisms in place to prosecute those violating these norms. Despite the continuing attention scholars devoted to laws and norms of war, no mechanisms of international criminal justice were established. This situation remained even when the main codifications of the norms of modern international humanitarian law took place in the late nineteenth and early twentieth century. The Geneva Conventions of 1864, 1906, 1929 and 1949 focused on protecting civilians and prisoners in war, and the First and Second Hague Peace Conferences in 1899 and 1907 led to the Conventions regulating the means and methods of warfare.[11] Yet the existence of a body of humanitarian law did not necessarily mean that attempts to prosecute individuals for violations of that law, in the first decades of the twentieth century, would be successful.[12]

In the aftermath of the First World War, a proposal to create an 'Allied High Tribunal' to try violations of the 'laws and customs of war' and 'the laws of humanity' failed because US and Japanese representatives doubted whether penal law was applicable.[13] The Treaty of Versailles provided for Kaiser Wilhelm II to be 'publicly arraigned' for 'a supreme offence against international morality and the sanctity of treaties' but this failed to materialise due to the refusal of the Netherlands, where he took exile, to hand him over to the Allies.[14] The Allies also demanded the extradition to military tribunals of 1590 German senior officers and political leaders 'accused of having committed acts in violation of the laws and customs of war'.[15] However, after nationalist street protests in Germany, extradition was suspended on request of the German government, and none of the accused were extradited.[16] Instead, the Leipzig War Crimes Trial was held before the German Supreme Court in 1921, only prosecuting 45 men. Ten of these were convicted and received short prison sentences.[17] For the Allies, the trial turned out to be wholly unsatisfactory, as the prosecution of a few low-ranking individuals for incidental crimes seemed to exonerate all others for collective crimes committed.[18] Similarly, the allied powers forced the post-war Turkish government to court-martial those responsible for the 'Armenian Massacre', which they had branded as 'crimes of Turkey against humanity and civilization' as early as 1915.[19] In both cases the Allies demanded an international tribunal, and in both cases this failed to materialise.[20] The failure of the Leipzig and Istanbul trials did, however, shape later prosecutions for war crimes.[21]

The Nuremberg precedent

After the Second World War, an important precedent for later mechanisms to prosecute human rights violations was set by the Nuremberg and Tokyo trials. The Holocaust and other atrocities committed by the Nazi regime called for the punishment of its military and civilian leaders.[22] The total victory of the allied powers, the occupation of Germany and Japan, the 'denazification' of Germany and the founding of the United Nations, made judicial tribunals feasible.[23] At the International Military Tribunal (IMT) for the Far East, 28 Japanese war criminals stood trial. The IMT at Nuremberg prosecuted 22 political, military and economic leaders of Nazi Germany for crimes against peace, war crimes and crimes against humanity. Despite accusations of imposing victor's justice, 'Nuremberg' set an important precedent for the later incarnation of international criminal justice. Most important, the IMT penetrated what Henry King called 'the veil of national sovereignty'.[24] According to King, the IMT did so by recognising that individuals have international human rights, even if the sovereign denies them those rights; that state authorisation provides no cover for the violations of those rights; and that, by judging that individuals have obligations under international law that go above, and might be contrary to, obligations to the sovereign state, they can be punished internationally for violating these obligations.[25] Moreover, the IMTs were 'international' in that the judges and prosecutors were nationals of the allied powers and prosecuted nationals of the axis powers, although the tribunals were not established internationally but by the allied powers after their victory over the axis powers.[26]

The aftermath of World War II and the procedures at Nuremberg and Tokyo also led to further codification of international norms, most notably those concerning crimes against humanity and genocide. In 1948, the General Assembly adopted the Genocide Convention in which genocide was defined and contracting parties agreed genocide would be a crime under international law.[27] The four Geneva Conventions of 12 August 1949 revised the three earlier treaties from 1864, 1906 and 1929, and adopted a fourth convention defining humanitarian protections for civilians in war.[28] Article 13 of the UN Charter states that the General Assembly 'shall initiate studies and make recommendations for the purpose of [...] encouraging the progressive development of international law and its codification'.[29] It was in that light that, in 1950, the International Law Commission (ILC) adopted the seven Nuremberg Principles on war crimes, of which principle VI sets out that crimes against peace, war crimes and crimes against humanity are crimes under international law.[30] In 1977, two additional protocols to the Geneva Conventions were adopted, relating to the protection of victims of international armed conflicts and non-international armed conflicts.[31]

The UN system

The horrors of the Second World War also led to the establishment of the UN itself. The UN Charter was signed on 26 June 1945 in San Francisco, reflecting a determination, among other things, to 'reaffirm faith in fundamental human rights' and 'establish conditions under which justice and respect for the obligations arising from treaties and other sources of international law can be maintained'.[32] However, both Dan Plesch and Mark Mazower argue that the actual birth of the UN was the adoption of the 'Declaration by United Nations' in Washington DC, on 1 January 1942, and that there is continuity between the wartime 'United Nations' and the post-war United Nations Organisation as created by the Charter.[33] The UN inherited the League of Nations institutions, but was 'above all a means of keeping the wartime coalition of Great Powers intact'.[34] The wartime origin of the new organisation was obscured so that it could start with a clean slate as a peace organisation, and be put on 'a pedestal of moral virtue'.[35] This was easily done as the losers of WWII rather forgot that part of history, and the USSR and United States soon started to dislike the idea that they established the UN together as allies.[36] Yet the origins of the UN as a fighting alliance can still be seen in the system of the Charter, which resonates that it was 'created as an organisation with an expectation both that compromise between the powerful was necessary and that violence might again have to be met with violence'.[37] The system of the Charter provides for force to be used in certain circumstances, but often only if agreement between the great powers can be reached.

The system of UN Security Council measures that the Charter provided for was instrumental in bringing international criminal justice into existence. The Charter codified the principle of state sovereignty – the principle on which the international state system had been built since the peace of Westphalia – in Article 2(4). But, in Chapter VII, it provided for a mechanism in case these norms were violated. The Charter codified the existing right of individual, or collective, self-defence in Article 51. Yet the Chapter VII mechanism, in Article 39, grants the Security Council the power to determine the existence of any 'threat to the peace, breach of the peace, or act of aggression'. Moreover, it gives the Council the possibility to ask members to take non-military (Article 41) and military (Article 42) measures to restore international peace and security.[38] Eventually, the Chapter VII system proved to be instrumental in the establishment of the first modern international criminal tribunals: in the 1990s the ICTY and ICTR would be established as measures to maintain and restore international peace and security.[39]

After the Nuremberg and Tokyo trials, the subsequent additions to the codified body of international criminal law and the establishment of the UN system, it took over 40 years before these mechanisms of international criminal justice were established, mainly because the ink of the UN Charter was not even dry when animosities between Eastern and Western blocs paralysed the Security Council and prevented the system from working as envisaged. This not only prevented actions taken under Chapter VII, it also made the prosecution of violations of humanitarian law through international judicial institutions virtually impossible.[40] The period between 1945 and 1990 was marked by countless acts of violence that could have been qualified as breaches of the peace, threats to the peace or acts of aggression, many of them involving violations of international humanitarian law. Yet, during the Cold War, the Security Council could only agree to determine a situation a 'threat to international peace and security' ten times, five of which contained an explicit reference to Chapter VII.[41]

A 'new world order': the UN Security Council and Iraq

With the end of the Cold War, 44 years after the signing of the Charter, the stalemate in the Security Council came to an end. The system was put to the test almost immediately. When Iraq invaded Kuwait in 1990, the Council for the first time in its existence was able to react in the manner foreseen in the Charter. It acted with speed and, only four days after the invasion, imposed a trade embargo under Article 41 of the Charter, and affirmed the right to collective self-defence in UN Security Council Resolution 661 of 6 August 1990.[42] Resolution 678 of 29 November 1990 set a deadline for Iraq to withdraw from Kuwait before 15 January 1991, and was the basis for large-scale military action led by the United States, Saudi Arabia, France and the United Kingdom (Operation Desert Storm), starting on 17 January 1991.[43] Forty days later, Saddam Hussein withdrew from Kuwait. It was also the first time the Council endorsed action purely to protect civilians nominally within the sovereign jurisdiction of a state when, in Resolution 688, the Council condemned 'the repression of the Iraqi civilian population in many parts of Iraq, including most recently in Kurdish populated areas, the consequences of which threaten international peace and security in the region'.[44]

The reaction of the Council to the invasion of Kuwait led to widespread optimism about its functioning. It renewed hope that the UN Charter would be taken seriously as an instrument of collective responsibility.[45] But the Gulf War also made clear that interstate conflicts such as this had become increasingly exceptional and that the main threat to international stability no longer came from states waging war against each other. It was in this light that, in January 1992, the UN Security Council heads of state and government recognised those changes when they stated that:

> The absence of war and military conflicts amongst States does not in itself ensure international peace and security. The non-military sources of instability in the economic, social, humanitarian and ecological fields have become threats to peace and security.[46]

This formal reinterpretation by the Security Council of what constituted a 'threat to international peace and security' meant that violations of international humanitarian law could be formally determined to be such a threat. The Council thereby widened the legal possibility for the UN Security Council to sanction measures to restore the peace, under Chapter VII of the Charter.

Widening the legal possibility to take measures against violations of humanitarian law alone did not lead to the establishment of mechanisms of international criminal justice. It created the possibility of doing so, but other factors that prompted the establishment of the first international tribunals were all consequences of the end of the Cold War. The international community was confronted with the horrendous violations of humanitarian law in conflicts in Yugoslavia, Rwanda and Somalia, and with 'blue helmets' who proved unable to prevent gross human rights violations and even genocide. Despite the hope for a 'new world order', the international community demonstrated its inability, and/or lack of political will, to prevent the most horrible atrocities committed in these conflicts.

The ICTY and ICTR and the era of reincarnation of international criminal justice

By 1993, the international community had proved unable to stop the war in Yugoslavia, and the horrible atrocities committed in it. The widespread violations of international humanitarian law included 'mass forcible expulsion and deportation of civilians', 'imprisonment and abuse of civilians in detention centres', deliberate attacks on non-combatants, hospitals and ambulances, and the massive, organised and systematic detention and rape of women.[47] The Security Council had expressed alarm and strongly condemned these acts, but it had been unable to stop them. In the belief that prosecuting the individuals responsible for violations of international humanitarian law 'would contribute to ensuring that such violations were halted and effectively redressed', the Security Council established an international tribunal in May 1993.[48] The Security

Council did so by Resolution 827, and acting under Chapter VII, as a tool to restore and maintain peace and security.[49]

In 1994, a year after the establishment of the ICTY, this time faced with its painful failure to prevent genocide in Rwanda, the Security Council used a Chapter VII resolution to establish the ICTR.[50] The genocide in Rwanda started when old conflicts between Hutu and Tutsi intensified after the plane of Hutu President Habyarimana was shot down in April 1994. While the conflict in Yugoslavia had an international dimension after the constituent republics declared independence, the external dimension of Rwanda was limited to refugees fleeing the country and militias regrouping across the borders. Yet, the Rwandan Genocide happened at an incredible speed: 250,000 people were killed in the first two weeks of the massacre, and during the 100 days the massacre continued an estimated 500,000–800,000 Tutsi and moderate Hutu were killed.[51] All this despite the presence in Rwanda of the United Nations Assistance Mission For Rwanda (UNAMIR) to aid the implementation of the Arusha Accords that had been signed less than a year earlier to end the Rwandan Civil War. UNAMIR Force Commander Roméo Dallaire, in his book *Shake Hands with the Devil: The Failure of Humanity in Rwanda*, described how an under-staffed UNAMIR (with only 270 soldiers left after the withdrawal of contingents of soldiers from several countries), uncertainty about their mandate and use of force to protect civilians, coupled with UN indecision, left him powerless to prevent atrocities on a massive scale.[52]

Both the ICTY and the ICTR came into being following failure to act and inability to prevent gross human rights violations by the international community, but these *ad hoc* tribunals also created momentum for further developments in the field of international criminal justice. The ILC took advantage of this by completing a draft statute for an international criminal court.[53] However, by the time the Rome Statute for the ICC was signed in 1998, the initial spirit of optimism about the collaboration between the five permanent members of the Security Council had already started to subside. By the late 1990s, *ad hoc* courts were no longer politically viable and the international community was suffering from tribunal fatigue.[54] The ICTY and ICTR had not always operated as quickly and effectively during their first years of existence as many had hoped. As *The Economist* had predicted, in 1990, 'the blessed unanimity of the Security Council' had ended, 'along with all that lovely talk about the new world order'.[55] The events of 11 September 2001 and the subsequent wars in Afghanistan and Iraq made the environment even less favourable for international criminal justice.

The Rome Statute and hybrid tribunals

While the ICTY and ICTR were established under Chapter VII, and redefined the limits of state sovereignty where human rights were violated, hybrid courts like the SCSL and the Extraordinary Chambers in the Courts of Cambodia, established in 2001 and 2003, were established at the request of the governments of the states in which the crimes were committed.[56] The STL, although established at the request of the government of Prime Minister Fouad Siniora, and pursuant to an agreement between the Lebanese government and the UN, was established by Resolution 1757 in May 2007.[57] The Council had to use its Chapter VII powers to establish a court because the Lebanese government could not reach agreement on ratification, but the narrow margin it passed showed hesitance among some of its members to use Chapter VII powers again to establish an international court.

The Rome Statute provided the ICC with jurisdiction to prosecute the 'most serious crimes of concern to the international community as a whole', encompassing war crimes, crimes against humanity and genocide.[58] While *ad hoc* tribunals depended directly on the political will among members of the Security Council to establish them, the ICC, being a permanent court, could initiate investigations, indict suspects and prosecute independently. In theory, this gives the court more ability to act on legal grounds instead of political considerations. This was an enormous step forward for international criminal justice, barring the fact that, for the foreseeable future, the Court would lack anything closely resembling universal jurisdiction.

Looking at what was accomplished, 122 states had by 2013 agreed that crimes taking place on their territory or committed by their nationals were subject to the jurisdiction of the ICC.[59] By Resolution 1593, the Security Council referred the crimes committed in Darfur to the ICC in 2005.[60] And by unanimously adopting Resolution 1970 in February 2011, the Security Council referred the crisis in Libya to the ICC.[61] Neier notes that while China, Russia and the United States are not themselves parties to the Rome Statute their vote in favour of the resolution on Libya reflected global acceptance of the role of the Court.[62]

The purpose of international criminal justice

It has been argued that the *ad hoc* tribunals, which spurred the developments made in international criminal justice since the early 1990s, were set up out of a sense of guilt and that they should, therefore, be seen as merely symbolic gestures.[63] It is true that the ICTY and ICTR were established after the inability, or lack of will, of the international community to prevent war crimes, crimes against humanity and genocide in the former Yugoslavia and Rwanda, and even some among those establishing the tribunals might not have expected them to have much effect.[64] Yet, the continuation of these courts and the establishment of new courts like the ICC suggest that they are more than very expensive symbolic gestures and they have some sort of desired effect.[65]

The high hopes and expectations many people have for the prosecution of war criminals and *génocidaires* give significant reason to devote attention to the potential efficacy of international criminal justice. Arguably, these high hopes and expectations are a better reason to look at the effectiveness of international criminal justice than the use of resources – in terms of time, money and expertise – it requires. Unsurprisingly, scholars have indeed studied the (potential) effectiveness of international criminal justice ever since the first modern *ad hoc* tribunals were established in the early 1990s. However, their conclusions differ as widely as the methods they use to reach these conclusions. This is not surprising, because to reach a conclusion about effectiveness one has to define what the desired results of international criminal justice should be, and also to determine whether the capability to produce these desired results is sufficient to be considered successful. Most arduous, even when merely assessing the effects of international criminal proceedings, one has to find a method to measure their results and establish a causal link between outcomes and the existence of international criminal justice.

Measuring the success of international criminal justice

First, different benchmarks for success lead to vastly different conclusions about effectiveness. Before looking at the complicated task of measuring the effects of international criminal justice, one could wonder at what point international prosecution can be considered a success. The ICC admits that the Rome Statute embodies high aspirations for the work of the Court.[66] Katherine Marshall argues that 'lofty goals have made it difficult for the ICC to meet expectations'.[67] Steven Freeland rightly remarks that:

> if success is to be regarded as a complete cessation of all wars, and an end to gross violations of human rights throughout the world, then it is obvious that the system of international criminal justice can never be effective.[68]

This would be an unfair expectation of international criminal justice. By its very nature, international criminal justice operates after the criminal act, so ending all human rights violations is more than can be expected of it. Alternatively, it has been suggested that assessing the 'numbers' can measure the success of international criminal justice. Lillian Barria and Steven Roper, for instance, suggest looking at the indictments handed down and the actual numbers of individuals apprehended to measure effectiveness.[69] By that standard, at least, the ICTY and ICTR eventually proved successful.[70] Aryeh Neier, among many others, indeed quotes the high numbers of indictees brought to trial to conclude that the *ad hoc* tribunals have been successful.

However, the numbers of indicted individuals, the percentages of those standing trial or the conviction rate of tribunals, do not paint a complete picture of the impact of the proceedings.[71] International tribunals are inherently selective; they are established to prosecute those 'most responsible' for the commission of 'the most heinous' crimes. This has not always been the case. The ICTY, in its early years, prosecuted many individuals who carried out, rather than ordered, murderous plans. Trials before any international court, by their very nature, will be complex, detailed and lengthy, and require large resources in terms of expertise, time and money.[72] International courts will therefore indict only a limited number of the individuals who committed crimes under international criminal law, and this will depend on the cooperation of states for successful prosecutions. In itself, the selectiveness of international tribunals does not say anything about their effectiveness; if the goal is to prosecute only those ordering crimes, they can still be effective in reaching these goals by prosecuting a limited number of individuals. But, even to prosecute only a few perpetrators successfully, the courts mainly depend on states – either directly or through the UN – for the funding of these expensive proceedings. These costs are often quoted in debates over its effectiveness, but where some argue that you cannot put a price on justice, others argue that nothing costing this much can be worthwhile.[73] A debate over the break-even point of international criminal justice eventually boils down to a political question. Or as Freeland put it: 'how much international criminal justice are we prepared to pay for?'[74]

The justifications and goals of international criminal justice

The political question of benchmarks for success aside, different studies also attribute different justifications and goals to international criminal justice. Success and effectiveness ultimately depend on the goals set. Some argue that the justifications and objectives of international criminal justice should be derived only from the establishing documents of international courts – that one should stick to the 'black letter of the law'.[75] Cedric Ryngaert, on the other hand, argues that the

> purpose and mission as interpreted by the tribunal's actors themselves [e.g. the prosecutor as opposed to the political operators behind the scenes] should be used as the primary point of reference for an effectiveness assessment of the work of the tribunals.[76]

There also is a wide range of other stakeholders, from victims to human rights advocates, from suspects to states and even the international community as a whole. At times, the objectives of stakeholders in international criminal justice may play a role in proceedings. It has been argued, for instance, that the objectives of victims should be taken into consideration by international tribunals.[77] Some stakeholders indeed exercise considerable influence on proceedings, e.g. States Party to the ICC, or members of the Security Council, when referring cases to the ICC.[78] Yet the justifications and objectives laid down by political operators in establishing documents, and their interpretation by practitioners, are the sources primarily shaping international justice and should therefore be the primary concern when assessing its impact.[79]

The establishing documents of the ICTY, ICTR and ICC show many similarities regarding their justifications and objectives. UN Security Council Resolution 827, establishing the ICTY, lists as its purpose 'to bring to justice the persons who are responsible [for serious violations of international humanitarian law]', to 'contribute to ensuring that such violations are halted and effectively redressed', and to 'contribute to the restoration and maintenance of peace'.[80]

Resolution 955, establishing the ICTR, uses the same phrasing but attributes to the court the additional aim to 'contribute to the process of national reconciliation'.[81] The Rome Statute justifies punishment by the ICC with the affirmation that 'the most serious crimes of concern to the international community as a whole must not go unpunished and that their effective prosecution must be ensured' and expresses the aim 'to put an end to impunity for the perpetrators of these crimes and thus to contribute to the prevention of such crimes'.[82]

The justifications and objectives of international tribunals, as described by the courts, generally follow the justifications laid down in their establishing documents. The Appeals Chamber of the ICTY, in *Prosecutor v. Aleksovski*, emphasises that 'a purpose of sentencing for international crimes' is 'to deter others from committing similar crimes'.[83] But the Appeals Chamber concurs with its own statement in *Prosecutor v. Tadic* that 'this factor must not be accorded undue prominence in the overall assessment of the sentences to be imposed on persons convicted by the International Tribunal'.[84] The Appeals Chamber explains that retribution is an equally important factor, but that this 'is not to be understood as fulfilling a desire for revenge but as duly expressing the outrage of the international community at these crimes'.[85] In this case, and in other cases before the ICTY and ICTR, it is expressed that one purpose of sentences, and by extension of the tribunal, is to 'make plain the condemnation of the international community' and show 'that the international community shall not tolerate the serious violations of international humanitarian law and human rights'.[86] The ICC expressed 'high aspirations' to contribute to 'an end to impunity for perpetrators of the most serious international crimes, the prevention of such crimes and lasting respect for and the enforcement of international justice'.[87]

The establishing documents and their interpretation by international courts reveal a hybrid system of justification for punishment analogous to most domestic justice systems. However, analogies between international criminal justice and national systems are also problematic because the former aims to combine the traditions of international law and criminal law.[88] While the former is horizontal, and relies on consensus between equal states, the latter is a vertical, coercive system ideally expressing the common values and norms of a community.[89] Yet, analogies are inevitable because international criminal justice relies on many of the same means, justifications and assumptions about punishment used in national systems.[90] As in domestic systems, punishment under international criminal justice is justified by both backward-looking and forward-looking considerations.[91] There are two classic theories of punishment – retribution and utilitarianism – and the purposes ascribed to the punishment of perpetrators of humanitarian violations generally fit within one of these.[92]

Backward- and forward-looking considerations for punishment

The retributive considerations of international criminal justice are based on restoring a moral wrong, or restoring a sense of justice. They are based on the belief that wrongdoing should be punished in a way appropriate to the criminal conduct.[93] Those believing that retribution is the only justification for punishment argue that the future conduct of the offender, or of society, is extraneous to the purpose of punishment.[94] Utilitarian justifications for punishment are forward-looking in that they are based on the possibility of desired effects in the future. They are based on a greater utility for the majority of people found in punishing an individual. As in domestic systems, the main utilitarian justifications of international criminal justice are general and special prevention, or deterrence of future criminal conduct.[95]

The objectives of international criminal tribunals regarding deterrence, the 'restoration and maintenance of peace', 'national reconciliation' and 'prosecuting and punishing those most responsible for the crimes committed' have been defined in very broad terms.[96] Moreover, there is a long list of subsidiary purposes that, at times, have been ascribed to international criminal prosecutions.[97] Minna Schrag lists those most commonly given as:

> To bring a sense of justice to war-torn places; to re-establish the rule of law; to provide a sound foundation for lasting peace; to bring repose to victims and provide an outlet to end cycles of violence and revenge; to demonstrate that culpability is individual, and not the responsibility of entire groups; to provide a safe forum for victims to tell their stories; to demonstrate fairness and the highest standards of due process; to provide exemplary procedures to serve as a model for rebuilding a legal system; to create an accurate historical record; public education in general; to develop and expand the application and interpretation of international law and norms; to provide a forum for considering restitution and reparations.[98]

However, most of these additional aims are primarily aims of international criminal justice procedures rather than aims of punishment.[99] For instance, the aim to produce a reliable historical record of the events and the background to the crimes committed to prevent future falsification or corruption of the facts for political gain.[100] It is also true of the often-named objective of international justice in which international tribunals are seen as a forum to give victims of atrocities a voice and to work towards reinforcement of rule of law norms, developing a culture of accountability and creating respect for judicial institutions and their influence on domestic justice.[101] At times, even the roles of international courts in the interpretation of international criminal law and the creation of case law have been described as objectives, rather than consequences, of rendering judgements.

Replacing collective responsibility with individual responsibility

Justification for punishment, often quoted in domestic systems – special prevention by rehabilitation for instance – is generally considered to play a less significant role in international criminal justice. In contrast to the rehabilitation of individuals, the rehabilitation of communities is considered to be an aim of international prosecutions and important in post-conflict state building and reconciliation. It is argued that, by holding individuals responsible for crimes, the perception is avoided that ethnic, religious or political groups are collectively responsible.[102] As the late Antonio Cassese explained to the UN General Assembly, 'Collective responsibility must be replaced by individual responsibility. Only international justice can dissolve the poisonous fumes of resentment and suspicion, and put to rest the lust for revenge.'[103]

Payam Akhavan correctly stated that crimes under international law should not be simplistically explained by 'myths of primordial "tribal" hatred' or 'expressions of spontaneous blood lust or inevitable historical cataclysms'.[104] These crimes are often the result of 'deliberate incitement of ethnic hatred and violence by which ruthless demagogues and warlords elevated themselves to positions of absolute power'.[105] The removal of individual leaders, and their punishment, is therefore likely to have a positive effect on post-conflict society. However, despite individual liability, expressed in international criminal justice, most acts that constitute crimes under international law are committed in, or by, an organised group. At least, in situations deemed grave enough to prosecute, the role of the individual can only be understood and explained within the framework of a state or QSE.[106]

War crimes are violations of the laws of armed conflict applicable to armed conflict between groups, and although a single individual can commit them, that individual has to be part of a group. For crimes against humanity, it is necessary that conduct was 'committed as part of a widespread, or systematic, attack directed against a civilian population' and that the perpetrator had knowledge of this wider plan.[107] Although, in theory, a single person could commit genocide, as a practical matter it almost always involves a *shared*, specific 'intent to destroy, in whole or in part, a national, ethnical, racial or religious group, as such'.[108] According to Kenneth Anderson, the emphasis on individual liability takes the emphasis away from the nature of how these crimes are committed, namely as part of a corporate activity.[109] Robert Sloane notes that international crimes also characteristically involve 'a collective or corporate mental state, a consciousness of action on behalf of or in furtherance of a collective project'.[110]

Because committing crimes under international law is usually an organised activity, tensions could arise between the desired preventive effect of international criminal courts and the perceived retributive effects. According to Mirjan Damaška, the individuals whose convictions are best suited to producing the preventive effects are seldom those from whose conviction the victims of crimes derive the greatest satisfaction.[111] Victims often have stronger retributive feelings towards the 'executioners' of crimes – as those are more recognisable, and who in Rwanda and Bosnia may well have been their neighbour – than towards the leaders who did not physically commit the crime.[112] But, in light of the preventive effects and other wider aims of international criminal justice, prosecuting political and military leaders is the primary aim of courts, not least because their convictions can be expected to contribute to a wider sense of accountability for gross human rights violations.[113]

A hierarchy of objectives of international criminal justice?

As there is no consensus on which goals of international prosecution should be prioritised, tensions may arise between them.[114] The establishing documents and the case law created by the courts do not create a hierarchy among the various objectives of international prosecution. For instance, tension may arise between providing 'utmost fairness to the accused' and 'special protections for victims'.[115] However, the examples most often given are when 'justice' and 'peace' are at odds, for instance when a leader that is prosecuted, or would be prosecuted when out of power, is unwilling to give up power, and when international criminal justice might hamper peace negotiations. Although this situation is not unthinkable, Neier argues that there is no example, yet, that can be cited, where holding officials accountable for war crimes, crimes against humanity and genocide has actually been proven to have negatively interfered with a peace settlement.[116] Creating an accurate historical record may at times be at odds with post-conflict peace building, or reconciliation, if it fails to avoid collective responsibility. For reconciliation the discourse that atrocities were incited by a small group of leaders (who can then be prosecuted) would be advantageous. Although this may be true, the inciting narratives of these leaders often fit pre-existing nationalist or ethnic tensions.[117]

Despite the hybrid system of justification for international criminal justice lacking a clear hierarchy between its retributive and utilitarian justifications and objectives, the establishing documents, the case law produced by tribunals and the statements of international law practitioners point towards three aims that resonate across the different existing mechanisms for international criminal prosecution. They are the retributive justification: (1) 'to do justice', and the utilitarian goals; (2) 'to deter further crimes'; and (3) 'to contribute to the restoration and maintenance of peace'.[118] Although retribution has been the dominant justification for punishment throughout history, and both establishing documents and practitioners use it as a justification for punishment under international law to assess the effectiveness of international criminal justice, focusing on the backward-looking considerations for punishment is problematic.[119] According to Immanuel Kant:

> Judicial punishment can never be used merely as a means to promote some other good for the criminal himself or for civil society, but instead it must in all cases be imposed on him only on the ground that he has committed a crime.[120]

When taking a purely retributionist standpoint like Kant's, retribution has no other legitimate goal than the punishment itself, making the measurement of any outcomes for the criminal himself, or for civil society, nonsensical. Even if retribution is not understood 'as fulfilling a desire for revenge but as duly expressing the outrage of the international community', it is impossible to gauge whether enough outrage has been expressed.[121]

In a hybrid system such as international criminal justice, it therefore makes more sense to focus on forward-looking goals than to attempt to measure whether 'justice is done'.[122] A wide range of studies conducted over the years used a variety of methods to prove the effects of international criminal justice towards its utilitarian justification.[123] Despite the different outcomes of these studies there seems to be agreement that measurement of the effects of international criminal justice is either very difficult or altogether impossible.[124] Practitioners also acknowledge this. For instance, former US Ambassador-at-Large for War Crimes Issues, David Scheffer, although of the opinion that there is 'a possible deterrence effect', sees proof for neither the existence of deterrence, nor for its absence, because '[h]ow do you prove the state of mind of a perpetrator of these crimes?'[125] It is even harder to prove the state of mind of a potential perpetrator who was deterred from committing human rights violations by the existence, or threat, of international criminal justice.

Measuring deterrence: looking into the heads of war criminals and génocidaires

While it is true that it is impossible to look inside the heads of (potential) perpetrators, Julian Ku and Jide Nzelibe argue that 'it is not clear that such proof is at all necessary to measure the likelihood of deterrence'.[126] They propose an approach utilising economic models of deterrence to assess the likelihood of a potential perpetrator being deterred by the risk of future prosecution by an international court.[127] According to their model, the certainty and severity of punishment and the individual's preference for risk have to be taken into consideration, as well as the likelihood and severity of other (extra-legal) sanctions.[128] They come to the conclusion that the influence of international criminal justice is marginal because likely perpetrators of atrocities (according to their study of African dictators and coup plotters) are likely to suffer a worse fate than being sent to The Hague.[129] Economic models of deterrence are problematic because they do not take other factors, such as the likelihood and severity of punishment, into consideration. Ku and Nzelibe depend on a predetermined pool of likely perpetrators and a lot of data is needed. In their research, the pool of perpetrators that is likely to be indicted by, *and* transferred to, international courts is composed of 'individuals in weak states who have been forced from political power', *in casu.* former African dictators, failed coup plotters and ex-leaders of QSEs.[130] The outcome that, for this group, extra-judicial punishment at home often proves more terrifying than the prospect of 'The Hague' was strengthened when Congolese war crimes suspect and rebel general, Bosco Ntaganda turned to the ICC in March 2013 in order to stay alive after his understanding with the Congolese government fell through and his M23 militia turned against him.[131] Yet, the potential cases on which they base their research is limited, looking solely at individual deterrence and disregarding the reality that international criminal justice does not lend itself to statistical analysis very well.

In national criminal justice systems, statistics are often used to measure the impact of criminal justice. The correlation between justice administered and the absence of crimes, or a drop in the crime rate, may be established by analysing data. However, Song Sang-Hyun, the president of the ICC, notes that while in national systems data with statistical relevance can be produced, a 'similar exercise is far more difficult with regard to atrocity crimes. Every situation is unique and each conflict has its specific historical and political setting'.[132] Similar problems arise when assessing the effect of international criminal justice on post-conflict state building. There is evidence to suggest that it has a positive effect on post-conflict societies, but relevant data cannot be produced. It is impossible to know how Bosnia would have fared today without the ICTY, or Rwanda without the ICTR. Song admits that causality is the greatest challenge as 'there are so many factors affecting the occurrence of atrocities that it is almost close to impossible to determine what the effect of deterrence is'.[133]

Song, like many others, nevertheless believes that a deterrent effect is slowly emerging, but relies on anecdotal evidence to come to that conclusion.[134] It is often pointed out that the likelihood of punishment has grown and with the indictments of sitting heads of state by the ICC and ICTY, and the conviction of Charles Taylor – the first head of state since Karl Dönitz – somewhat ended impunity.[135] Akhavan, among others, believes that:

> [T]he symbolic effect of prosecuting even a limited number of the perpetrators, especially the leaders who planned and instigated the genocide, would have considerable impact on national reconciliation, as well as on deterrence of such crimes in the future.[136]

Antonio Cassese suggests that the failed efforts to punish the perpetrators of the Armenian genocide 'gave a nod and a wink to Adolf Hitler and others to pursue the Holocaust some twenty years later'.[137]

After his former protégé, Charles Taylor, was handed over to the SCSL in July 2007, *The Economist* quoted Libya's Colonel Gaddafi as saying: 'This means that every head of state could meet a similar fate. It sets a serious precedent'.[138] Freeland notices that the precedents set by international criminal justice gave rise to a 'Pinochet syndrome' and that 'the senior political and military leaders of today and tomorrow can no longer ignore the rule of law and the reach of the various systems of national and international criminal justice'.[139] Neier also concludes that high-ranking officials and state leaders have to take international prosecution into account, but he admits that: 'We do not know enough yet to be able to say for certain that this is acting as a deterrent. But it seems likely that it is a factor in some cases'.[140] The reality is that it remains incredibly difficult to establish a causal link between international criminal justice and deterrence. Or, as Ryngaert puts it: 'From an empirical perspective, clearly, the causal link between international criminal justice and a durable peace, political reconciliation, and the entrenchment of the rule of law has not yet been conclusively proven'.[141]

General prevention may work in different ways, by internalisation and deterrence. International criminal justice addresses leaders who operate on a programmatic level – 'the leaders responsible for planning, ordering, and instigating the crimes' – and those who carry out criminal plans.[142] According to Immi Tallgren, the latter group has:

> little or no influence on those features of the crimes that actually make them international; "with the intent to destroy, in whole or in part, a group", "as part of a widespread or systematic attack", "as part of a plan or policy or as part of a large-scale commission of such crimes".[143]

Adolf Hitler, Charles Taylor and Slobodan Milošević on the one hand, and Adolf Eichmann, Duško Tadić and Dražen Edermović on the other, all committed horrible crimes, but they did so in very different ways. The former as instigators, as the 'roots of evil', while the latter are what Harry Mulisch during the Eichmann trial called '*de kleinste mens*' or 'the smallest person'.[144] For the second group especially, the norms and values of the group they belong to are likely to carry more weight than those of the international community, and/or, the threats from within their own group may be greater than those posed to them by international criminal justice.[145] Internalisation of norms of international criminal law through international criminal justice is problematic too.

Every system of norms works on the basis that people believe in them, not because they are enforced. Although more international criminal proceedings may lead to more people believing that upholding the norms of international humanitarian law is important, the effect of group processes is likely to be stronger. Law, including international criminal law, has a function as a basis for punishment but, more important, it:

> matters as a legitimacy device, as a device for providing the social structure by which the law is accepted *by* one, rather than merely as a command backed by a threat *against* one.[146] It is sociological, insofar as it is Weberian in its appeal to legitimacy.[147]

The violation of law often has a delegitimating effect. As David Wippman observes, international criminal prosecutions may 'strengthen whatever internal bulwarks help individuals obey the rules of war, but the general deterrent effect of such prosecutions seems likely to be modest and incremental, rather than dramatic and transformative'.[148]

The impact international criminal justice has on legitimacy is more likely to affect those who take decisions, rather than those who execute orders. Those who led the organisations or entities in whose name international crimes are committed are typically directly affected by international criminal justice. Akhavan describes this phenomenon:

> Stigmatizing delinquent leaders through indictment, as well as apprehension and prosecution, undermines their influence. Even if wartime leaders still enjoy popular support among an indoctrinated public at home, exclusion from the international sphere can significantly impede their long-term exercise of power.[149]

It is this effect of international criminal justice, the impact on legitimacy, which is underestimated and deserves more attention. It is the point where the impact of the changing discourse – the use of an international criminal justice discourse – can be seen to create critical legitimacy moments for those implicated, or the entities that they represent.

Notes

1 R. Cryer *et al.*, *An Introduction to International Criminal Law and Procedure*, Cambridge: Cambridge University Press, 2007, p. 4, pp. 5–6.
2 UN Security Council Resolution 827, 25 May 1993.
3 The Rome Statute of the International Criminal Court, 17 July 1998, in force on 1 July 2002, United Nations Treaty Series, vol. 2187, no. 38544, Preamble.
4 R.C. Kerr, *The International Criminal Tribunal for the Former Yugoslavia: An Exercise in Law, Politics and Diplomacy*, Oxford: Oxford University Press, 2004, p. 21.
5 The legal maxim that a crime can only exist and can only be punished if a previously existing penal law is violated was first codified in the Bavarian Code of 1813 by Paul von Feuerbach, and has been incorporated into international criminal law.
6 Although it could be argued that the trial of Peter von Hagenbach in 1474, for atrocities committed during the occupation of Breisach, by a tribunal of the Holy Roman Empire, was the first case of international criminal justice. See: W.A. Schabas, *An Introduction to the International Criminal Court*, Cambridge: Cambridge University Press, 2007, p. 1; and E. Greppi, 'The Evolution of Individual Criminal Responsibility under International Law', *International Review of the Red Cross*, no. 835, September 1999, p. 1.
7 M.C. Bassiouni, 'Perspectives on International Justice', *Virginia Journal of International Law*, vol. 50, no. 2, 2010, pp. 269–323 at p. 285. See more generally on the history of international humanitarian law: M.C. Bassiouni, 'The Evolution of International Humanitarian Law and Arms Control Agreements'. In: M.C. Bassiouni (ed.), *A Manual on International Humanitarian Law and Arms Control Agreements*, Ardsley-on-Hudson, NY: Transnational Publishers, 2000.
8 A. Neier, 'International Criminal Justice: Developing into a Deterrent', *Openspace*, Open Society Initiative for Southern Africa, 5 March 2012, pp. 6–10, p. 8. Bassiouni, 'Perspective on International Justice', p. 285. See also: S. Neff, 'A Short History of International Law', in: M. Evans (ed.), *International Law*, 2nd edn, Oxford: Oxford University Press, 2006, pp. 29–55.
9 Grotius, *The Rights of War and Peace*, vol. 1, Preliminary Discourses.
10 H. Grotius, *De Iure Belli ac Pacis*, Leiden: E.J. Brill, 1939, (ed. B.J.A. de Kantervan Hettinga Tromp), (first published 1625) Prolegomena X, p. 17; Translation: H. Grotius, *The Rights of War and Peace*, edited and with an Introduction by R. Tuck, from the edition by J. Barbeyrac, Indianapolis: Liberty Fund, 2005, vol. 1, Preliminary Discourses.
11 Cryer, *An Introduction to International Criminal Law and Procedure*, p. 222.
12 Kerr, *The International Criminal Tribunal for the Former Yugoslavia*, p. 22.
13 Commission on the Responsibility of the Authors of the War and on Enforcement of Penalties, Report of the Commission on the Preliminary Peace Conference, 29 March, 1919. Reprinted in *American Journal of International Law*, vol. 14, no. 1, 1920, pp. 95–154, p. 128. Cryer, *An Introduction to International Criminal Law and Procedure*, p. 92. Bassiouni, 'Perspective on International Justice', pp. 302–303.
14 Cryer, *An Introduction to International Criminal Law and Procedure*, p. 92. Treaty of Versailles, 28 June 1919, Part VII 'Penalties', Art. 227.

15 Treaty of Versailles, Part VII 'Penalties', Art. 229. A. Kramer, 'The First Wave of International War Crimes Trials: Istanbul and Leipzig', *European Review*, vol. 14, no. 4, 2006, pp. 441–455, p. 446.
16 Ibid., p. 442.
17 Ibid.
18 Ibid., pp. 449–450.
19 Ibid., p. 441. Telegram sent by the US Department of State to the US Embassy in Constantinople, 29 May 1915, containing the Allied joint declaration of 24 May 1915.
20 Kramer, 'The First Wave of International War Crimes Trials', p. 442, p. 444.
21 Ibid., p. 451.
22 Kerr, *The International Criminal Tribunal for the Former Yugoslavia*, p. 23.
23 R. Overy, 'The Nuremberg Trials: International Law in the Making', in: P. Sands (ed.), *From Nuremberg to The Hague: The Future of International Criminal Justice*, Cambridge: Cambridge University Press, 2003, p. 5. Kerr, *The International Criminal Tribunal for the Former Yugoslavia*, p. 23.
24 H.T. King, 'Nuremberg and Sovereignty', *Case Western Reserve Journal of International Law*, vol. 28, 1996, pp. 135–140, p. 137.
25 Ibid.
26 J. Gow, *War and War Crimes: The Military, Legitimacy and Success in Armed Conflict*, London: Hurst and Co., 2013, pp. 51–54, 59.
27 UN General Assembly Resolution 260 of 9 December 1948.
28 Geneva Convention relative to the Protection of Civilian Persons in Time of War, Geneva, 12 August 1949.
29 Charter of the United Nations, San Francisco, 26 June 1945, Art. 13(1).
30 Principles of International Law Recognized in the Charter of the Nürnberg Tribunal and in the Judgment of the Tribunal, 1950, Principle VI.
31 Protocol Additional to the Geneva Conventions of 12 August 1949, and relating to the Protection of Victims of International Armed Conflicts (Protocol I), 8 June 1977. Protocol Additional to the Geneva Conventions of 12 August 1949, and relating to the Protection of Victims of Non-International Armed Conflicts (Protocol II), 8 June 1977.
32 Charter of the United Nations, Preamble.
33 D. Plesch, 'How the United Nations Beat Hitler and Prepared the Peace', *Global Society*, vol. 22, no. 1, 2008, pp. 137–158, p. 137. D. Plesch, *America, Hitler and the UN: How the Allies Won World War II and Forged Peace*, London: I.B. Taurus, 2011, pp. 8–9. M. Mazower, *Governing the World: The History of an Idea*, New York: Penguin Press, 2012, p. 206.
34 Mazower, *Governing the World*, p. 212.
35 Ibid.
36 Plesch, *America, Hitler and the UN*, pp. 8–9.
37 Ibid., p. 158.
38 Charter of the United Nations, Chapter VII.
39 For a discussion on the ICTY as a measure to 'restore and maintain' rather than 'restore', 'maintain' or 'restore or maintain' international peace and security, see: M. Futamura and J. Gow, 'The Strategic Purpose of the ICTY and International Peace and Security', in: J. Gow, R. Kerr and Ž. Pajić, (2013) *Prosecuting War Crimes*, London: Routledge, pp. 15–28, p. 17.
40 A. Cassese, 'On the Current Trends towards Criminal Prosecution and Punishment of Breaches of International Humanitarian Law', *European Journal of International Law*, vol. 9, 1998, pp. 2–17, p. 7.
41 For a detailed description of Chapter VII actions during the Cold War, see: P. Fifoot, 'Functions and Powers, and Inventions: UN Action in Respect of Human Rights and Humanitarian Intervention', in: N.S. Rodley (ed.), *To Loose the Bands of Wickedness: International Intervention in Defence of Human Rights*, London: Brassey's, 1992, pp. 133–164, at pp. 148–155.

42 UN Security Council Resolution 661, 6 August 1990.
43 UN Security Council Resolution 678, 29 November 1990.
44 UN Security Council Resolution 688, 5 April 1991.
45 Schachter, 'United Nations Law in the Gulf Conflict', p. 452.
46 Note by the President of the Security Council, S/25300, 31 January 1992, p. 3.
47 UN Security Council Resolution 771, 13 August 1992. UN Security Council Resolution 780, 6 October 1992. UN Security Council Resolution 798, 18 December 1992, UN Security Council Resolution 808, 22 February 1993.
48 UN Security Council Resolution 827, 25 May 1993.
49 For a more detailed account of the establishment of the ICTY, see Chapter 4, this book.
50 S/RES/955, 8 November 1994.
51 A. Des Forges, *Leave No One to Tell the Story: Genocide in Rwanda*, New York: Human Rights Watch, 1999, p. 15; Barria and Roper, 'How Effective are International Criminal Tribunals?' p. 353.
52 R. Dallaire, *Shake Hands with the Devil: The Failure of Humanity in Rwanda*, London: Random House, 2003.
53 Kerr, *The International Criminal Tribunal for the Former Yugoslavia*, pp. 25–26. For more on the establishment of the ICC, in Chapter 6 this book, see The International Criminal Court: a decisive blow for impunity?
54 R.P. Alford, 'Proceedings of the Annual Meeting', American Society of International Law, vol. 94, 2000, pp. 160–165, p. 160. R. Kerr and E. Mobekk, *Peace and Justice: Seeking Accountability after War*, Cambridge: Polity, 2007, p. 30. R. Kerr, 'Introduction: Trials and Tribulations at the ICTY', in: J. Gow, R. Kerr and Z. Pajić (eds), *Prosecuting War Crimes: Lessons and Legacies of the International Criminal Tribunal for the Former Yugoslavia*, London: Routledge, 2013, pp. 1–14, p. 6.
55 *The Economist* (UK edition) 'New World Order Inc.', 10 November 1990, Issue 7680, p. 12.
56 Hybrid (or internationalised) courts combine both international and national features; they apply elements of both systems in their procedural and applicable law, and consist of international and local registrars, prosecutors and judges.
57 S/RES/1757, 30 May 2007. For more on the establishment of the STL, see: Chapter 5 this book, The Special Tribunal for Lebanon.
58 In future, the crime of aggression may be added to that list. See Chapter VI.
59 For more on the ratification of the Rome Statute, see Chapter VI.
60 S/RES 1593, 31 March 2005.
61 S/RES 1970, 26 February 2011.
62 Neier, 'International Criminal Justice: Developing into a Deterrent', p. 10.
63 C. Ryngaert (ed.), *The Effectiveness of International Criminal Justice*, Antwerp: Intersentia, 2009, p. ix. I. Tallgren, 'The Sensibility and Sense of International Criminal Law', *European Journal of International Law*, vol. 13, no. 3, 2002, pp. 561–595, p. 581.
64 Ryngaert, *The Effectiveness of International Criminal Justice*, p. ix.
65 'About ICTR': General Information. 'About the ICTY': The Cost of Justice. J. Silverman, 'Ten years, $900m, one verdict: Does the ICC cost too much?' *BBC News*, 14 March 2012.
66 Strategic Plan of the International Criminal Court, 4 August 2006, ICC-ASP/5/6, p. 2.
67 K.A. Marshall, 'Prevention and Complementarity in the International Criminal Court: A Positive Approach', *Human Rights Brief*, vol. 17, no. 2, 2010, pp. 21–26, p. 21.
68 S. Freeland, 'The "Effectiveness" of International Criminal Justice', *ALTA Law Research Series*, no. 16, 2008, pp. 1–9, p. 2.
69 Barria and Roper, 'How Effective are International Criminal Tribunals?' p. 349.

70 The ICTY, at long last, was able to apprehend the 161 individuals indicted that were still at large. After the arrest of Ladislas Ntaganzwa in March 2016, only 8 of the 92 individuals indicted by the ICTR remain at large. By mid-2016, of the 39 individuals publicly indicted by the ICC, 8 remain at large, most notably Joseph Kony and Omar al-Bashir. All five suspects indicted by the STL remained at large, and the STL made the unprecedented step (in international criminal justice) of undertaking proceedings *in absentia.*

71 Although the ICTY apprehended all individuals who remained at large, and the ICTR most of them, it took the better part of two decades to bring Ratko Mladić and Radovan Karadžić to The Hague.

72 Freeland, 'The "Effectiveness" of International Criminal Justice', p. 3.

73 See: Neier, 'International Criminal Justice: Developing into a Deterrent'.

74 Freeland, 'The "Effectiveness" of International Criminal Justice', p. 5.

75 Barria and Roper, 'How Effective are International Criminal Tribunals?' p. 349.

76 Ryngaert, *The Effectiveness of International Criminal Justice*, pp. ix–x.

77 See: R. Roth and M. Henzelin, 'The Appeal Procedure of the ICC', in: Cassese, Gaeta and. Jones (eds), *The Rome Statute of the International Criminal Court, A Commentary*, Oxford: Oxford University Press, 2002, p. 1551. M. Rauschenbach and D. Scalia, 'Victims and International Criminal Justice: A Vexed Question?' *International Review of the Red Cross*, vol. 90, no. 870, 2008, pp. 441–459.

78 Rome Statute Article 13.

79 Ryngaert, *The Effectiveness of International Criminal Justice*, p. x.

80 UN Security Council Resolution 827, 25 May 1993.

81 UN Security Council Resolution 955, 8 November 1994.

82 Rome Statute, Preamble.

83 *Prosecutor v. Aleksovski*, Case No. IT-95-14/1, 'Judgment', 24 March 2000, § 185.

84 Ibid.

85 Ibid. *Prosecutor v. Tadic*, Case N0: IT-94-1-A and A bis, Appeals Chamber, 26 January 2000, § 48.

86 *Prosecutor v. Aleksovski*, Judgment, 24 March, § 185. *Prosecutor v. Erdemovic*, Case No. IT-96-22-T, 'Sentencing judgement', 24 December 1996, §§ 21–24 and 64–65.

87 Strategic Plan of the International Criminal Court, 4 August 2006, ICC-ASP/5/6, p. 2.

88 Tallgren, 'The Sensibility and Sense of International Criminal Law', p. 562. R. Sloane, 'The Expressive Capacity of International Punishment', *Columbia Public Law and Legal Theory Working Papers*, Paper 06100, 2006, p. 2.

89 Tallgren, 'The Sensibility and Sense of International Criminal Law', p. 562. Sloane, 'The Expressive Capacity of International Punishment', p. 2. L. Arbour, 'Progress and Challenges in International Criminal Justice', *Fordham International Law Journal*, vol. 21, 1997, pp. 531–540, p. 531. R. Higgins, *Problems and Process: International Law and How We Use It*, Oxford: Clarendon Press, 1994, p. 1.

90 Tallgren, 'The Sensibility and Sense of International Criminal Law', p. 565.

91 If the backward-looking considerations prevail a system is called deontological, and if the forward-looking considerations prevail it is called consequentialist. International criminal justice considers both and is therefore 'hybrid'.

92 G.S. Yacoubian, 'Sanctioning Alternatives in International Criminal Law: Recommendations for the International Criminal Tribunals for Rwanda and Yugoslavia', *World Affairs*, vol. 161, no. 1, 1998, pp. 48–54.

93 Tallgren, 'The Sensibility and Sense of International Criminal Law', p. 579.

94 For more on retributive justifications of punishment, see A von Hirsch, *Doing Justice: The Choice of Punishments. Report of the Committee for the Study of Incarceration*, Boston: Northeastern University Press, 1976. I. Kant, *Metaphysics of Morals: Metaphysical Elements of Justice*, London: Hackett, 1887 (ed. John Ladd,

1999). Tallgren, 'The Sensibility and Sense of International Criminal Law'. Sloane, 'The Expressive Capacity of International Punishment'. G.S. Yacoubian, 'Evaluating the Efficacy of the International Criminal Tribunals for Rwanda and the Former Yugoslavia: Implications for Criminology and International Criminal Law', *World Affairs*, vol. 165, no. 3, 2003, pp. 133–141.

95 Tallgren, 'The Sensibility and Sense of International Criminal Law', p. 569.
96 M. Fedorova, S. Verhoeven, and J. Wouters, 'Safeguarding the Rights of Suspects and Accused in International Criminal Proceedings', *Institute for International Law Working Paper*, no. 27, June 2009, p. 5.
97 Ibid., p. 56.
98 M. Schrag, 'Lessons Learned from ICTY Experience', *Journal of International Criminal Justice*, vol. 2, no. 2, 2004, pp. 427–434, p. 428.
99 M.R. Damaška, 'What is the Point of International Criminal Justice?' *The Chicago-Kent Law Review*, vol. 83, no. 1, 2008, pp. 329–365, p. 331.
100 Damaška, 'What is the Point of International Criminal Justice?' p. 331 and 337–339.
101 J. Pejic, 'Creating a Permanent International Criminal Court: The Obstacles to Independence and Effectiveness', *Human Rights Law Review*, vol. 29, 1998, pp. 291–354.
102 Damaška, 'What is the Point of International Criminal Justice?' p. 330. J.E. Stromseth, 'Goals and Challenges in the Pursuit of Accountability', in: J.E. Stromseth (ed.), *Accountability for Atrocities: National and International Responses*, Ardsley, NY: Transnational Publishers, 2003, p. 7. Also see: UN Security Council Resolution 955, 8 November 1994, establishing the ICTR. *Prosecutor v. Nikolic*, Case No. IT-02-60/1-S, Sentencing Judgement, 2 December 2003. President of the ICTY, Annual Report of the ICTY, p. 16, UN Doc. A/49/342, (29 August 1994).
103 A. Cassese, President of the ICTY, Address to the General Assembly of the United Nations, 14 November 1994.
104 P. Akhavan, 'Beyond Impunity: Can International Criminal Justice Prevent Future Atrocities?' *American Journal of International Law*, vol. 95, 2001, pp. 7–31 at p. 7.
105 Ibid.
106 A. Nollkaemper, 'Systemic Effects of International Responsibility for International Crimes', *Santa Clara Journal of International Law*, vol. 8, no. 1 (2010) pp. 313–352, p. 314.
107 'Elements of Crimes', published by the ICC (2011). Rome Statute, Article 7.
108 Sloane, 'The Expressive Capacity of International Punishment', p. 23. The Trial Chamber of the ICTY deemed the case of the lone génocidaire theoretically possible in *Prosecutor v. Goran Jelisic*, IT-95-10-T, 'Judgment', 14 December 1999 Trial Chamber I, §§100–101.
109 K. Anderson, 'The Rise of International Criminal Law: Intended and Unintended Consequences', *European Journal of International Law*, vol. 20, no. 2, 2009, pp. 331–358, pp. 347–348.
110 Sloane, 'The Expressive Capacity of International Punishment', p. 23.
111 Damaška, 'What is the Point of International Criminal Justice?' pp. 334–335.
112 Ibid.
113 Ibid.
114 Schrag, 'Lessons Learned from ICTY Experience', p. 428.
115 Ibid.
116 Neier, 'International Criminal Justice: Developing into a Deterrent', p. 9.
117 Damaška, 'What is the Point of International Criminal Justice?' p. 332.
118 First Annual report of ICTY, 29 August 1994, UN Doc. A/49/342, §11.
119 See: H. Arendt, *The Human Condition*, Chicago: University of Chicago Press, 1958, p. 241. Sloane, 'The Expressive Capacity of International Punishment', p. 47.
120 Kant, *Metaphysics of Morals: Metaphysical Elements of Justice*, p. 138.

121 *Prosecutor v. Aleksovski*, Case No. IT-95-14/1, Judgment, (24 March 2000) Para. 185. *Prosecutor v. Tadic*, Case N0: IT-94-1-A and A bis, Appeals Chamber, 26 January 2000, § 48.
122 H. Arendt, *Eichmann in Jerusalem: A Report on the Banality of Evil*, New York: Penguin, 1963, p. 277.
123 See: Damaška, 'What is the Point of International Criminal Justice?' Sloane, 'The Expressive Capacity of International Punishment'. Akhavan, 'Beyond Impunity'. Tallgren, 'The Sensibility and Sense of International Criminal Law'. Anderson, 'The Rise of International Criminal Law'. Yacoubian, 'Evaluating the Efficacy of the International Criminal Tribunals for Rwanda and the Former Yugoslavia'. Ryngaert, *The Effectiveness of International Criminal Justice.* Song, 'From Punishment to Prevention'. Freeland, 'The "Effectiveness" of International Criminal Justice'. Barria and Roper, 'How Effective Are International Criminal Tribunals?'
124 Barria and Roper, 'How Effective are International Criminal Tribunals?' p. 349. J. Ku and J. Nzelibe, 'Do International Criminal Tribunals Deter or Exacerbate Humanitarian Atrocities?' *Washington University Law Review*, vol. 84, no. 4, 2006, pp. 777–833 at p. 791.
125 D. Scheffer, 'Should the United States Join the International Criminal Court?' *U.C. Davis Journal of International Law and Policy*, vol. 9, 2002, pp. 45–52, p. 51.
126 Ku and Nzelibe, 'Do International Criminal Tribunals Deter or Exacerbate Humanitarian Atrocities?' p. 791.
127 Ibid., p. 777.
128 Ibid.
129 Ibid., p. 832.
130 Ibid., p. 778.
131 'DR Congo: Bosco Ntaganda appears before ICC', *BBC News*, 26 March 2013.
132 Sang-Hyun Song, 'From Punishment to Prevention'.
133 Ibid.
134 Ibid.
135 Karl Dönitz, who had been Germany's *Reichspräsident* for less than a month following Adolf Hitler's suicide, was convicted by the IMT in Nuremberg and was sentenced to ten years imprisonment in 1946.
136 P. Akhavan, 'The International Criminal Tribunal for Rwanda: The Politics and Pragmatics of Punishment', *American Journal of International Law*, vol. 90, 1996, pp. 501–510, p. 509. M.C. Bassiouni, 'Justice and Peace: The Importance of Choosing Accountability over Realpolitik', *Case Western Reserve Journal of International Law*, vol. 35, 2003, pp. 191–204, at p. 192.
137 A. Cassese, 'Reflections on International Criminal Justice', *The Modern Law Review*, vol. 61, no. 1, 1998, pp. 1–10, p. 2.
138 'How the Mighty Are Falling: The Beginning of the End of Impunity for the World's Once All-Powerful Thugs', *The Economist*, 5 July 2007.
139 Freeland, 'The "Effectiveness" of International Criminal Justice', p. 8.
140 Neier, 'International Criminal Justice: Developing into a Deterrent', p. 10.
141 Ryngaert, *The Effectiveness of International Criminal Justice*, p. vii.
142 Tallgren, 'The Sensibility and Sense of International Criminal Law', p. 572.
143 Ibid.
144 H. Mulisch, *De Zaak 40/61: Een Reportage*, Amsterdam: De Bezige Bij, 1962, p. 183.
145 See, for instance: *Prosecutor v. Erdemovic*, Case No. IT-96-22-T.
146 Anderson, 'The Rise of International Criminal Law', p. 341.
147 Ibid.
148 D. Wippman, 'Atrocities, Deterrence, and the Limits of International Justice', *Fordham International Law Journal*, vol. 23, no. 2, 1999, pp. 473–488, p. 488.
149 Akhavan, 'Beyond Impunity', p. 7.

Bibliography

Akhavan, P. (1996) 'The International Criminal Tribunal for Rwanda: The Politics and Prag-matics of Punishment'. *American Journal of International Law*, 90(3), pp. 501–510. doi: 10.2307/2204076.

Akhavan, P. (2001) 'Beyond Impunity: Can International Criminal Justice Prevent Future Atrocities?'. *American Journal of International Law*, 95(1), pp. 7–31. doi: 10.2307/2642034.

Alford, R.P. (2000) 'Proceedings of the Annual Meeting'. *American Society of International Law*, 94, pp. 160–165.

Ambos, K. (2011) 'Judicial Creativity at the Special Tribunal for Lebanon: Is There a Crime of Terrorism Under International Law?' *Leiden Journal of International Law*, 24(03), pp. 655–675. doi: 10.1017/s0922156511000215.

Anderson, Kenneth (2009) 'The Rise of International Criminal Law: Intended and Unin-tended Consequences'. *European Journal of International Law*, 20(2), pp. 331–358. doi: 10.1093/ejil/chp030.

Anderson, K. (2009) 'The Rise of International Criminal Law: Intended and Unintended Consequences'. *European Journal of International Law*, 20(2), pp. 331–358. doi: 10.1093/ejil/chp030.

Arbour, L. (1997) 'Progress and Challenges in International Criminal Justice'. *Fordham International Law Journal*, 21, pp. 531–540.

Arendt, H. (1958) *The Human Condition*. Chicago: University of Chicago Press.

Arendt, H. (1963) *Eichmann in Jerusalem: A Report on the Banality of Evil*. New York: Penguin.

Bassiouni, M.C. (2000) 'The Evolution of International Humanitarian Law and Arms Control Agreements'. In Bassiouni, M.C. (ed.), *A Manual on International Humanitarian Law and Arms Control Agreements*. Ardsley-on-Hudson, NY: Transnational Publishers.

Bassiouni, M.C. (2003) 'Justice and Peace: The Importance of Choosing Accountability over Realpolitik'. *Case Western Reserve Journal of International Law*, 35, pp. 191–204.

Bassiouni, M.C. (2010) 'Perspectives on International Justice'. *Virginia Journal of International Law*, 50(2), pp. 269–323.

BBC News (2013) 'DR Congo: Bosco Ntaganda appears before ICC'. *BBC News*, 26 March.

Cassese, A. (1994) *Address to the General Assembly of the United Nations* [by the President of the ICTY], 14 November.

Cassese, A. (1998) 'On the Current Trends towards Criminal Prosecution and Punishment of Breaches of International Humanitarian Law'. *European Journal of International Law*, 9(1), pp. 2–17. doi: 10.1093/ejil/9.1.2.

Commission on the Responsibility of the Authors of the War and on Enforcement of Pen-alties (1919) *Report of the Commission on the Preliminary Peace Conference*. *American Journal of International Law*, vol. 14, no. 1, 1920, pp. 95–154.

Cryer, R., Friman, H. and Robinson, D. (2007) *An Introduction to International Criminal Law and Procedure: Principles, Procedures, Institutions*. Cambridge: Cambridge University Press.

Dallaire, R. (2003) *Shake Hands with the Devil: The Failure of Humanity in Rwanda*. London: Random House.

Damaška, M. (2008) 'What is the Point of International Criminal Justice?' *The Chicago-Kent Law Review*, 83(1), pp. 329–365.

Des Forges, A. (1999) *Leave None Left to Tell the Story: Genocide in Rwanda*, 2nd edn. New York, NY: Human Rights Watch [u.a.].

The Economist (2007) 'How the Mighty Are Falling: The Beginning of the End of Impunity for the World's Once All-Powerful Thugs'. *The Economist*, 5 July.

Fedorova, M., Verhoeven, S. and Wouters, J. (2009) 'Safeguarding the Rights of Suspects and Accused in International Criminal Proceedings'. *Institute for International Law Working Paper*, (27).

Fenrick, W.J. (2001) 'Targeting and Proportionality During the NATO Bombing Campaign Against Yugoslavia'. *European Journal of International Law*, 12(3), pp. 489–502. doi: 10.1093/ejil/12.3.489.

Fifoot, P. (1992) 'Functions and Powers, and Inventions: UN Action in Respect of Human Rights and Humanitarian Intervention'. In: Rodley, N.S. (ed.), *To Loose the Bands of Wickedness: International Intervention in Defence of Human Rights*. London: Brassey's, pp. 133–164.

Freeland, S. (2008) 'The "Effectiveness" of International Criminal Justice'. *ALTA Law Research Series*, (16), pp. 1–9.

Futamura, M. and Gow, J. (2013) 'The Strategic Purpose of the ICTY and International Peace and Security'. In Gow, J., Kerr, R., and Pajić, Z. (eds), *Prosecuting War Crimes*. London: Routledge, pp. 15–28.

Geneva Convention (1949) *Geneva Convention Relative to the Protection of Civilian Persons in Time of War*.

Gow, J. (2013) *War and War Crimes: The Military, Legitimacy and Success in Armed Conflict*. London: Hurst and Co.

Greppi, E. (1999) 'The Evolution of Individual Criminal Responsibility under International Law'. *International Review of the Red Cross*, (No. 835).

Grono, N. and de Courcy Wheeler, A. (2012) 'The Deterrent Effect of the ICC on the Commission of International Crimes by Government Leaders'. *Presentation for the conference The Law and Practice of the International Criminal Court: Achievements, Impact and Challenges*. At the Peace Palace, The Hague, 2012.

Grotius, H. (1625) *De Iure Belli ac Pacis*. Edited by B.J.A. de Kanter-van Hettinga Tromp (1939). Leiden: Brill.

Grotius, H. (2005) *The Rights of War and Peace*. (Vol. I). Indianapolis: Liberty Fund. De Iiure Belli ac Pacis, first published 1625.

Habermas, J. (1973) *Legitimation Crisis*. London: Heinemann.

Habermas, J. (1976) *Communication and the Evolution of Society*. London: Heinemann.

Higgins, R. (1994) *Problems and Process: International Law and How We Use It*. Oxford: Clarendon Press.

ICC. (2006) *Strategic Plan of the International Criminal Court*. (ICC-ASP/5/6).

ICTY (1994) *First Annual report of the ICTY*. UN Doc. (A/49/342).

ICC. (2011) *Elements of Crimes*. Available at: www.icc-cpi.int/NR/rdonlyres/336923D8-A6AD-40EC-AD7B-45BF9DE73D56/0/ElementsOfCrimesEng.pdf.

Kant, I. (1887) *The Metaphysics of Morals: Metaphysical Elements of Justice*. Edited by John Ladd (1999). London: Hackett.

Kerr, R. (2013) 'Introduction: Trials and Tribulations at the ICTY'. In: Gow, J., Kerr, R., and Pajić, Z. (eds), *Prosecuting War Crimes: Lessons and Legacies of the International Criminal Tribunal for the Former Yugoslavia*. London: Routledge.

Kerr, R.C. (2004) *The International Criminal Tribunal for the Former Yugoslavia: An Exercise in Law, Politics and Diplomacy*. Oxford: Oxford University Press.

Kerr, R. and Mobekk, E. (2007) *Peace and Justice: Seeking Accountability after War*. Cambridge: Polity Press.

King, H.T. (1996) 'Nuremberg and Sovereignty'. *Case Western Reserve Journal of International Law*, 28, pp. 135–140.

Kramer, A. (2006) 'The First Wave of International War Crimes Trials: Istanbul and Leipzig'. *European Review*, 14(4), pp. 441–455. doi: 10.1017/s1062798706000470.

Ku, J. and Nzelibe, J. (2006) 'Do International Criminal Tribunals Deter or Exacerbate Humanitarian Atrocities?' *Washington University Law Review*, 84(4), pp. 777–833.

Marshall, K.A. (2010) 'Prevention and Complementarity in the International Criminal Court: A Positive Approach'. *Human Rights Brief*, 17(2), pp. 21–26.

Mulisch, H. (1962) *De Zaak 40/61: Een Reportage*. Amsterdam: De Bezige Bij.

Neff, S. (2006) 'A Short History of International Law'. In: Evans, M. (ed.), *International Law*. Oxford: Oxford University Press, pp. 29–55.

Neier, A. (2012) 'International Criminal Justice: Developing into a Deterrent', *Openspace*. Open Society Initiative for Southern Africa, pp. 6–10.

Nollkaemper, A. (2010) 'Systemic Effects of International Responsibility for International Crimes'. *Santa Clara Journal of International Law*, 8(1), pp. 313–352.

Nuremberg Principles (1950) *Principles of International Law Recognized in the Charter of the Nürnberg Tribunal and in the Judgment of the Tribunal*.

Overy, R. (2003) 'The Nuremberg Trials: International Law in the Making'. In: Sands, P. (ed.), *From Nuremberg to The Hague: The Future of International Criminal Justice*. Cambridge: Cambridge University Press.

Pejic, J. (1998) 'Creating a Permanent International Criminal Court: The Obstacles to Independence and Effectiveness'. *Human Rights Law Review*, 29, pp. 291–354.

Pettifer, J. (2012) *The Kosova Liberation Army: Underground War to Balkan Insurgency, 1948–2001*. London: Hurst and Co.

Plesch, D. (2008) 'How the United Nations beat Hitler and Prepared the Peace'. *Global Society*, 22(1), pp. 137–158. doi: 10.1080/13600820701740779.

Plesch, D. (2011) *America, Hitler and the UN: How the Allies Won World War II and Forged a Peace*. London: I. B. Tauris.

Prosecutor v. Aleksovski [2000] ICTY Judgment IT-95-14/1.

Prosecutor v. Nikolic [2003] ICTY Sentencing Judgment IT-02-60/1-S.

Prosecutor v. Erdemovic [1996] ICTY Sentencing Judgment IT-96-22-T.

Prosecutor v. Tadic [no date] Appeals Chamber ICTY IT-94-1-A.

Protocol I to the Geneva Conventions (1977) *Protocol Additional to the Geneva Conventions of 12 August 1949, relating to the Protection of Victims International Armed Conflicts (Protocol I), 8 June 1977*.

Protocol II to the Geneva Conventions (1977) *Protocol Additional to the Geneva Conventions of 12 August 1949, and relating to the Protection of Victims of Non-International Armed Conflicts (Protocol II), 8 June 1977*.

Rauschenbach, M. and Scalia, D. (2008) 'Victims and International Criminal Justice: A Vexed Question?' *International Review of the Red Cross*, 90(870), p. 441. doi: 10.1017/s1816383108000398.

Rome Statute (1998) *The Rome Statute of the International Criminal Court*. Entry into force on 1 July 2002, United Nations Treaty Series, vol. 2187.

Roth, R. and Henzelin, M. (2002) 'The Appeal Procedure of the ICC'. In: Cassese, A., Gaeta, and Jones (eds), *The Rome Statute of the International Criminal Court, A Commentary*.

Ryngaert, C. (ed.), (2009) *The Effectiveness of International Criminal Tribunals*. Antwerp: Intersentia Uitgevers.

Schabas, W. (2007) *An Introduction to the International Criminal Court*. Cambridge: Cambridge University Press.

Scheffer, D.J. (2002) 'Should the United States Join the International Criminal Court?' *U.C. Davis Journal of International Law and Policy*, 9, pp. 45–52.

Schrag, M. (2004) 'Lessons Learned from ICTY Experience', *Journal of International Criminal Justice*, 2(2), pp. 427–434. doi: 10.1093/jicj/2.2.427.

Silverman, J. (2012) 'Ten years, $900m, one verdict: Does the ICC cost too much?' *BBC News*, 14 March.

Sloane, R. (2006) 'The Expressive Capacity of International Punishment' *Columbia Public Law and Legal Theory Working Papers*, 06100.

Stromseth, J.E. (2003) 'Goals and Challenges in the Pursuit of Accountability'. In: Stromseth, J.E. (ed.), *Accountability for Atrocities: National and International Responses*. Ardsley, NY: Transnational Publishers.

Tallgren, I. (2002) 'The Sensibility and Sense of International Criminal Law'. *European Journal of International Law*, 13(3), pp. 561–595. doi: 10.1093/ejil/13.3.561.

The Economist (1990) 'New World Order Inc.' *The Economist*, 10 November, Issue 7680.

Prosecutor v. Goran Jelisic [1999] ICTY Judgment IT-95-10-T.

United Nations (1945) *Charter of the United Nations, 1 UNTS XVI.*

(1915) *Telegram sent by the US Department of State to the US Embassy in Constantinople containing the Allied joint declaration of 24 May 1915.*

Von Hirsch, A. (1985) *Doing Justice: The Choice of Punishments: Report of the Committee for the Study of Incarceration.* Boston: Northeastern University Press.

Wippman, D. (1999) 'Atrocities, Deterrence, and the Limits of International Justice'. *Fordham International Law Journal*, 23(2), pp. 473–488.

Yacoubian, G.S. (1998) 'Sanctioning Alternatives in International Criminal Law: Recommendations for the International Criminal Tribunals for Rwanda and Yugoslavia'. *World Affairs*, 161(1), pp. 48–54.

Yacoubian, G.S. (2003) 'Evaluating the Efficacy of the International Criminal Tribunals for Rwanda and the Former Yugoslavia: Implications for Criminology and International Criminal Law', *World Affairs*, 165(3), pp. 133–141.

4 The International Criminal Tribunal for the former Yugoslavia and the impact on legitimacy in Kosovo[1]

The ICTY was the first international criminal tribunal since the IMTs in Nuremberg and Tokyo and, therefore, the embodiment of the reincarnation of international criminal justice. The establishment of the Tribunal embodied the hope of many people for an end to impunity for war criminals in the post-Cold War era. In many ways, expectations of the outcomes of the Tribunal were way too high, and such high hopes were bound to disappoint some. It is therefore no wonder that much has been written about the ICTY, as a body and regarding the development of international law, as well as the Tribunal in relation to Croatia, Bosnia and Serbia. Yet, consideration of Kosovo has been limited in the literature on the ICTY.

It is in Kosovo, after all, where the impact of the Tribunal on legitimacy can be distinguished most clearly, albeit not by design but by accident. The existing literature predominantly focuses on the legal procedures and juridical merits of cases, not on how these procedures influenced the outcome of the conflict over Kosovo. Sonja Boelaert-Suominen and Marc Weller have each discussed legal aspects of the Tribunal's engagement with Kosovo.[2] Laura Dickinson focused on the relationship between the ICTY and the domestic-hybrid court in Kosovo.[3] Michael Scharf examined the ICTY's handling of the Milošević case, including those parts relating to Kosovo,[4] while David Gowan, a former British diplomat who had been responsible for war crimes liaison between London and The Hague, explained the role the United Kingdom played regarding Kosovo.[5] Various authors have considered the ICTY investigation of NATO action over Kosovo during 1999.[6] None of these, mostly legal, analyses concern the impact of international criminal justice on Kosovo itself. There are studies that focused on the ICTY's impact on Kosovo. Mirko Klarin examines the effect of the Tribunal on public opinion there.[7] Majbritt Lyck, concerned with the implications of executing arrest warrants for suspects in post-conflict peacekeeping situations, considers the case of former KLA commander, and then prime minister, Ramush Haradinaj and its implications for the NATO-led security force in Kosovo.[8] Fred Cocozzelli considers how Kosovo's fate might have been different had events at critical junctures after 1999 taken a different course, one of which concerns the Tribunal: the indictment of then Kosovo prime minister Haradinaj.[9]

The indictment of Haradinaj is indeed a significant moment, especially where it contributes to the legitimacy-building process affecting the KLA and Kosovo's quest for recognition of independent international personality. Cocozzelli notes the significant moment as part of a path-dependency study, but he does not develop the analysis of that critical juncture into a wider understanding of critical legitimacy regarding Kosovo. More significantly, the critical moment for Kosovo's legitimacy – the point from which later ones flowed – is not the indictment, or subsequent acquittal, of Haradinaj and other Kosovar leaders, but the indictment of Serbian leader Slobodan Milošević, in May 1999. The purpose of this present chapter is to show how, despite a somewhat accidental character, the Tribunal's most significant activity regarding Kosovo was this indictment, which transformed the course of the Kosovo project and the prospects that the KLA would achieve its ambition of a new state in international society.

The ICTY: the reincarnation of international criminal justice

The Yugoslav War played an important role in the rise of international criminal justice for many reasons. First, the breakup of the Socialist Federal Republic of Yugoslavia (SFRY) gave rise to a conflict that, at its core, had a strategy of war crimes.[10] Second, the Yugoslav War was the 'first truly television war'.[11] Through satellite TV networks, images of refugees, the shelling of civilian targets and the concentration camps at Omarska and Trnopolje reached a wider audience than the horrors of previous wars. Televised human rights violations changed public opinion, especially in the West, and 'concern shifted to condemnation' in relation to human rights violations.[12]

The inability of the international community to prevent atrocious war in Yugoslavia

As well as international audiences watching the events in Yugoslavia unfold on their televisions, so did a swathe of international and regional organisations. The UN, the European Community (EC) (after 1993 the European Union (EU)), the Western European Union (WEU) and the Conference on Security and Cooperation in Europe (CSCE) (after 1995, the OSCE) all expressed growing concern about the war that started to unfold on their doorstep. The newly reinvigorated Security Council, strengthened by its success in Iraq, launched a string of initiatives and resolutions on Yugoslavia from September 1991 onwards. In Resolution 713 of 25 September 1991, the Council expressed its concern that continuation of the situation would constitute a threat to international peace and security and commended the efforts undertaken by the EC, its member states and the CSCE to restore peace and dialogue in Yugoslavia, and to implement ceasefires.[13] When those ceasefires were broken, the UN established an arms embargo, in Resolution 721 of 11 December 1991.[14] In the course of 1992, the Council established The United Nations Protection Force (UNPROFOR) in Resolution 743 of 21 February 1992,[15] in which it expressed its concern about the daily violations of the ceasefire,[16] demanded that all parties stopped the fighting in Bosnia-Hercegovina and noted the urgent need for humanitarian assistance.[17] In Resolution 757, the Council installed sanctions against the Federal Republic of Yugoslavia (Serbia and Montenegro).[18] Later in the year, the Council first acted under Chapter VII of the Charter and condemned violations of international humanitarian law, including those involved in the practice of 'ethnic cleansing'.[19] The Resolution reaffirmed that those persons who committed or ordered the commission of grave breaches of the Geneva Conventions of 12 August 1949 were individually responsible, although at the time no international mechanism to hold them responsible existed. Resolution 781 of 9 October 1992 established a no-fly zone over Bosnia and Hercegovina. Most significant for later formation of an international tribunal was the establishment of a 'commission of experts to investigate and collect evidence on "grave breaches" of the Geneva Conventions and other violations of international humanitarian law'.[20]

By the beginning of 1993, the Council had repeatedly expressed alarm at continuing reports of widespread violations of international humanitarian law. It had mentioned horrors ranging from 'mass forcible expulsion and deportation of civilians' to 'imprisonment and abuse of civilians in detention centres' and deliberate attacks on non-combatants, hospitals and ambulances.[21] It had strongly condemned 'ethnic cleansing' and the massive, organised and systematic detention and rape of women. But, despite all the measures it had taken, the Security Council, and the wider international community, had been unable to stop or prevent these atrocities.[22] The Commission of Experts issued its first Interim Report on 22 February 1993, which stated that the establishment of an *ad hoc* international criminal tribunal was necessary.[23] In May 1993, Resolution 827 established an international tribunal in the belief that prosecuting the individuals responsible for violations of international humanitarian law 'would contribute to ensuring that such violations were halted and effectively redressed'.[24] The Security Council did so under Chapter VII, as a tool to restore and maintain peace and security. However, in clear view of the entire world, including that of the Security Council, the killing, raping and ethnic cleansing continued, despite continued condemnation of those violations of international law and previous resolutions by the Council and the international community.

UNSC Resolution 827 and the establishment of the ICTY

Resolution 827 provided the ICTY with a Statute determining its jurisdiction, a basic structure and very general procedural rules. The jurisdiction of the Tribunal defined in the Statute was little more than an expanded version of its official name: 'The International Tribunal for the Prosecution of Persons Responsible for Serious Violations of International Humanitarian Law Committed in the Territory of the Former Yugoslavia since 1991'. Besides defining the court's jurisdiction *ratione temporis* as open-ended from 1 January 1991 onwards, and its jurisdiction *ratione loci* as extending to the entire territory of the former Yugoslavia, it also gave the Tribunal primacy over all competing domestic jurisdictions.[25] The jurisdiction *ratione personae* of the Tribunal was not limited by the official position of an individual or by immunities applying to heads of state.[26] Moreover, the Statute identified four categories of crimes falling within the jurisdiction of the ICTY: grave breaches of the Geneva Conventions of 1949; violations of the laws or customs of war; genocide; and crimes against humanity.[27] However, apart from a Statute and jurisdiction, when Resolution 827 passed unanimously in the Security Council, the newly found court lacked everything else a court needed, and the ICTY was a long way from being a functioning international criminal tribunal. The tribunal had no judges, prosecutors or registrar; there were no courtrooms or prison facilities, and there were no means to conduct investigations.[28] Moreover, for guidance, besides 'Nuremberg', the Tribunal had little precedent it could fall back on. Although an extensive body of substantive international criminal law existed, and the Statute defined some of the norms applicable, in terms of procedural law and jurisprudence the ICTY had to start with an almost blank slate.

According to Resolution 827, the ICTY had its seat in The Hague, and the Headquarters Agreement between the Government of the Netherlands and the United Nations of 27 May 1994 solved some of the practical issues such as premises of the Tribunal, use of detention facilities in Scheveningen and the legal position of the Tribunal and its staff, such as the personality of the court and immunities applying to its employees.[29] However, one of the biggest challenges the ICTY had to overcome in those early days was a lack of funding. While, within the UN, a debate was active about whether an initiative by the Security Council could be financed by the regular UN budget, the Tribunal only received $5.6 million, a fraction of the estimated costs (excluding detention and housing costs) of $31.2 million for the first year of operations.[30]

That the ICTY was so underfunded was also a sign, or a symptom, of the fact that few really believed an international criminal tribunal could work. Such scepticism was based on the fact that the Tribunal was established on the presumption that the Security Council could do so under Chapter VII, but then in many ways was left to its own devices to establish itself, its legality under international law and its legitimacy. Even among those who had supported the establishment of the Tribunal, many doubted whether it was feasible to conduct investigations and prosecutions, and expected it to remain little more than a political statement. Not least, this was because the ICTY lacked a police force to track down, arrest and transport accused to The Hague. Nevertheless, by July 1994, the Office of the Prosecutor was sufficiently staffed to begin field investigations and in November 1994 the first indictment, against Dragan Nikolić, was issued and confirmed. By July 1995, two years after its establishment and after a year of being operational, the Tribunal had indicted 46 individuals.[31] However, the individuals accused by the ICTY in its first years were not those 'most responsible' for the crimes committed. With the exception of Radovan Karadžić and Ratko Mladić, most of the accused were lower-ranking individuals who were accused of executing orders to commit atrocities, rather than of having ordered them. Nikolić, for instance, was commander of Sušica camp, in eastern Bosnia, and

Duško Tadić, the first to stand trial at the ICTY, commencing in May 1996, also had a low rank in the hierarchy of the Serb paramilitary forces. This was in part because the ICTY had difficulty apprehending suspects and could only undertake proceedings in the cases of Dražen Erdemović, a member of the Bosnian Serb Army, who had been indicted for participating in killing Bosnian Muslims at Pilica Farm, and pleaded guilty, and Tadić, who had been arrested in Germany. Not all the countries that had come out of the former Yugoslavia were willing to work with the Tribunal. The prosecution of 'small fry' did however make the 'Tribunal look rather impotent when it came to the "big fish"'.[32]

Prosecuting war criminals

The first Prosecutor at the Tribunal, Richard Goldstone, and the first president, Antonio Cassese, made way, in 1996 and 1997 respectively, for Louise Arbour and Gabrielle Kirk McDonald, as the Tribunal entered a new phase. The two had been driving forces in establishing the Tribunal and turned a 'lofty – some might have said nebulous – idea to a living reality'.[33] However, now that the ICTY was a real, functioning court, it also had to deal with the practical realities of a real court. These ranged from dealing with accused in detention to developing procedural law. The ICTY had to develop a victims and witnesses programme, a legal aid system and had to deal with defence attorneys.[34] Moreover, the Tribunal created a judicial database of all its jurisprudence, trial records and evidence presented to the court, in order to deal with vast amounts of information. Besides practical and legal issues, the ICTY aimed to prosecute those higher up the chain of command, and by issuing indictments under seal the new Prosecutor's strategy made it more likely that the accused would be apprehended. It was Arbour who did not relent when under pressure not to go all the way to the top of the command chain, indicting Slobodan Milošević for crimes committed in Kosovo, in 1999. Moreover, she was able to persuade those with boots on the ground in the former Yugoslavia, in particular members of NATO, to cooperate with the Tribunal in arresting suspects.[35]

Although the first arrests by international forces on the territory of the former Yugoslavia meant a turning point for the Tribunal and gave a symbolic boost to the court, some high-profile indictees remained unaccounted for in the years that followed.[36] Moreover, the cases of those who were present in The Hague often moved slowly. In part, this was due to the procedural law that had to be developed as the Tribunal went along. In part, it was due to the court's sometimes broad scope in the charges against the accused and the desire to create a historical record of the crimes committed in the former Yugoslavia.[37] But the Tribunal's desire to give those it accused a fair trial, and to let them exercise the right to represent themselves also contributed to lengthy proceedings that were sometimes misused as a political stage. Especially Milošević, while defending himself, sometimes used this right for rants against the court and to make political accusations. Nevertheless, it was a huge setback for the Tribunal that the proceedings against Milošević, which had started after his arrest and transfer to

The Hague in June 2001 and had 'always been the trial for which the ad hoc Court was created', came to a premature end with the death of the accused in March 2006.[38]

In those early years, a huge amount of work was done in developing procedures and both legal and institutional frameworks for international criminal justice, but the focus was on The Hague and, as Kerr points out, there was a lack of dialogue with the Tribunal's core constituents in the former Yugoslavia and the late start of the ICTY's outreach programme was a mistake.[39] Moreover, the ICTY, throughout its existence, had to deal with an image of anti-Serb bias, which it never managed to overcome. The acquittal by the Appeals Chamber of Croatian general Ante Gotovina and security chief Mladen Markač for their roles in Operation Storm, after having been found guilty and sentenced to 24 and 18 years respectively in the first instance, enforced this image. Only two weeks after the acquittal of Gotovina and Markač, Ramush Haradinaj, the former leader of the KLA and prime minister of the Republic of Kosovo, was acquitted for the second time for crimes against humanity and violations of the laws or customs of war. This only exacerbated the negative perception of the Tribunal among the Serb population.

The ICTY had an enormous impact on the development of international criminal justice. This was not only at the procedural level of international law, but also in terms of a vast body of jurisprudence and institutional development. The ICTY played a pivotal role in the evolution of international criminal law and procedure. Moreover, against all odds, the ICTY eventually managed to apprehend all individuals at large. In May 2011, Mladić was finally apprehended, after being on the run for 16 years and, on 20 July 2011, Goran Hadžić was the last of the 161 ICTY indictees at large to be arrested and transferred to The Hague.

The KLA and Kosovo

While Kosovo had statehood questions dating back to the Second World War and before, and so represented the QSE phenomenon already, this took on a new dimension with the emergence of the KLA in the course of the 1990s. On 22 April 1996, four simultaneous attacks on Serbian security forces were claimed by a mysterious and, until then, little-known organisation calling itself the *Ushtria Çlirimtare e Kosovës (UÇK)* or Kosovo Liberation Army – the KLA. While in Kosovo a majority had supported the Democratic League of Kosovo (LDK) of Dr Ibrahim Rugova throughout the early 1990s, in the diaspora and among exiles in Western Europe the idea that the Serb leadership would only bend under force was taking hold. They linked up with radicals in Kosovo and, during meetings in August and December 1993, the Popular Movement for Kosovo (LPK) set up a special branch, the Kosovo Liberation Army, to prepare for a guerrilla war against the Serbs.[40] Although the KLA carried out some successful attacks on Serbian policemen between 1993 and 1996, it had a very limited supply of arms and ammunition. This changed in early 1997, when the collapse of a pyramid scheme in Albania led to the collapse of the economy and civil unrest in the entire country.[41] The govern-ment of President Berisha fell and with him governmental control over the weapons in army depots. Some weaponry from the border area with Kosovo disappeared and gave a boost to local rebels in Kosovo, not necessarily part of the KLA at that stage, although, broadly, the KLA was to get most of its material from Serbian sources.[42] However, the KLA and its supporting com-munities were boosted and began to attract both funds and recruits, enabling it to step up its campaign of attacks against the Serbian police and ethnic Albanians who it regarded as collaborators.

Contested Kosovo

Kosovo has been contested territory since the collapse of the Roman Empire, and probably before that. The territory of what is now Kosovo has changed hands often and violently over the last centuries, usually accompanied by a shift of the ethnic composition of the population. There is disagreement about the numbers of both Albanian and Serbian refugees that fled the territory during, or after, the 1999 war, and about the number that returned. The fact that the 1991 and 2011 censuses were boycotted by either one side or the other only added to the uncertainty about the pre- and post-war percentages of the population identi-fying as Serbian or Albanian.[43] However, it is usually assumed that around 90 per cent of the population of Kosovo is ethnic Albanian, a percentage that is unlikely to be too far off.[44] Nevertheless, both Serbs and Albanians claim Kosovo as their home.[45]

Since the declining Ottoman Empire lost Kosovo in the Balkan Wars in 1912, it was as part of Serbia that Kosovo became part of the Kingdom of Yugoslavia and later the SFRY. Although Kosovo's autonomy increased during Tito's rule, ethnic Albanian aspirations to be recognised as a full member republic of the Yugoslav federation were denied but never disappeared. Throughout the 1980s, growing ethnic tension between the Albanian majority and Serb minority led to numerous violent outbreaks.[46] This provided Slobodan Milošević, then chairman of the League of Communists of Serbia, with a chance to boost his political career by openly supporting the Serbs in Kosovo. On 24 April 1987, after a riot with the Kosovo police, Milošević told a crowd of Serbs and Montenegrins: 'Nobody must be allowed to beat you'.[47] Televised that same evening in Serbia, the event became a turning point in Milošević's career. In early 1989, strikes and demonstrations against the reforms of the Serbian constitution that removed most of the autonomous powers Kosovo had enjoyed since 1974 were violently repressed.[48] When Milošević became president of Serbia in May 1989, he pressed on with installing allies in the leadership of Kosovo in an 'anti-bureaucratic revolution'. On 28 June, at an event remembering the 600th anni-versary of the Battle of Kosovo, in front of a crowd of an estimated one million Serbs that had come down to the heart of Kosovo, Milošević warned: 'Six centu-ries later, now, we are being again engaged in battles and are facing battles. They are not armed battles, although such things cannot be excluded yet'.[49]

Violent resistance under Dr Rugova

In July 1990, the Assembly of Serbia passed a decision to suspend the Assembly of Kosovo, shortly after 114 of the 123 Kosovo Albanian delegates from that Assembly had passed an unofficial resolution declaring Kosovo to be an equal and independent entity within the SFRY. In a reaction to the loss of autonomy and increasing control by Belgrade, the Kosovo Assembly first declared Kosovo a republic within Yugoslavia, but then on 22 September 1991 declared Kosovo independent. In May 1992, in an election that was deemed illegal, null and void by the Serbian authorities that retained effective control over Kosovo, Dr Rugova of the LDK was elected president of Kosovo.

Soon after the 1991 declaration, Rugova was running parallel institutions, and a shadow parliament existed in parallel to the Serbian legislature. The LDK in many ways was a very successful QSE, offering many of the services usually provided by the state. But, while the rest of Yugoslavia was burning, Rugova remained a proponent of a non-violent strategy towards statehood and against oppression by Serbia. Although this strategy was more based on Serb military superiority and a fear of being ethnically cleansed than on anything else, the misunderstanding in the international community about the non-violence of the Kosovo Albanians – that earned Rugova the nickname 'the Ghandi of the Balkans' – was a fortunate one for the Kosovo Albanians.[50] By 1995, when the desperation of the EC and other international actors to come to a solution for Bosnia kept Kosovo off the agenda at Dayton, 'the Kosovo Albanians realized that passive resistance had failed as a strategy'.[51] As Tim Judah puts it, they felt themselves 'penalized for eschewing violence'.[52]

KLA and the Kosovo War

As pressure built among the ethnic Albanian population and Serbian repression and provocation continued, a low-level armed conflict began. The conflict intensified when, after the shooting of a police officer in February 1998, the Yugoslav Army (VJ) took revenge by killing 27 residents of Drenica. A week later, 58 people were killed in the shelling of the compound of the family of Adem Jashari, creating a martyr and momentum for the KLA, in terms of support among the population.[53] As the KLA started to take territory, Kosovo Albanians started to believe in the KLA, and donations and recruits started to come in. Initially, they took areas dominated by Albanians, but as they tried their luck at areas with mixed populations and near the *Trepça/Trepča* mines, the Serbs started a serious counteroffensive.[54] 'Milošević' forces, as they had done in Bosnia and Croatia, pushed streams of terrified refugees straight into the cameras of the international media, losing the war for public opinion even before it really started'.[55]

On 16 January, the executed bodies of 45 farmers and their children were found near the village of Račak. The massacre 'was widely perceived in Europe and Washington as the final warning bell, and was so portrayed by the media'.[56]

The international community, with the failure to prevent ethnic cleansing and atrocities in Bosnia fresh in its memory, wanted to end the armed conflict in Kosovo as soon as possible and with all means at their disposal.[57] The images of displaced people and refugees that the conflict started to produce provided the international media with images similar to those of Bosnia, only a few years earlier. Moreover, the same narratives were used that were used in the Bosnian War. Kosovo was different in many respects, but what matters was that the depiction and the narratives were the same, and the images available to Western audiences were images that were associated with the death and destruction of Bosnia and the role of the Serbs in those crimes.

The Rambouillet negotiations and NATO's Operation Allied Force

All attempts failed to negotiate a settlement that would keep Kosovo within Serbia, but would guarantee the impossibility of ethnic cleansing. In a last surge of coercive diplomacy the Contact Group, comprising the United States, United Kingdom, France, Germany, Italy and Russia, organised a final round of talks at Chateau de Rambouillet just outside Paris, in February 1999. On 21 January, President Clinton and Prime Minister Blair had already agreed that force should be used if the Contact Group proved unsuccessful; a NATO activation order had been approved as early as October 1998, and on 30 January 1999 the Alliance had sent out a press statement: 'The NATO Secretary General may authorise air strikes against targets on FRY territory'.[58] The Russians, wanting to keep the initiative with the Contact Group they were part of, had given tacit approval to threatening with the use of force, yet continued to insist that the actual use of force by NATO against Yugoslavia would be unacceptable.[59] The negotiation process at Rambouillet was not only putting pressure on the Serbs, but the agreement also proposed that Kosovo would remain part of Serbia, and the KLA would have to disarm. However, US Secretary of State Madeleine Albright made clear to the Kosovo delegation, consisting of KLA members and Rugova, and headed by Hashim Thaçi, that if they would not sign, there would be no air strikes against Serbia.[60] *Nolens volens*, the Kosovo Albanians eventually signed the Rambouillet Accords on 18 March. Milošević, possibly out of fear of being handed over to the ICTY, had stayed in Belgrade, where US envoy Richard Holbrooke visited him in a last attempt to make him sign the agreement. He refused and 36 hours later NATO commenced 'Operation Allied Force'.

The NATO bombing of Yugoslavia lasted from 24 March 1999 to 10 June 1999, and was a first in many ways. The campaign was the first sustained use of armed force by NATO; the first time NATO used massive armed force with the stated purpose of implementing UN Security Council resolutions, but without authorisation of the Council; and the first major bombing campaign intended to bring a halt to crimes against humanity.[61] Belligerents usually have different expectations of the outcome of an armed conflict, but Milošević and NATO had widely diverging expectations of the outcome of the bombing campaign. Milošević initially had reason to believe that the unity within the alliance would not last long.

NATO also expected a short bombing campaign. Its leaders relied on experience from Bosnia, when it only took 13 days of air strikes to get Milošević to Dayton – albeit that the two situations were quite distinct, from the Serbian leader's perspective.[62] When three days, or one week, and not even 13 days of air operations failed to alter Milošević's position, a protracted stalemate emerged, which ended abruptly and surprisingly after 78 days. Throughout that period, Kosovo remained very firmly within the embrace of Serbian sovereignty, in the international perspective, despite the NATO action. The KLA, while more prominent than ever before, remained a largely ineffectual phenomenon, even with NATO air power at work. The armed conflict was suddenly ended, Serbia's sovereign grip on Kosovo was loosened, and the KLA was transformed from irritant to victorious combatant by international judicial intervention, albeit that this was entirely unexpected. The publication of the indictment against Milošević and others inverted the bases of legitimacy and revolutionised the environments of support. The next section will discuss the indictment, ahead of later analysis of its impact.

The Milošević indictment

On 27 May 1999, 64 days into Operation Allied Force, the NATO bombing campaign against Serbia, the ICTY announced the indictment, and issued arrest warrants against Slobodan Milošević and four other senior members of the leadership of Serbia and the Federal Republic of Yugoslavia.[63] The indictment, submitted five days earlier by Chief Prosecutor Louise Arbour, was directed against Milošević as President of the FRY, and against Milan Milutinović, President of Serbia; Nikola Šainović, Deputy Prime Minister of the FRY; Colonel General Dragljub Ojdanić, Chief of the General Staff of the Yugoslav Armed Forces; and Vlajko Stojiljković, Minister of the Interior of Serbia. According to the Prosecutor, Milošević *et al.* had 'planned, instigated, ordered, committed or otherwise aided and abetted in a campaign of terror and violence directed at Kosovo Albanian civilians living in Kosovo in the FRY'.[64] The Prosecutor claimed that this campaign was executed by forces of the FRY and Serbia acting at the direction, with the encouragement, or with the support of Milošević *et al.*, and that they were 'undertaken with the objective of removing a substantial portion of the Kosovo Albanian population from Kosovo in an effort to ensure continued Serbian control over the province'.[65] Besides a general description of the events in Kosovo, the indictment also described details of 20 operations that were executed in a systematic manner and together resulted in the forced deportation of approximately 740,000 Kosovo Albanian civilians and the killing of hundreds of Kosovo Albanian civilians including women and children.[66] The Serbian leaders were charged with three counts of crimes against humanity; deportation (punishable under Article 5(d) of the Statute of the Tribunal); murder (Article 5 [a]); persecutions on political, racial and religious grounds (Article 5[h]); and one count of a violation of the law or customs of war; murder (punishable under Article 3 of the Statute of the Tribunal and recognised by Article 3[1] [a] [murder] of the Geneva Conventions).[67]

Before the indictment against Milošević *et al.*, the Tribunal had focused mainly on the perpetrators of specific atrocities or criminal acts. The first indictments were against people such as Dragan Nikolić, the Serbian commander of the Sušica camp, Duško Sikirica the commander of the Keraterm camp, and other commanders, guards and interrogators of camps in Bosnia, as well as members of paramilitaries and local politicians. However, the responsibility for these crimes was extended to their commanding officers and the leadership of the Republika Srpska by the indictment of Ratko Mladić and Radovan Karadžić.[68] Up until March 1999, the leadership of Serbia, or the FRY, had not been indicted. This was not because the Prosecutor did not want to, but because she had no possibility of doing so. As Deputy Chief Prosecutor Graham Blewitt of the ICTY later explained: 'We were given a task by the Security Council and it was our job to bring the indictment if the evidence was sufficient'.[69] The indictment over Kosovo was a result of the ability of the Prosecutor to gather evidence of violations of humanitarian law in Kosovo. It was a result of the ability to establish command responsibility of the Serb and FRY leadership over those executing the executions, a connection between those masterminding, and the foot soldiers doing the dirty work of ethnic cleansing.

Going after the 'big fish': the timing of the indictment of Milošević

In the Kosovo case, instead of prosecuting the individuals that pulled the trigger, the Prosecutor could refer both to individual responsibility, under Article 7(1), and to command responsibility, under Article 7(3), of the Statute of the ICTY.[70] By describing the official functions of the accused, the indictment claimed they had 'had authority or control' over the individuals committing crimes. Command responsibility was more straightforward to address for crimes committed in Kosovo than it had been for crimes committed in Bosnia, as Kosovo was considered a purely internal matter and there was no entity like the Republika Srpska acting as a buffer. Moreover, the indictment pointed out that Milošević was the Supreme Commander of the Yugoslav Army (VJ) as he chaired the Supreme Defence Council.[71] Although we can assume that Milošević also had de facto control over all Serbian forces, including the forces of the Serbian Ministry of Internal Affairs (*Ministarstvo Unutrasnjih Poslova*, MUP) and other paramilitary and police forces, in peacetime the formal chain of command of these forces was less straightforward than that of the VJ. However, a state of war was declared in Yugoslavia on 24 March 1999, increasing Milošević's control over domestic media and parliament, which also went beyond the de facto control he already wielded, to give him *de jure* control over all forces for the first time since war broke out in the Yugoslav lands at the start of the 1990s.[72]

At the same time, the ability of the Tribunal to gather evidence increased. The ICTY had already claimed jurisdiction in relation to Kosovo in early 1998,[73] and the Security Council had affirmed its jurisdiction in November 1998.[74] However, as a result of Yugoslavia's persistent denial of this claim to jurisdiction, the ICTY had no access to Kosovo. The Chief Prosecutor was denied access to

Kosovo after the Račak massacre of January 1999, and at the time of the indictments the Tribunal had no access to the sites of the atrocities it described.[75] With a lack of forensic evidence, the prosecution had to depend on the witness statements it gathered itself from refugees in camps outside of Kosovo and on testimonies transmitted through NGOs.[76] Not only had the Tribunal's abilities to collect evidence improved, but governments could also provide information, and the United States and United Kingdom, both of which had been hesitant to share information during the early years of the ICTY, now handed over evidence in the form of satellite images and telephone intercepts to the Prosecutor to make the case against Milošević.[77]

Milošević was indicted because it was the first time the ICTY was able to do so, but the timing of publication of the indictment was also prompted by fear of a deal between Holbrooke and Milošević. Although Holbrooke's promising Milošević immunity of prosecution by the ICTY in itself would have held no real legal value, it would have undermined the work of the Tribunal. This illustrates how the diplomats and NATO did not foresee the impact that the indictment would have. On the contrary, when Washington and London found out about the imminent indictment they tried to persuade Chief Prosecutor Arbour to delay the indictment, or keep it under seal, as they expected it could hamper negotiations to end the NATO campaign.[78] Madeleine Albright describes in her memoirs how there were those in the US administration and NATO who were nervous about the indictment, feeling that it would mean they could not negotiate with Milošević anymore.[79] However, she personally was gratified by the indictments because of the message it sent. According to Albright: 'those who perpetrate ethnic cleansing will end up failing to gain what they seek and lose what they have', but she was unsure whether the indictments would make Milošević less or more likely to accept NATO's terms.[80] It turned out to be the latter. The indictment of Milošević also proved to be a turning point for the future status of Kosovo and shaped its transition to statehood, as is demonstrated in the final part of this analysis.

The pivotal moment: the indictment transforms armed conflict and the Serbia–Kosovo legitimacy equation

At the beginning of 1998, the KLA was designated as a terrorist organisation by the US State Department. In 1999, it was a legitimate negotiating party. In 1998, Kosovo was nowhere in terms of statehood. In terms of military capabilities at that time, the KLA had no chance of enforcing anything against the VJ and Serbian security troops. In terms of political support for its objective, the KLA had little prospect of mustering international support as the instinctive reaction of the international community was protecting the principles of territorial integrity. After 1999, Kosovo was put on a path towards statehood. By 2012, Kosovo was a self-declared republic which had de facto control over most of the territory it claimed and a government that formally executed most of the functions usually attributed to statehood. Following a unilateral declaration of independence in

February 2008, by July 2016, 111 UN Member States had recognised Kosovo as a sovereign state having international legal personality independent from Serbia.[81] Its direct neighbours – Montenegro, Macedonia and Albania – as well as 23 of the 28 members of the EU, recognised Kosovo's independence, although the European Union lacks the unanimity to express a common foreign policy towards Kosovo's independence. From transitional administration under the UN, Kosovo moved on to become a transitional state with more and more qualities of complete statehood.[82]

From transitional statehood to Olympic Gold

Although blocked from membership of the UN by states that objected to its independence, most notably Russia, Kosovo became a member of the International Monetary Fund (IMF) and the World Bank in June 2009, and it became a member of the European Bank for Reconstruction and Development (EBRD) in December 2012.[83] While the government of Kosovo exercised most statehood functions, since becoming responsible for its own governance in 2012, transitional support and administration of Kosovo were still in place by mid-2016. The United Nations Interim Administration Mission in Kosovo (UNMIK) and European Union Rule of Law Mission in Kosovo (EULEX) still existed and were both operating in Kosovo, under UN Security Council Resolution 1244.[84] The EULEX mandate had been extended until 2018, and had largely taken over the functions of UNMIK.[85] By 2016, the NATO-led international peace implementation force, KFOR, had been scaled down but was also still necessary, and roughly 4600 troops provided by 31 countries continued to work towards 'maintaining a safe and secure environment and freedom of movement for all citizens and communities in Kosovo'.[86] The International Civilian Office (ICO), a parallel body to UNMIK founded by the International Steering Group for Kosovo (ISG) involving states backing Kosovo's independence to oversee the Comprehensive Proposal for the Kosovo Status Settlement (CSP) – known as the Ahtisaari Plan – closed in September 2012, ending a period of 'supervised independence'.[87] A Stabilisation and Association Agreement between the EU and Kosovo entered into force in early 2016, marking a closer EU–Kosovo relationship and cooperation and making Kosovo a potential future candidate for membership of the EU.[88] Within months of the 2008 declaration of independence, Kosovo applied to become a member of a number of international sports federations. At long last the Olympic Committee of Kosovo became a full member of the International Olympic Committee in December 2014. Judoka Majlinda Kelmendi won Kosovo's first ever medal (gold) at the 2016 Rio de Janeiro Olympics[89] More important even than UN membership, according to many Kosovars, was membership of the Fédération Internationale de Football Association (FIFA), which was finally obtained in May 2016.[90]

In the grand scheme of independent statehood for Kosovo, Kosovars representing Kosovo at the Olympic Games, or participation of its football team in the qualifying rounds for the 2018 World Cup, might seem trivial. Yet, for Kosovo it carries a highly symbolic meaning to see its athletes representing Kosovo competing against other national teams, especially as this was almost unthinkable not so long ago. That Kosovo would take the route of transitioning statehood, becoming a functioning de facto or quasi-state was not a foregone conclusion. On the contrary, in early 1998, Kosovo was absolutely nowhere in terms of statehood. Militarily, it faced an uphill battle against a superior opponent, and politically it was not in a position to take any major steps towards statehood. The KLA was no match for the Serb security forces and the Yugoslav Army, in terms of arms and military capabilities. In terms of international support, the outlook was bleak, at best. The KLA was listed as a terrorist organisation by the US State Department.[91] Moreover, the KLA, according to NATO, was 'the main initiator of the violence'; the reason for the violence was given that it had 'launched what appears to be a deliberate campaign of provocation'.[92] With the very limited degree of NATO support at the time, aimed at preventing ethnic cleansing, the Kosovo Albanians had very limiting prospects of enforcing anything against the Yugoslav Army.[93]

An uphill battle and territorial integrity

In 1998, there were no real prospects of political achievement either. The sovereignty principle and the protection of states, their status and borders, favoured Belgrade as far as the international community was concerned. The international community generally adheres to those sovereignty principles, even while some of the parties involved with the former Yugoslavia at that time, the United States in particular, were to a certain extent sympathetic to the Kosovo Albanians. There was a widespread consensus that the territorial integrity of states is limited by humanitarian concerns, and that this might trump the non-intervention principle, but few were willing to go any further than that.

UN Security Council Resolution 1160, of 31 March 1998, expressed the position of the international community at the time by affirming 'the commitment of all Member States to the sovereignty and territorial integrity of the Federal Republic of Yugoslavia', although it also expressed support for 'a substantially greater degree of autonomy and meaningful self-administration'.[94] The Resolution condemned 'use of excessive force by Serbian police forces against civilians and peaceful demonstrators in Kosovo', but in the same sentence the Security Council also condemned 'all acts of terrorism by the Kosovo Liberation Army'.[95] All diplomatic efforts focused on preventing ethnic cleansing stressed the territorial integrity of the Federal Republic of Yugoslavia. The proposals, or negotiations, by the international community, the Yeltsin–Milošević agreement, in June 1998, the negotiations by Christopher Hill, or the Holbrooke–Milošević agreements, were all based on the basic presumption of Serbia's sovereignty over Kosovo,[96] and so was the more harshly worded UN Security Council Resolution 1199 of 23 September 1998. Even when, in 1999, the international community became firmer with Serbia, the Rambouillet Accords only foresaw establishing democratic self-governance, granting Kosovo substantial autonomy.

Milošević refused to sign the Rambouillet Accords: self-governance in itself would have been a bitter pill to swallow for most Serbs, but allowing NATO forces to restore order and oversee that self-governance, while granting NATO troops immunity and right of passage through the entire territory of the Federal Republic of Yugoslavia was definitely too much to bear.[97] Yet, even these proposed provisions did not nearly go as far in terms of a road towards transitional administration and transitional statehood as the highway that Kosovo eventually took after the war. Although the Rambouillet Accords stipulated that Serbia was to remove forces from Kosovo, they included a commitment to the sovereignty and territorial integrity of the Federal Republic of Yugoslavia and, for instance, gave the FRY the power to control international border crossings.[98] In essence it proposed self-governance and in turn asked a commitment from the KLA to stop fighting and the Kosovo Albanians to give up the quest for independence.

Shifting legitimacy in Kosovo after the indictment

The road of transitional statehood towards de facto independence that Kosovo took was the result of a combination, or chain, of events. But, in that chain of events, war crimes were the key, and the indictment of Slobodan Milošević was the most important link. The NATO bombings indisputably played a central role in turning the events that followed, as did the KLA and a myriad of other factors. But it was the reaction of the Serbs, which involved more ethnic cleansing and war crimes, resulting in a stream of refugees and displaced people, and ultimately the indictment of Milošević for war crimes committed in Kosovo, that changed the game. If war crimes and the indictment of Milošević are seen as the pivot, or fulcrum, on which Kosovo's future turned, Serbia applied continuous resistance to the lever, on one side, and effort was applied, on the other, by the KLA and later the Kosovo government, NATO and the international community, to turn that future. However, the more resistance Serbia applied, the more war crimes it committed, the more legitimacy it lost, thereby adding length to the lever of the KLA and the Kosovo Albanians and to the force that was applied by NATO against Serbia.

The human rights violations by the Serb security forces and the Yugoslav Army, most notably the Račak massacre in January 1999, meant that the international community could not sit back. NATO also justified the air strikes that followed the failed negotiations and ceasefire by just that – preventing further humanitarian disaster in Kosovo. However, it was the indictment against Milošević that created a critical legitimacy moment. It became the pivotal event by which Milošević found himself in a downward spiral of legitimacy loss that could no longer be turned around. Milošević lost legitimacy in the international community as a whole but, most important, also in Russia, and it was a spiral that eventually led to legitimacy loss in Serbia as well. At the same time, it was a pivotal moment for the KLA, which gained legitimacy for its actions and aspirations. The KLA that had been designated a terrorist organisation less than a year earlier had the principle of the international community, and the legitimacy in that community for their aim of self-determination. It had legitimacy for resisting the repressive action and eventually war crimes, albeit that it also helped to trigger some of them, and committed crimes itself. But the key principle of legitimacy, in this context, that of sovereignty, turned in that moment and so the support nexus in Kosovo aligned more with the support nexus outside Kosovo. The new-found legitimacy outside Kosovo enabled the KLA to be more successful in providing statehood functions and become the primary QSE in Kosovo, further strengthening its legitimacy inside Kosovo. By the time the talks at Rambouillet took place in early 1999, the KLA had surpassed the LDK. It was Hashim Thaçi who led the representation of the Kosovar Albanians at the negotiations and Dr Rugova was there as his deputy.[99] This legitimacy of the KLA, also expressed in its position as negotiating entity, was eventually endorsed by Security Council Resolution 1244, which still implied that sovereignty stayed with Serbia and that, although this was not yet complete statehood, it set the path towards it.[100]

Multiple actors seeking legitimacy in multiple constituencies simultaneously

All parties in the Kosovo War depended on legitimacy for success in attaining their goals. The KLA not only needed legitimacy within its home constituencies, but also in the international community. NATO needed to maintain a level of legitimacy within 19 home constituencies. Milošević needed legitimacy, both internally while his population was bombed and, to a certain extent, externally, in the international community. For all of the actors in the Kosovo conflict, critical challenges and spurs to legitimacy evolved around war crimes. The legitimacy crises these actors had to overcome and the messages that they had to convey to various constituencies simultaneously have to be seen in conjunction with each other. Legitimacy is not a zero-sum game, but if the narrative of one belligerent is more successful in a constituency, its opponent will likely lose legitimacy.

NATO legitimacy and its 19 home constituencies

NATO ostensibly went to war for humanitarian reasons. Its leaders made sure that the narratives they used focused on the protection of human rights. The alliance made its aims clear in a list of demands, to which Milošević had to accede, in order to stop the air strikes. Milošević would have to: end violence and repression; withdraw all Serb forces from Kosovo; agree to the deployment of international forces in Kosovo; agree to the safe return of refugees and access for humanitarian aid organisations; and agree to work on the basis of the Rambouillet agreement.[101] Milošević did not take the threats seriously, and ongoing debate in NATO capitals seemingly indicated that he could doubt the alliance's credibility.[102] While the message, or the narrative of the alliance had to impact the various Serb constituencies in a way that it conveyed unity and its willingness to continue to use force, it also had to deal with home constituencies. In fact, NATO had to deal with 19 home constituencies, that it had to reach with one effective narrative, and each of the various home constituencies had to continue to believe in the legitimacy of its actions against the Serbs, even when those actions went on longer than expected and led to more casualties and destruction. In addition, it had to seek legitimacy in the wider international community, especially as it was not acting under a UN Security Council resolution.[103]

However, besides a moral argument that atrocities committed by the Serbs were a good reason to go to war, it had to find a narrative justifying the means it deployed to reach its goals. Freedman noted that the moral paradox of the Kosovo War lay there, 'for it was always easier to proclaim the morality of the ends pursued than of the means deployed'.[104] As the campaign lasted longer, other effects also had to be taken into account. War, inevitably, involves bloodshed and innocent casualties. Public opinion, or what some might call the 'CNN effect', may call for actions against atrocities, but it could also easily be turned in the opposite direction, and Western audiences are believed to have a low tolerance for their own casualties.[105] The refusal of President Clinton to put boots on the ground in Kosovo indicates that he took this 'body bag effect' into account. Finally, NATO had to convey a message that its chosen strategy worked, which, as long as Milošević was holding out and NATO failed to stop the intensifying campaign of the Serbs against Albanians in Kosovo, was complicated. However, Milošević, by stepping up his campaign of ethnic cleansing, simultaneously strengthened the basis of NATO action while weakening its claim to success.

The KLA and the game of 'comparative victimology'

As Tim Judah has so appositely expressed it, the KLA 'has to rank as one of the most successful military organizations in history'.[106] This success though, Judah admits, 'had nothing to do with its military prowess', but depended on being in the right place at the right time, and having NATO able to win its war for it.[107] The belief among the Albanians in Kosovo that the KLA was doing the right thing in taking up arms after years of a strategy of non-violence, could only take hold after the Serbian forces retaliated vengefully after KLA provocation. Moreover, what looked like success, taking territory at the beginning of the war, strengthened the legitimacy of the armed resistance. International condemnation for attacks on Serb forces, and on Albanians seen as collaborators, and being labelled as a terrorist organisation by the United States, could have created a legitimacy crisis. However, the KLA strategy worked in that the reprisals by Serbian forces were fierce. They won, in what Freedman calls the battle of 'comparative victimology'.[108] The Kosovo Albanians, who are the KLA's home constituency, felt the reaction of Serbian security forces but euphoria that something was finally happening was often stronger than fear within the population.[109] Summarising the KLA's miraculous triumph this way, of course, misses the impact of the ICTY indictment against Milošević which, while not sufficient in determining the course of events, was decisive to the extent that it completely stripped almost all his, and Serbia's, legitimacy in the contest.

The narrative of the KLA fitted with the images of refugees shown on satellite news networks and with pre-existing ideas within Western constituencies about Milošević's Serbia and its role in the genocide in Bosnia. Kosovo differed in many ways from Bosnia, but these were harder to distinguish for a television audience.[110] Western audiences saw death and destruction in the Balkans again; they did not see that Kosovo was not a sovereign state, as Bosnia had been. Also, little noted, was the difference that, unlike in Bosnia, the Serbs could not employ a proxy army in Kosovo. What provided the basis for KLA legitimacy in its home constituency, fighting for full independence, hampered its ability to be successful with international constituencies. The Badinter Commission had not considered Kosovo as having a right to independence and the international community followed that line.[111] NATO did not want to be seen as fighting to change borders and create new states.

Milošević's spiral of legitimacy loss

It could be argued that Milošević was unable to sign the Rambouillet agreement because being seen as giving away Kosovo would have led to his ouster in Serbia. NATO boots on the ground, in the whole of Yugoslavia, was not an appealing prospect for Milošević either. Although the population of Serbia proper suffered under NATO bombing, a common enemy also boosted the legitimacy of those fighting it. Moreover, as Milošević controlled most of the media in Serbia, he managed to get across his message of fighting American imperialism.[112]

Although the Serb population was suffering from air strikes, and mistakes were made and innocent people killed, these images hardly reached outside constituencies:

> Although Serbs deliberately tried to present themselves as victims, however, the harsh methods used to suppress Kosovar Albanian aspirations ensured that it was they who appeared as the victims. The Serb effort was also counter-productive in that it made the KLA harder, instead of easier, to defeat.[113]

Milošević clearly had to deal with a legitimacy crisis in the international community. He had done so for years, but this time it led to a continuing bombing campaign. Now the Serb leadership had to deal with a situation in which it would have been very hard to find a narrative that would send a legitimating message to both international and home constituencies simultaneously. Giving in to NATO would have lost him legitimacy at home and would have given the KLA (and the Kosovar Albanians) a green light to continue their fight for independence. The opposite tack – not giving in to the demands made by NATO but at the same time failing to be seen as the victim – created a loss of legitimacy in the international community.

The indictment of Milošević *et al.* turned out to be a pivotal moment in the Kosovo War. There is little doubt that the timing of the indictment was a significant factor in this. However, this impact was neither foreseen by those making the decision to indict, nor by those who were affected by it. During his later trial, Milošević pointed out the timing of the indictment as evidence of the political influence of the United States on the Tribunal.[114] He was wrong, but the indictment, indeed, came at a crucial moment for NATO. By 27 May, the bombing campaign had been going on for much longer than Milošević had foreseen, but it had also lasted much longer than anyone at Supreme Headquarters Allied Powers Europe (SHAPE), Brussels and Washington – or any other NATO capital for that matter – had foreseen. During the air strikes, the Chinese Embassy in Belgrade had accidentally been bombed and in the press in most of its home constituencies NATO faced fierce criticism over the use of cluster bombs.[115] If NATO had been forced to end the bombing campaign before Milošević had given in, either by internal criticism in the 19 home constituencies or by pressure from non-member states, it would have done severe damage to the credibility of the alliance, damage that might have been irrevocable and thus had to be avoided at any cost with the 50th anniversary of NATO coming up.[116] According to Scharf, the United States was suddenly pressing for charges to be issued against Milošević, as they knew that 'it would bolster the political will of NATO countries to continue the bombing campaign, and would ultimately force Milošević to accept NATO's terms for Kosovo'.[117] However, James Gow, citing senior US and British sources, argues that just the opposite was at work and that Richard Holbrooke, the US Special Envoy, was offering Milošević immunity from prosecution if he were to end hostilities,[118] reflecting concerns that the operations had no end in sight and that Washington, and perhaps other capitals, were looking for a way out, short of deploying ground troops, even though President Bill Clinton had just agreed to that, in principle.

Gow also maintains that it was the impact of the indictment on Milošević that prompted him suddenly to sue for peace.[119] This is a position backed by US Ambassador-at-Large for War Crimes, David Scheffer, and others. Scheffer argued:

> when Milošević was actually indicted, in late May 1999, during the Kosovo campaign, that indictment by the War crimes Tribunal may have had some influence on his concession a couple of weeks later in conjunction with the bombing, of course, to basically back down on Kosovo.[120]

The moment had come for Milošević to save himself.[121] On 4 June an independent Belgrade news analyst commented that:

> This time around, Milošević did not have much choice. He could have continued the war, which would result in the complete destruction of the country and enormous casualties as well as his probable overthrow at the end of the campaign. Instead, he decided to accept the peace plan, giving

himself a little more manoeuvring space in a bid to present his defeat as victory and to remain in power, together with his cronies, as long as possible.[122]

In a similar vein, the private Belgrade news agency *BETA*, in its commentary of 9 June 1999, reported that the government 'was faced with a choice to either continue to resist and risk a complete destruction of the country's infrastructure, or to accept NATO's demands'. *BETA* went on to say that Milošević, being a pragmatist, decided 'to salvage what could be salvaged, that being his power in Serbia'. It also suggested that the Tribunal's indictment of Milošević gave the FRY president an important additional incentive to stop the bombing, in that he realised that he could best postpone an appearance before the Tribunal in The Hague only if he preserved at least a partially stable country in which his word remained decisive.[123]

The unexpected and unintended impact of international criminal law on legitimacy

Contrary to what most expected, the indictment turned out contingently to help NATO's strategic purpose.[124] Or, as Weller put it, the Tribunal 'played a strategic role, as its action effectively denied to Belgrade any hope of achieving its principal aims'.[125] A day after the publication of the indictment, Milošević announced that he would accept the G8 principles and that he would withdraw unilaterally. In the week that followed, it became clear to Milošević that he could not count on support from Moscow and that he was losing control of the information that reached the Serbian population, as more critical messages about the war in Kosovo were spreading by word of mouth.[126] The indictment marked a point at which the downward spiral of the Serbian leadership, losing legitimacy, especially in the eyes of the international community, reached a point of no return. Legitimacy is not a zero-sum game, but Milošević's loss of legitimacy did influence the legitimacy of the NATO action: 'It transformed NATO's use of force from an exercise in coercive diplomacy into an action which approximated an actual "war" in a more traditional sense'.[127] At the same time, it further legitimised the actions of the KLA against the VJ and Serbian security forces. The KLA, still labelled as a terrorist organisation, a year earlier had increasingly become a legitimate negotiating partner, while the consequence of the indictment was that Milošević was no longer a partner to talk to. He was no longer part of the solution; rather he became part of the problem. That happened, not by means of NATO propaganda, but by means of an international, UN sanctioned, Tribunal.[128]

Milošević conceded to the five demands of NATO: (1) to ensure a verifiable stop to all military action and the immediate ending of violence and repression; (2) to ensure the withdrawal from Kosovo of the military, police and paramilitary forces; (3) to agree to the stationing in Kosovo of an international military presence; (4) to agree to the unconditional and safe return of all refugees and displaced persons and unhindered access to them by humanitarian aid organisations; and (5) to provide credible assurances of his willingness to work on the basis of the Rambouillet Accords in the establishment of a political framework agreement for Kosovo, in conformity with international law and the Charter of the United Nations.[129] He agreed to terms that had been completely unacceptable for him at Rambouillet.

The indictment by the ICTY for crimes against humanity and violations of the laws or customs of war, committed in Kosovo, marked the beginning of the end of Milošević's career. It did not take Milošević out of the game immediately, but it was a pivotal moment because it created a legitimacy crisis he was not to overcome. After Milošević lost elections in 2000, elections he tried to steal, it was on St Vitus Day, 28 June 2001 that he was transferred by the Serbian Government to Scheveningen jail and the Tribunal. The terms on which he conceded went way beyond anything that had been offered, or discussed, even, at Rambouillet.[130]

In June 1999, Milošević had to agree to withdraw all his forces from Kosovo immediately, instead of keeping border guards, police and customs agents in Kosovo, as proposed in the Rambouillet agreement.[131] Moreover, the ending of hostilities was cemented by Security Council Resolution 1244 that, while formally bolstering Serbian sovereignty, also, crucially, confirmed the de facto separation of Kosovo, with a *de jure* underpinning.[132] While Rambouillet had foreseen 'areas of competence' that the FRY would continue to enjoy in Kosovo – such as a common market within the FRY, monetary policy, defence, foreign policy, customs services, federal taxation and federal elections – Resolution 1244 did not provide for 'areas of competence'.[133] This set Kosovo on a path through transitional administration and, then, transitional statehood, towards eventual, independent, fully legitimate, international statehood – and, so, to success for the KLA's project. The war crimes issue was decisive in this outcome.

The impact of the ICTY on legitimacy and Kosovo's statehood project

Although international criminal justice is by no means the only factor in legitimacy crises, it can be particularly salient, whether by accident or design. Legitimacy is not created in court, and definitely not by court procedures alone. But the narratives international criminal justice uses can, in conjunction with other legitimating messages, have an effect on the ability of an entity to create and maintain the idea that its actions and institutions are the right ones. International criminal justice has an impact on legitimacy, not in the least because, in contemporary conflict, the morality of force is defined by its legality. War crimes are seen by the international community and condemned by the public, and procedures before an international tribunal make war crimes and crimes against humanity even more visible. International justice influences legitimacy – and legitimacy is a prerequisite for success. The history of Kosovo and the KLA exemplifies this.

On several occasions, international criminal justice, in the form of the ICTY, through the indictment of individual leaders, had an impact on the legitimacy of the parties to the conflict. In combination with other factors, international criminal justice procedures influenced the beliefs held in various constituencies. Therefore, it had an impact on both parties' chances of successfully attaining their statehood goals. War crimes were in the forefront of minds in the West, repeatedly and continually: in 1999; during the war; in the direct aftermath of the war; and during the extended process that one could call the 'final status debate' (a 'debate' that was not only fought in Priština and Belgrade, but also in Brussels, Washington and other capitals and which, at times, was more heated than a mere debate of words, and was not complete at time of writing).

After the ICTY indictment against Milošević, something vital shifted. What shifted was legitimacy. The war crimes issue was decisive. It was a turning point because it affected the legitimacy of Milošević and the Serbian cause and, at the same time, it boosted the legitimacy of the KLA. In the KLA's position of having no chance of achieving anything meaningful militarily (in the sense of achieving statehood), even with some degree of NATO support, the prospects of success were very limited. Physically, at least, at that point the KLA had no chance of defeating the Belgrade forces. There was no prospect of achieving its political goals because the sovereignty principle, as well as armed force, favoured Belgrade and the protection of states, their status and borders – even if some of those involved, particularly the Americans, were sympathetic to the idea of a new and democratic Kosovo. Milošević, in the contra-flow, rejected various terms that would have seen Kosovo clearly as part of Serbia (even if this might have entailed more autonomy than Milošević, at that point, was willing to give), but under terms that would have prevented the ethnic cleansing.

Although unforeseen, at the time, the indictment had an acute impact on the legitimacy of Milošević and his actions in Kosovo. More important, in the chain of events that led to the de facto independence of Kosovo, the indictment of Milošević was a pivotal moment in that it rearranged the bases of legitimacy and changed the environments of support. By deepening a legitimacy crisis to the point where it could no longer be turned around, it changed the outcome of the war. But it also had a long-term effect on the future status of Kosovo, shifting beliefs in the West about the legitimacy of the Serbian leadership and increasing its belief in the justice of a Kosovar statehood project, while there had been, at least up until then, some legitimacy for maintaining the territorial integrity of Serbia. Under the pressure of international criminal justice, Milošević was forced to give in to NATO demands to salvage what was left of his power in Serbia. For NATO, the indictment against Milošević *cum suis* added weight to the human rights narratives it used. In the 19 home constituencies it had to influence it added legitimacy to the bombing campaign that had already lasted much longer than expected. In terms of critical legitimacy, the KLA had both the principle of justice in the face of gross abuses of human rights against its constituency and also legitimacy in the community for its aim of self-determination. It had legitimacy from resisting repressive action and, eventually, war crimes (albeit that it also helped in triggering some of those, and committed some itself). The indictment turned the KLA into a force fighting an enemy of the international community. The key principle of legitimacy, in this context of sovereignty, turned on that moment. The support nexus in Kosovo aligned more with the support nexus outside Kosovo, and was endorsed by a UN Security Council resolution. Although this was not complete statehood, it set the path towards it.

Notes

1 Parts of this chapter were published in Ernst Dijxhoorn, 'International Criminal Justice and Kosovo: Critical Legitimacy and Impact on a Quasi-State Entity', in R. Kerr, J. Gow and Z. Pajić (eds), *Prosecuting War Crimes: Lessons and Legacies of the International Criminal Tribunal for the Former Yugoslavia*, (Routledge, 2013). Reproduced by permission of the publisher.
2 S. Boelaert-Suominen, 'The International Criminal Tribunal for the Former Yugoslavia and the Kosovo Conflict', *Revue Internationale de la Croix-Rouge/International Review of the Red Cross*, no. 82, 2000. M. Weller, 'The Kosovo Indictment of the International Criminal Tribunal for Yugoslavia', *International Journal of Human Rights*, vol. 4, no. 3–4, 2000.
3 L.A. Dickinson, 'The Relationship between Hybrid Courts and International Courts: The Case of Kosovo', *New England Law Review*, vol. 37, no. 1059, 2003.
4 M.P. Scharf, 'The Legacy of the Milosevic Trial', *New England Law Review*, vol. 37, no. 915, 2003.
5 D. Gowan, 'Commentary: Kosovo: The British Government and ICTY', *Leiden Journal of International Law*, vol. 13, no. 4, 2000.
6 W.J. Fenrick, 'Targeting and Proportionality during the NATO Bombing Campaign Against Yugoslavia', *European Journal of International Law*, vol. 12, no. 3, 2001, and its expanded version 'The Law Applicable to Targeting and Proportionality After Operation Allied Force: A View From the Outside', in: *Yearbook of International Law*, vol. 3, 2000. A. Laursen, 'NATO, the War over Kosovo, and the ICTY Investigation', *American University International Law Review*, vol. 17, no. 4, Article 3, 2002. D. Kritsiotis, 'The Kosovo Crisis and NATO's Application of Armed Force Against the Federal Republic of Yugoslavia', *The International and Comparative Law Quarterly*, vol. 49, no. 2, 2000. M. Roscini, 'Targeting and Contemporary Aerial Bombardment', *International and Comparative Law Quarterly*, vol. 54, no. 2, 2005.
7 M. Klarin, 'The Impact of the ICTY Trials on Public Opinion in the Former Yugoslavia', *Journal of International Criminal Justice*, vol. 7, 2009.
8 M. Lyck, 'International Peace Enforcers and Indicted War Criminals: The Case of Ramush Haradinaj', *International Peacekeeping*, vol. 14, no. 3, 2007.
9 F. Cocozzelli, 'Critical Junctures and Local Agency: How Kosovo Became Independent', *Southeast European and Black Sea Studies*, vol. 9, issue 1–2, 2009.
10 For more on the strategic use of war crimes in the breakup of the SFRY, see: J. Gow, *The Serbian Project and Its Adversaries: A Strategy of War Crimes*, London: Hurst and Co., 2003.
11 M. Michalski and J. Gow, *War, Image and Legitimacy: Viewing Contemporary Conflict*, Abingdon: Routledge, 2007, p. 118. Michalski and Gow acknowledge that the Vietnam War and the Gulf Conflict both have a claim to be the first 'television war' but, while at the end of the Vietnam War same-day broadcasts became possible, yet reports remained limited and isolated, the Yugoslav War was 'the first war in which television was everywhere'. Neier, 'International Criminal Justice: Developing into a Deterrent', p. 8.

12 F. Kalshoven and L. Zegveld, *Constraints on the Waging of War*, Geneva: ICRC, 2001, p. 185.

13 UN Security Council Resolution 713, 25 September 1991.

14 Resolution 721, 11 December 1991. L.R. Barria and S.D. Roper, 'How Effective Are International Criminal Tribunals? An Analysis of the ICTY and the ICTR', *International Journal of Human Rights*, vol. 9, no. 3, 2005, pp. 349–368, at p. 354.

15 UN Security Council Resolution 743, 21 February 1992. UN Security Council Resolution 780, 6 October 1992.

16 UN Security Council Resolution 749, 7 April 1992.

17 UN Security Council Resolution 752, 15 May 1992.

18 UN Security Council Resolution 757, 30 May 1999.

19 UN Security Council Resolution 780, 6 October 1992.

20 Ibid.

21 UN Security Council Resolution 771, 13 August 1992.

22 UN Security Council Resolution 771, 13 August 1992. UN Security Council Resolution 780, 6 October 1992. UN Security Council Resolution 798, 18 December 1992. UN Security Council Resolution 808, 22 February 1993.

23 Barria and Roper, 'How Effective Are International Criminal Tribunals?' p. 354.

24 UN Security Council Resolution 827, 25 May 1993.

25 Statute of the ICTY, Articles 8 and 9 (2).

26 Ibid., Article 7 (2).

27 Ibid., Articles 2–5.

28 R. Kerr, *The International Criminal Tribunal for the Former Yugoslavia: An Exercise in Law, Politics and Diplomacy*, Oxford: Oxford University Press, 2004, p. 42.

29 Ibid., p. 43. Agreement between the United Nations and the Kingdom of the Netherlands Concerning the Headquarters of the International Tribunal for the Prosecution of Persons Responsible for Serious Violations of International Humanitarian Law Committed in the Territory of the Former Yugoslavia since 1991, New York, 27 May 1994.

30 Kerr, *The International Criminal Tribunal for the Former Yugoslavia*, p. 42. R. Kerr, 'Introduction: Trials and Tribulations at the ICTY', in: J. Gow, R. Kerr and Z. Pajić (eds), *Prosecuting War Crimes: Lessons and Legacies of the International Criminal Tribunal for the Former Yugoslavia*, London: Routledge, 2013, pp. 1–14, p. 2.

31 ICTY, 'Timeline'.

32 Kerr, 'Trials and Tribulations at the ICTY', pp. 3–4.

33 Address of Antonio Cassese, President of the International Criminal Tribunal for the former Yugoslavia, to the General Assembly of the United Nations, 7 November 1995. Quoted in: Kerr, *The International Criminal Tribunal for the Former Yugoslavia*, p. 58.

34 ICTY, 'Developing International Law'.

35 Kerr, *The International Criminal Tribunal for the Former Yugoslavia*, p. 159.

36 Ibid., p. 212.

37 M.I. Khan, 'Historical Record and the Legacy of the International Criminal Tribunal for the Former Yugoslavia', in: J. Gow, R. Kerr and Z. Pajić (eds), *Prosecuting War Crimes: Lessons and Legacies of the International Criminal Tribunal for the Former Yugoslavia*, London: Routledge, 2013, pp. 88–102.

38 M.P. Scharf, 'The Legacy of the Milosevic Trial', *New England Law Review*, vol. 37, no. 915, 2003, p. 916.

39 R. Kerr, 'Lost in Translation: Perceptions of the ICTY in the Former Yugoslavia', in: J. Gow, R. Kerr and Z. Pajić (eds), *Prosecuting War Crimes: Lessons and Legacies of the International Criminal Tribunal for the Former Yugoslavia*, London: Routledge, 2013, pp. 102–114, p. 112.

40 T. Judah, *Kosovo, War and Revenge*, New Haven: Yale University Press, 2000, p. 66.

41 C.J. Jarvis, *The Rise and Fall of the Pyramid Schemes in Albania*, Washington: IMF Working Paper, 1999.
42 J. Gow, *The Serbian Project and its Adversaries: A Strategy of War Crimes*, London: Hurst and Co., 2002, p. 260.
43 T. Judah, *Kosovo: What Everyone Needs to Know*, Oxford: Oxford University Press, 2008, pp. 2–3. Kosovo Population and Housing Census 2011, Final Results, p. 94. H. Brunborg, *Report on the Size and Ethnic Composition of the Population of Kosovo*, Oslo, 14 August 2002.
44 Judah, *Kosovo, War and Revenge*, pp. 2–3.
45 N. Malcolm, *Kosovo: A Short History*, 2nd edn, Basingstoke: Pan Macmillan, 2002, p. xlvii.
46 J. Ker-Lindsay, *Kosovo: The Path to Contested Statehood in the Balkans*, London: I.B. Tauris, 2009, p. 10.
47 ICTY Trial Transcript, Wednesday, 9 February 2005, 050209IT, pp. 35946–35949.
48 *The Prosecutor Of The Tribunal v. Slobodan Milosevic, Milan Milutinovic, Nikola Sainovic, Dragoljub Ojdanic, Vlajko Stojiljkovic*, ICTY Case No. IT-99-37, Indictment of 22 May 1999, §9.
49 Speech by Slobodan Milošević, delivered at the central celebration marking the 600th anniversary of the Battle of Kosovo, held at Gazimestan on 28 June 1989. See, H. Krieger (ed.), *The Kosovo Conflict and International Law: An Analytical Documentation 1974–1999*, Cambridge: Cambridge University Press.
50 Judah, *Kosovo, War and Revenge*, p. 71.
51 T. Judah, 'Kosovo's Road to War', *Survival*, vol. 41, no. 2, 1999, pp. 5–18, at p. 12, cited in L. Freedman, 'Victims and Victors: Reflections on the Kosovo War', *Review of International Studies*, vol. 26, no. 3, 2000, pp. 335–358, at p. 341.
52 Ibid.
53 Judah, *Kosovo, War and Revenge*, pp. 110–111.
54 Ibid., p. 82.
55 Ibid., p. 83.
56 R.A. Falk, 'Kosovo, World Order, and the Future of International Law', *American Journal of International Law*, vol. 93, no. 4, 1999, p. 849.
57 Ker-Lindsay, *Kosovo*, p. 1.
58 A.J. Bellamy, *Kosovo and International Society*, Basingstoke: Palgrave Macmillan, 2002, p. 98, p. 124. NATO Press Release (99) 12, 30 January 1999.
59 Bellamy, *Kosovo*, pp. 125–126.
60 M. Albright, *Madam Secretary: A Memoir*, New York: Miramax, 2003, p. 513.
61 A. Roberts, 'NATO's Humanitarian War over Kosovo', *Survival*, vol. 41, no. 3, 1999, pp. 102–123, p. 102.
62 Marc Weller suggests that the scenario was not without reason: Weller, 'The Kosovo Indictment' pp. 213–214.
63 'President Milosevic and Four Other Senior FRY Officials Indicted for Murder, Persecution and Deportation in Kosovo', press release by the Registry of the ICTY, The Hague, 27 May 1999, JL/PIU/403-E.
64 *The Prosecutor Of The Tribunal v. Slobodan Milosevic, Milan Milutinovic, Nikola Sainovic, Dragoljub Ojdanic, Vlajko Stojiljkovic*, ICTY Case No. IT-99–37, Indictment of 22 May 1999, § 97–98.
65 Ibid.
66 Ibid.
67 Ibid., § 100.
68 Press Release by the Registry of the ICTY, The Hague, 27 May 1999.
69 *Australian Broadcasting Corporation*, Graham Blewitt speaks to Tony Jones, Broadcast: 14/07/2008, Transcript.
70 Article 7(1), Article 7(3).

71 *The Prosecutor Of The Tribunal v. Slobodan Milosevic, et al.*, ICTY Case No. IT-99-37, Indictment of 22 May 1999, §30.
72 Gow, *Serbian Project*, p. 88.
73 Prosecutor's Statement Regarding the Tribunal's Jurisdiction over Kosovo, The Hague, 10 March 1998, CC/PIO/302-E.
74 UN Security Council Resolution 1207, 17 November 1998.
75 Weller, 'The Kosovo Indictment', p. 210.
76 Ibid.
77 Ibid.
78 Gow, *Serbian Project*, p. 295.
79 Albright, *Madam Secretary*, pp. 533–534.
80 Ibid.
81 Ministry of Foreign Affairs, Republic of Kosovo, countries that have recognised the Republic of Kosovo. Although the declaration of independence was unilateral, as it was against Serbia's wishes, it was coordinated with Brussels and Washington.
82 J. Gow, 'Kosovo – The Final Frontier? From Transitional Administration to Transitional Statehood', *Journal of Intervention and Statebuilding*, vol. 3, no. 2, 2009, pp. 239–257, at p. 255.
83 EBRD (2013) The EBRD in Kosovo: Overview. Available at: www.ebrd.com/where-we-are/kosovo/overview.html (Accessed: 16 August 2016).
84 UN Security Council Resolution 1244, 10 June 1999.
85 EULEX Press Office (2016) *EULEX new mandate.* Available at: www.eulex-kosovo.eu/?page=2,10,437&sqr=extend (Accessed: 16 August 2016).
86 KFOR (2016) *NATO's Role in Kosovo.* Available at: http://jfcnaples.nato.int/kfor/about-us/welcome-to-kfor/natos-role-in-kosovo (Accessed: 16 August 2016). NATO (2016) *NATO's Role in Kosovo.* Available at: www.nato.int/cps/en/natolive/topics_48818.htm# (Accessed: 16 August 2016).
87 Deutsche Welle (2012) *International Steering Group Passes Sovereignty to Kosovo news DW.COM 10.09.2012.* Available at: www.dw.com/en/international-steering-group-passes-sovereignty-to-kosovo/a-16230752-1 (Accessed: 16 August 2016).
88 COMM (2016) Stabilisation and Association Agreement (SAA) between the European Union and Kosovo Enters into Force. Available at: http://europa.eu/rapid/press-release_IP-16-1184_en.htm (Accessed: 16 August 2016).
89 BBC (2016) Rio 2016 Olympics: Majlinda Kelmendi Wins Kosovo's First Ever Gold. Available at: www.bbc.co.uk/sport/olympics/37006027 (Accessed: 8 August 2016).
90 FIFA.com www.fifa.com/associations/association=kvx/index.html.
91 J. Pettifer, *The Kosova Liberation Army: Underground War to Balkan Insurgency, 1948–2001*, London: Hurst 2012, p. 140.
92 Hammond, P. (2004) 'Humanizing War: The Balkans and Beyond', in Allan, S. and Zelizer, B. (eds), *Reporting War: Journalism in Wartime*, Abingdon: Routledge, pp. 174–189. P.178.
93 Madeleine Albright, in her memoir, stated:

> I wanted to stop Milošević from marauding through Kosovo, but I didn't want that determination exploited by the KLA for purposes we opposed. We therefore took pains to insist that we would not operate as the KLA's air force or rescue the KLA if it got into trouble as a result of its own actions.
> Albright, *Madam Secretary*, p. 386, cited in Judah, *Kosovo: What Everyone Needs*, p. 83

94 UN Security Council Resolution 1160, 31 March 1998.
95 Ibid.
96 Bellamy, *Kosovo and International Society*, pp. 57, 67, 81–83.
97 Interim Agreement for Peace and Self-Government in Kosovo (Rambouillet Agreement), Appendix B: Status of Multi-National Military Implementation Force.

98 Rambouillet Agreement, Preamble. Article VI: Security on International Borders.
99 Judah, *Kosovo: What Everyone Needs to Know*, p. 24
100 The Preamble to the document and the Annexes, including the G8 principles, formally embedded Serbian sovereignty. The Preamble and Annexes are full parts of agreements under the governing doctrine of international law.
101 Statement Issued at the Extraordinary Ministerial Meeting of the North Atlantic Council held at NATO Headquarters, Brussels, on 12th April 1999.
102 Bellamy, *Kosovo and International Society*, p. 124.

103   Most operations these days are multinational in nature, and require the sponsorship of an international organization, preferably the United Nations. So account must be taken of the impression being made on the wider international community. These issues become even more important when there can be no guarantee that a war can be settled by a decisive battle.

Freedman, 'Victims and victors', p. 340

104 Freedman, 'Victims and Victors', p. 341.
105 'Public opinion can be so moved by images of suffering humanity that it demands action, even where inappropriate'. Freedman, 'Victims and Victors', p. 338.
106 Judah, *Kosovo: What Everyone Needs to Know*, p. 75.
107 Ibid.
108 Freedman, 'Victims and Victors', pp. 356–358.
109 Judah, *Kosovo: What Everyone Needs to Know*, p. 81.
110 Michalski and Gow, *War, Image and Legitimacy*, pp. 119–120.
111 The Arbitration Commission of the Conference on Yugoslavia (commonly known as Badinter Arbitration Committee) was a commission set up by the Council of Ministers of the European Economic Community on 27 August 1991 to provide the Conference on Yugoslavia with legal advice.
112 J. Armatta, 'Milosevic's Propaganda War', Institute for War and Peace Reporting, *TRI Issue* 301, 22 February 2005.
113 Freedman, 'Victims and Victors', p. 335.
114 Scharf, 'The Legacy of the Milosevic Trial', p. 923.
115 Ibid.
116 See: M.K. Albright, 'We won't let war criminals walk; with or without a Balkan peace deal, the U.S. won't relent', *Washington Post*, 19 November 1995.
117 Scharf, 'The Legacy of the Milosevic Trial', p. 924. This belief seems to be based more on the outcome of the indictment than on anything else, although Scharf insinuates that Louise Arbour was rewarded for the indictment by getting a seat on the Canadian Supreme Court.
118 Gow, *Serbian Project*, pp. 295–297.
119 Ibid.
120 D.J. Scheffer, Killing fields and "Kangaroo" Courts: Symposium on an emerging international criminal justice system, *Davis Journal of International Law and Policy*, vol. 45, no. 9, 2002, pp. 45–52, p. 51.
121 S.T. Hosmer, 'Why Milosevic Decided to Settle When He Did', RAND, 2001, p. 106.
122 *V.I.P. Daily News Report*, No. 1521, 4 June, 1999, p. 5.
123 'Kosovo and Politics in FRY – A New Round Starts', BETA Commentary, 9 June 1999, FBIS-EEU-1999-0609.
124 Gow, *Serbian Project*, p. 296.
125 Weller, The Kosovo Indictment', p. 207.
126 Gow, *Serbian Project*, pp. 296–297.
127 Weller, 'The Kosovo Indictment', p. 207.
128 Ibid., p. 214.
129 Statement issued at the Extraordinary Ministerial Meeting of the North Atlantic Council Brussels, Belgium 12 April 1999.

130 Hosmer, 'Why Milosevic Decided to Settle When He Did', p. 106.
131 Hosmer, 'Why Milosevic Decided to Settle When He Did', pp. 116–117.
132 UN Security Council Resolution 1244, 10 June 1999.
133 Hosmer, 'Why Milosevic Decided to Settle When He Did', p. 117, Rambouillet Agreement, Chapter 8, Article I, (3).

Bibliography

NATO (2016) *NATO's Role in Kosovo*. Available at: www.nato.int/cps/en/natolive/topics_48818.htm# (Accessed: 16 August 2016).

Albright, M. (1995) 'We won't let war criminals walk; with or without a Balkan peace deal, the U.S. won't relent', *Washington Post*, 19 November.

Albright, M. (2003) *Madam Secretary*. New York: Miramax.

Armatta, J. and Institute for War and Peace Reporting (2005) 'Milosevic's Propaganda War'. *TRI*, 301.

Barria, L.A. and Roper, S.D. (2005) 'How Effective Are International Criminal Tribunals? An Analysis of the ICTY and the ICTR'. *International Journal of Human Rights*, 9(3), pp. 349–368. doi: 10.1080/13642980500170782.

BBC (2016) *Rio 2016 Olympics: Majlinda Kelmendi Wins Kosovo's First Ever Gold*. Available at: www.bbc.co.uk/sport/olympics/37006027 (Accessed: 17 August 2016).

Bellamy, A.J. (2002) *Kosovo and International Society*. New York: Palgrave Macmillan.

BETA (1999) 'Kosovo and Politics in FRY – A New Round Starts'. *BETA Commentary*, June. FBIS-EEU-1999-0609.

Boelaert-Suominen, S. (2000) 'The International Criminal Tribunal for the Former Yugoslavia and the Kosovo Conflict'. *International Review of the Red Cross*, 82.

Brunborg, H. (2002) *Report on the Size and Ethnic Composition of the Population of Kosovo*.

Cassese, A. (1994) *Address to the General Assembly of the United Nations* [by the President of the ICTY], 14 November.

Cocozzelli, F. (2009) 'Critical Junctures and Local Agency: How Kosovo Became Independent'. *Southeast European and Black Sea Studies*, 9(1–2), pp. 191–208. doi: 10.1080/14683850902723603.

COMM (2016) *Stabilisation and Association Agreement (SAA) between the European Union and Kosovo Enters into Force*. Available at: http://europa.eu/rapid/press-release_IP-16-1184_en.htm (Accessed: 16 August 2016).

Daily News Report No. 1521 (1999) *V.I.P.*, 4 June.

Deutsche Welle (2012) *International Steering Group Passes Sovereignty to Kosovo news DW.COM 10.09.2012*. Available at: www.dw.com/en/international-steering-group-passes-sovereignty-to-kosovo/a-16230752-1 (Accessed: 16 August 2016).

Dickinson, L.A. (2003) 'The Relationship between Hybrid Courts and International Courts: The Case of Kosovo'. *New England Law Review*, 37(1059).

EBRD (2013) *The EBRD in Kosovo: Overview*. Available at: www.ebrd.com/where-we-are/kosovo/overview.html (Accessed: 16 August 2016).

EULEX Press Office (2016) *EULEX new mandate – EULEX press releases – EULEX, Kosovo, European Union Rule of Law Mission in Kosovo, EU, European Union, European Union External Action*. Available at: www.eulex-kosovo.eu/?page=2,10,437 &sqr=extend (Accessed: 16 August 2016).

Falk, R.A. (1999) 'Kosovo, World Order, and the Future of International Law', *American Journal of International Law*, 93(4), p. 847. doi: 10.2307/2555350.

Fenrick, W.J. (2000) 'The Law Applicable to Targeting and Proportionality after Operation Allied Force: A View From the Outside'. *Yearbook of International Humanitarian Law*, 3, pp. 53–80. doi: 10.1017/s1389135900000581.

Fenrick, W.J. (2001) 'Targeting and Proportionality during the NATO Bombing Campaign Against Yugoslavia'. *European Journal of International Law*, 12(3), pp. 489–502. doi: 10.1093/ejil/12.3.489.

FIFA, 2016 (2016) *Associations*. Available at: www.fifa.com/associations/association=kvx/index.html (Accessed: 17 August 2016).

Freedman, L. (2000) 'Victims and Victors: Reflections on the Kosovo War', *Review of International Studies*, 26(3), pp. 335–358. doi: 10.1017/s0260210500003351.

Gow, J. (2003) *The Serbian Project and Its Adversaries: A Strategy of War Crimes.* London: Hurst and Co.

Gow, J. (2009) 'Kosovo – The Final Frontier? From Transitional Administration to Transitional Statehood'. *Journal of Intervention and Statebuilding*, 3(2), pp. 239–257. doi: 10.1080/17502970902830034.

Gowan, D. (2000) 'Commentary: Kosovo: The British government and ICTY'. *Leiden Journal of International Law*, 13(4), pp. 913–929. doi: 10.1017/s0922156500000534.

Graham Blewitt speaks to Tony Jones (2008) Australian Broadcasting Corporation, 14 July. Transcript.

Hammond, P. (2004) 'Humanizing War: The Balkans and Beyond'. In: Allan, S. and Zelizer, B. (eds), *Reporting War: Journalism in Wartime*. Abingdon: Routledge, pp. 174–189.

Hosmer, S.T. (2001) 'Why Milosevic Decided to Settle When He Did', *RAND*.

Prosecutor's Statement Regarding the Tribunal's Jurisdiction over Kosovo [1998] ICTY CC/PIO/302-E.

The Prosecutor v. Slobodan Milosevic, et al. [1999] ICTY Indictment IT-99-37.

Prosecutor vs Naser Oric [2005] ICTY Trial Transcript, pp. 35946-9. Case IT-03-68-T. 050209IT.

ICTY Headquarter Agreement (1994) *Agreement between the United Nations and the Kingdom of the Netherlands Concerning the Headquarters of the International Tribunal for the Prosecution of Persons Responsible for Serious Violations of International Humanitarian Law Committed in the Territory.*

Jarvis, C.J. (1999) 'The Rise and Fall of the Pyramid Schemes in Albania'. *IMF Working Papers*, 99(98), p. 1. doi: 10.5089/9781451852127.001.

Judah, T. (1999) 'Kosovo's Road to War'. *Survival*, 41(2), pp. 5–18. doi: 10.1093/survival/41.2.5.

Judah, T. (2000) *Kosovo: War and Revenge*, 2nd edn. New Haven, CT: Yale University Press.

Judah, T. (2008) *Kosovo: What Everyone Needs to Know.* Oxford: Oxford University Press.

Kalshoven, F. and Zegveld, L. (2001) *Constraints on the Waging of War: An Introduction to International Humanitarian Law*, 3rd edn. Geneva: ICRC.

Ker-Lindsay, J. (2009) *Kosovo: The Path to Contested Statehood in the Balkans (library of European studies).* London, United Kingdom: I.B.Tauris.

Kerr, R. (2013a) 'Introduction: Trials and Tribulations at the ICTY'. In: Gow, J., Kerr, R., and Pajić, Z. (eds), *Prosecuting War Crimes: Lessons and Legacies of the International Criminal Tribunal for the Former Yugoslavia.* London: Routledge.

Kerr, R. (2013b) 'Lost in Translation: Perceptions of the ICTY in the Former Yugoslavia'. In: Gow, J., Kerr, R., and Pajić, Z. (eds), *Prosecuting War Crimes: Lessons and Legacies of the International Criminal Tribunal for the Former Yugoslavia.* London: Routledge, pp. 102–114.

Kerr, R.C. (2004) *The International Criminal Tribunal for the Former Yugoslavia: An Exercise in Law, Politics and Diplomacy*. Oxford: Oxford University Press.

KFOR (2016) *NATO's Role in Kosovo*. Available at: http://jfcnaples.nato.int/kfor/about-us/welcome-to-kfor/natos-role-in-kosovo (Accessed: 16 August 2016).

Khan, M.I. (2013) 'Historical Record and the Legacy of the International Criminal Tribunal for the Former Yugoslavia'. In: Gow, J., Kerr, R., and Pajić, Z. (eds), *Prosecuting War Crimes: Lessons and Legacies of the International Criminal Tribunal for the Former Yugoslavia*. London: Routledge, pp. 88–102.

Klarin, M. (2009) 'The Impact of the ICTY Trials on Public Opinion in the Former Yugoslavia'. *Journal of International Criminal Justice*, 7(1), pp. 89–96. doi: 10.1093/jicj/mqp009.

Kosovo Census (2011) *Kosovo Population and Housing Census 2011, Final Results*.

Krieger, H. (ed.), (2012) *The Kosovo Conflict and International Law: An Analytical Documentation 1974–1999*. Cambridge, UK: Cambridge University Press.

Kritsiotis, D. (2000) 'The Kosovo Crisis and NATO's Application of Armed Force against the Federal Republic of Yugoslavia'. *International and Comparative Law Quarterly*, 49(02), pp. 330–359. doi: 10.1017/s0020589300064186.

Laursen, A. (2002) 'NATO, the War over Kosovo, and the ICTY Investigation'. *American University International Law Review*, 17(4).

Lyck, M. (2007) 'International Peace Enforcers and Indicted War Criminals: The Case of Ramush Haradinaj'. *International Peacekeeping*, 14(3), pp. 418–432. doi: 10.1080/13533310701422968.

Malcolm, N. (2002) *Kosovo: A Short History*. Basingstoke: Macmillan.

Michalski, M. and Gow, J. (2007) *War, Image and Legitimacy: Viewing Contemporary Conflict*. London: Routledge.

Milošević, S. (1989) *Speech by Slobodan Milošević, delivered at the central celebration marking the 600th anniversary of the Battle of Kosovo, held at Gazimestan* 28 June.

NATO (1999) *Statement Issued at the Extraordinary Ministerial Meeting of the North Atlantic Council held at NATO Headquarters, Brussels* 12 April.

Pettifer, J. (2012) *The Kosova Liberation Army: Underground War to Balkan Insurgency, 1948–2001*. London: C. Hurst and Co.

Rambouillet Accords (1999) *Interim Agreement for Peace and Self-Government in Kosovo*.

Registry of the ICTY (1999) *President Milosevic and Four Other Senior FRY Officials Indicted for Murder, Persecution and Deportation in Kosovo*. The Hague: Press Release. (JL/PIU/403-E).

Roberts, A. (1999) 'NATO's "Humanitarian War" over Kosovo'. *Survival*, 41(3), pp. 102–123. doi: 10.1093/survival/41.3.102.

Roscini, M. (2005) 'Targeting and Contemporary Aerial Bombardment'. *International and Comparative Law Quarterly*, 54(02), pp. 411–444. doi: 10.1093/iclq/lei006.

Scharf, M.P. (2003) 'The Legacy of the Milosevic Trial'. *New England Law Review*, 37(915).

Scheffer, D.J. (2002) 'Killing Fields and "Kangaroo" Courts: Symposium on an Emerging International Criminal Justice System'. *Davis Journal of International Law and Policy*, 45(9), pp. 45–52.

Weller, M. (2000) 'The Kosovo Indictment of the International Criminal Tribunal for Yugoslavia'. *International Journal of Human Rights*, 4(3–4), pp. 207–222. doi: 10.1080/13642980008406900.

5   The Special Tribunal for Lebanon and the legitimacy of Hezbollah

On 14 February 2005, the detonation of a truck filled with approximately 2500 kilograms of TNT ripped to pieces the armoured car of former Lebanese Prime Minister Rafik Hariri, killing him and 22 others. The explosion left a crater three metres deep and could be heard all over Beirut, but it was its aftershock that changed the political map of Lebanon. The 'Cedar Revolution' that followed the attack ended almost three decades of Syrian suzerainty in Lebanon and produced two rival blocs, the pro-Syrian March 8 Alliance and the anti-Syrian March 14 movement, that have since dominated Lebanese politics. The Sunni–Shia divide, deepening across the Muslim world, 'replaced the civil war's Muslim–Christian divide to become the dominant schism' in Lebanon.[1] The STL – a criminal court of an international character – was established to bring the perpetrators of the attack to justice, and the issue of the Court dominated Lebanese politics thereafter. Combined, these factors pushed tension in the multi-sectarian system to dangerous levels and paralysed the government on several occasions. Moreover, the staunch resistance to the STL by Hezbollah and the debate on disarming its militia further exacerbated animosity between pro- and anti-Syrian parties in Lebanon.[2]

Literature and research on the STL has largely focused on the legal foundation and jurisdiction of the Tribunal, and on the legal implications of the STL for international justice and law. Analysis on the impact of the STL on Lebanon is often limited to the crisis of the day. However, as part of a wider analysis of post-2005 Lebanese politics, Are Knudsen and Michael Kerr considered the domestic impact of the Tribunal in depth, including the impact on Hezbollah. The existing literature generally agrees that the STL is the odd one out in the field of international criminal justice because of the way it was established, its application of domestic law and ability to conduct full trials *in absentia*. But what most distinctively sets apart the STL from other mechanisms of international criminal justice is that its stated purpose is very narrowly defined as 'bringing to justice those responsible for the terrorist bombings of 14 February 2005'; a limited purpose that is reflected in its limited jurisdiction. The STL Statute remained silent regarding an aim to end impunity, even though it can be assumed the Tribunal has an implied purpose beyond mere retribution. Although none of the mechanisms of international criminal justice established so far have been free from critique, even from those who, in principle, support international criminal justice, the STL has met particularly heavy criticism. Criticism not only aimed at the limited jurisdiction, but also at the functioning of the Tribunal. The timing of its establishment, and the manner in which it was set up, exposed the STL to allegations that it was a political tool against Syria. Yet, this does not mean the Tribunal cannot have an impact. Changing narratives, indeed, reveal it has an effect on the legitimacy of various actors in Lebanon, including on what is arguably the most powerful QSE in the region – Hezbollah – whose members the Tribunal indicted for the murder of Hariri.

Much has been written on Hezbollah as a militia, a terrorist organisation or a political party. At times, or to some, it may be all of those things, but in this chapter the organisation is treated like a QSE as described in Chapter 2 and used as an example of an evolving QSE, at times a very successful one. The actions of the Hezbollah leadership, especially when under pressure of legitimacy crises, indicate that it understands the success of the organisation depends on creating legitimacy in various constituencies simultaneously. The present chapter will consider how Hezbollah creates and maintains legitimacy in various constituencies and how the investigation into the murder of Hariri and the subsequent indictments by the STL impacted on that ability. In addition, how the set-up of the Tribunal, its jurisdiction, actions and leaks from within the UN investigation, or the STL, combined with Hezbollah's strong bases of legitimacy, in the Shia community, and experience dealing with critical legitimacy moments, gave the organisation the opportunity to mitigate some of the negative effects that the implication of its members for the murder of Hariri could have had on its abilities to maintain legitimacy in certain constituencies. By providing counter narratives that fitted better with pre-existing ideas in its core constituencies, and with increased Sunni–Shia tension in Lebanon, Hezbollah managed to make the STL, and the indictment of four, and later five, of its members, at times as much a problem of the government of Saad Hariri, the 'March 14' parliamentary bloc, and the rest of Lebanon, as it was their own. Moreover, these counter narratives gave the organisation and its allies the chance to prevent the Tribunal from getting much closer to reaching its primary goal of bringing the perpetrators of the murder of Hariri to justice, or to justify its existence by representing a step towards ending political violence and 'ending impunity' for political assassinations in Lebanon.

The Special Tribunal for Lebanon

Hariri dominated post-civil war Lebanese politics, and the charismatic billionaire was about to run for a third term as prime minister when he was killed. Hariri was not the first victim of a high-profile political murder in Lebanon, nor would he be the last. It was not the first political assassination in Lebanon that led to outrage in the international community, nor was it the first time the UN Secretary-General and the Security Council condemned the assassination of a political figure in Lebanon – both had happened after the assassination of

President-elect Bashir Gemayel 23 years earlier.[3] However, the attack on Hariri would change the political balance in Lebanon and the region. Moreover, this time the UN, and especially permanent Security Council members France and the United States, seemed determined to identify and punish the perpetrators. The establishment of an international criminal tribunal to bring those who killed Hariri to justice illustrates, even more so than other international tribunals, that international criminal justice is effectively encircled by politics. The establishment of courts is highly political. Their funding is political. Their outcomes have political consequences. However, the courts themselves are expected to function purely juridically, judging on the legal merits of a case.

A culture of impunity for political assassinations

The day after the attack, the UN Security Council called on the Lebanese government to 'bring to justice the perpetrators, organizers and sponsors of this heinous terrorist act'.[4] Lebanese prosecutors briefly suspected four men who had allegedly fled to Australia and, 30 minutes after the attack, a video was released to *Al Jazeera*, in which a group calling itself 'Victory and Jihad in the Greater Syria' claimed responsibility for the attack and named Ahmad Abu Adass as the suicide bomber.[5] However, both notions were dismissed soon afterwards, and what remained was suspicion of Syrian involvement, despite a lack of credible evidence on who ordered and executed the assassination of Hariri.[6] Nevertheless the UN fact-finding mission stopped short of accusing Syria, but found that 'it is clear that the assassination took place in a political and security context marked by acute polarization around the Syrian influence in Lebanon' and that the Lebanese investigation had 'neither the capacity nor the commitment to reach a satisfactory and credible conclusion'.[7] As a result, the Council established the UN International Independent Investigation Commission (UNIIIC) to gather evidence and to assist the authorities in their investigation.[8]

That the Lebanese had not produced a credible investigation into the murder was not surprising. The security apparatus at the time was closely interwoven with the Syrian security services and had no tradition of thoroughly investigating political assassinations. Moreover, the premise of Lebanese politics was the proverbial 'no victor, no vanquished', and internal conflicts were usually defused by inter-sect compromise followed by collective amnesia rather than judicial processes,[9] despite Lebanon's long history of political murders – since the 1950s a president, a president-elect and three prime ministers had been assassinated, as well as (former) ministers, journalists, clerics, army officers and other political figures.[10] As political violence continued after the civil war, so did impunity. There were more than 30 high-profile assassinations since 1990, but in the few cases that justice was pursued, it was obstructed by politicised trials and few led to credible convictions.[11]

Often, changing alliances in Lebanon required political leaders to be forgiving of the crimes their new allies had committed against them. To facilitate this collective amnesia, Lebanon repeatedly turned to general amnesties.[12] The most far-reaching, the General Amnesty Law at the end of the civil war, granted amnesty for all political crimes committed by Lebanese citizens before 28 March 1991. Thus, nobody was held responsible for the most horrible atrocities committed and the estimated 100,000–150,000 Lebanese killed in the conflict.[13] On the contrary, the law ensured immunity from prosecution for war crimes for militia leaders-turned-politicians and furthered an existing culture of impunity for political crimes.[14]

UNSC Resolution 1757 on the establishment of the Special Tribunal for Lebanon

Contrary to tradition, the murder of Hariri was thoroughly investigated, albeit by the UN. To prosecute those responsible for his murder the STL was established. This was the result of a combination of factors: the power of Hariri's legacy united a large part of the Lebanese Sunni in the Future Movement; and the stance of France and the United States. Moreover, by 2005 the ICTY, ICTR and the SCSL had proved their utility.[15] Although Lebanon was not a signatory to the Rome Statute, the Security Council could have referred the case to the ICC, were it not for the fact that it was highly doubtful that the murder of Hariri constituted one of the international crimes over which the Court has jurisdiction, as described in Article 6–8 of the Rome Statute. It was, therefore, that the government of Fouad Siniora asked the UN to create a tribunal 'of an international character'.[16]

Unsurprisingly, pressing for an international tribunal led to a government crisis when, in November 2006, all Shia ministers resigned.[17] The Speaker of Parliament, Nabih Berri, refused to convene parliament to hold a vote on the ratification of the 'agreement for the Special Tribunal for Lebanon' that the UN and the Lebanese government had signed on 23 January 2007. The conflicting views on the Tribunal of the pro-Syrian 'March 8' bloc and the anti-Syrian 'March 14' coalition provoked an 18-month political stalemate.[18] To circumvent the stalemated parliament the Tribunal was established by UNSC Resolution 1757 of 30 May 2007.[19] That the Security Council was willing to use Chapter VII, its most far-reaching powers, to go beyond state sovereignty had to do with the standing of the victim, the existence of a precedent for establishing an international court and the fact that the case could not be brought before the ICC, but that the prime suspect (Syria) was targeted by Western countries and the UN undoubtedly played a role as well.[20]

On 1 March 2009, the STL opened in Leidschendam, a suburb of The Hague, as an independent judicial organisation, not a UN Court. The location was chosen to 'ensure justice, fairness and security', but the distance to the *locus delicti* is a problem for the judicial process and its legitimacy in Lebanon.[21] The Tribunal's international judges outnumbered the Lebanese judges and, like the prosecutor and registrar, are all appointed by the UN Secretary-General, with the Lebanese judges being chosen from a list of nominees submitted by the Lebanese government.[22] The expenses of the Tribunal (between 2009 and 2016 about €60 million per year) are shared.[23] Fifty-one per cent comes from voluntary contributions by UN Member States and although the Lebanese government is legally bound to pay its 49 per cent share, Hezbollah and other pro-Syrian parties made sure that the funding of the Tribunal became a highly contentious issue.[24]

The jurisdiction of the STL

The Statute of the STL provided 'jurisdiction over persons responsible for the attack of 14 February 2005 resulting in the death of former Lebanese Prime Minister Rafiq Hariri',[25] but if the Tribunal were to find that other attacks that occurred in Lebanon between 1 October 2004 and 12 December 2005 were connected to this attack, its jurisdiction would be extended to those responsible for those attacks.[26] The begin and end dates limiting the jurisdiction were not random, being the dates of the assassination attempt on Marwan Hamadeh, and the assassination of Gibran Tueni.[27] Although a number of attacks occurred during that period, the pre-trial judge ruled that there was only *prima facie* evidence that the attacks on Marwan Hamadeh, George Hawi and Elias el-Murr were connected to the attack of 14 February 2005, thereby establishing jurisdiction of the Tribunal over these cases.[28] In the years that followed, a number of political and army figures were assassinated, including Internal Security Forces (ISF) Captain Wissam Eid, who led investigations into five interconnected mobile phone groups that were used prior to the attack on Hariri and that later proved to be the backbone of the evidence against the individuals indicted by the STL.[29] Broadening the jurisdiction to include crimes connected with the assassination of Hariri that occurred after 12 December 2005 would require agreement between the Security Council and the Lebanese government.[30]

Applicable law

While the ICTY and ICTR were limited to prosecuting crimes under international law and other hybrid tribunals have jurisdiction over both crimes under municipal law and crimes under international law, the STL was unique in that there were no provisions in the Statute for prosecuting a crime under international law.[31] While Article 2 of the Statute stated that the substantive laws applicable were the relevant provisions in the Lebanese Criminal Code, Article 3 added modes of criminal liability found in international law, most notably joint criminal enterprise and command responsibility.[32] This made the Tribunal well suited to prosecuting high-ranking officials who failed to stop subordinates from executing the plot, but might conflict with the *nullum crimen sine lege* principle, as joint criminal enterprise and command responsibility do not exist in this form under Lebanese criminal law.[33] In a decision on the applicable law, the Appeals Chamber interpreted the provisions that: 'under the Tribunal's Statute the Judges are called upon primarily to apply Lebanese law to the facts coming within the purview of the Tribunal's jurisdiction'.[34] This stipulated that the definition of the crime of terrorism, as described under Lebanese law, should be applied, but it also held that it would do so 'in consonance with international conventional and customary law that is binding on Lebanon'.[35] The Appeals Chamber further held that:

> [A]lthough it is held by many scholars and other legal experts that no widely accepted definition of terrorism has evolved [...] a customary rule of international law regarding the international crime of terrorism, at least *in time of peace*, has indeed emerged.[36]

This decision has been heavily discussed, and is not without critics. The lack of consensus in the international community on the crime of terrorism, and the Appeals Chamber's reliance on domestic laws to establish *opinio juris*, make it doubtful such an *opinio* exists, or existed in February 2005.[37] Moreover, there is no need for an internationalist interpretation of the crime of terrorism by the STL, as terrorism is sufficiently described under Lebanese law.[38]

Trial in absentia

Article 22 of its Statute allows the STL to conduct a full trial *in absentia*. While prosecutors at the ICTY had to wait 16 years to start proceedings against Ratko Mladić while he evaded arrest and the ICC is waiting for someone to arrest Sudanese President al-Bashir, the STL could start trial proceedings when all reasonable steps had been taken to secure the appearance of the accused.[39] In February 2012, the Trial Chamber decided to proceed to try four accused *in absentia*.[40] The first trial of the Tribunal, *The Prosecutor v. Ayyash et al.*, started on 16 January 2014 without any of the five accused in custody. While some commentators noted that the conditions in which to hold a trial before the STL without the defendant present are stringent enough,[41] others argued that it could prevent a fair trial and did not live up to the 'highest standard of justice' the STL was established to uphold.[42]

Critique on the STL

It is not surprising that the Tribunal has been under constant attack from pro-Syrian factions in Lebanon, including Hezbollah, but while they often did not get further than resorting to various conspiracy theories, the set-up of the STL also made it vulnerable to substantial criticism. It is 'prone to allegations of being a political tool and not a legal body', not only because its setting up was supported by the West, but also because it went against Lebanese political tradition by making liability for a political crime a legal question rather than something up for negotiation.[43]

Much of the legal criticism focused on the Tribunal's limited jurisdiction. It could be argued that the selectivity in setting the mandate of the Tribunal was unjustifiable, as Lebanon had been confronted by many other violent incidents before and afterwards, some claiming more casualties than attacks that fall within the jurisdiction of the STL.[44] Moreover, the limited purpose of the Tribunal, as reflected in its jurisdiction, was not in line with the wider justification of international justice to end impunity.

Discussions about the impact of the STL on Lebanese sovereignty, specifically the idea that the UNSC resolution bypassed Lebanese democracy, were not limited to Lebanon.[45] The Council adopted Resolution 1757 with ten votes in favour, but permanent members China and Russia, as well as South Africa, Qatar and Indonesia abstained, fearing that 'Lebanese sovereignty was being unduly encroached on'.[46] In the Resolution, the Council, acting under Chapter VII, decided that the annex to the Resolution would enter into force on 10 June 2007. Bardo Fassbender argues that what 'the Security Council in fact sought to accomplish with Resolution 1757 was to put the Agreement into effect, despite the absence of ratification by Lebanon'.[47]

The timing of the establishment of the Tribunal has led to allegations that the STL had been 'tailor-made to further a certain view of recent Lebanese history'.[48] It came at a moment when both the investigations of the UN and Lebanese authorities pointed towards the involvement of high-ranking Syrian officials. One could argue that some of the provisions in the Statute of the STL could be best explained by expectations of the outcomes at the time of its establishment, and that its limited jurisdiction was not in line with the aims of international criminal justice towards 'putting an end to impunity' for serious crimes regardless of where, when and by whom they were committed.[49]

From the beginning, the Tribunal was also plagued by leaks. Following the publication of a list of witnesses the registrar even appointed a special investigator to probe 'unauthorised disclosures'.[50] Finally, three top officials and six senior staff members of the Tribunal quit during the first 18 months after it opened, and rumours that they resigned after outside attempts to influence their work weakened the Tribunal.[51] On 10 October 2013 the indictment against a fifth suspect was made public, this time – and in contrast to the indictments that were issued against four individuals in 2011 – the indictment was not leaked while under seal.

Hezbollah and Lebanon

In order to see how the actions of the STL impacted the legitimacy of Hezbollah, to assess the narratives that Hezbollah used to counter the challenges to its legitimacy, it is important to first understand Hezbollah, its rise, organisation and strategy. As a QSE-cum-political party, Hezbollah differs from most other QSEs in that, besides running a Shia militia, it also entered politics as a political party using the democratic process to change the status quo. Hezbollah has statehood aspirations in that it wants to change the system of the state, not to separate a part of Lebanon to create a different state. Despite claims to the contrary by its opponents, Hezbollah acknowledged that not all of their original aims, such as establishing an Islamic state, are attainable in multi-sectarian Lebanon. Nevertheless, the organisation took over many state functions in large parts of the country. It continued to run parallel institutions even when its representatives became part of the government. Hezbollah withstood numerous demands from both the Lebanese government and the UN to disarm its militia. It showed that, when pressured, it was willing to use its advanced military and security apparatus within Lebanon against the Lebanese.

The emergence of Hezbollah

To understand how present-day Hezbollah became one of the most complex organisations of all Islamist movements, one has to look at how it came about. In 1982, the year its leader Hassan Nasrallah refers to as the year of its establishment, Hezbollah was, at most, an amalgamation of various radical clandestine Shia activists.[52] Yet, the young Shia clerics that founded it proved adept at providing a narrative that fitted with pre-existing ideas of its core constituents, the Lebanese Shia. Ignored by the government and led by feudal leaders – who primarily took care of their own interests – the Shia, as a group, had been trailing behind the rest of the country for years. The living conditions in Lebanon's rural areas, like the Bekaa Valley and southern Lebanon, where the Shia were concentrated, had not improved during Lebanon's periods of prosperity and lacked most basic facilities.[53] Growing political and economic inequality reinforced the lack of a framework for individual and collective identity for the Lebanese Shia, while the all-encompassing life system of Islam, that includes religion, state and law, provided a framework of identity that the multi-confessional state could not provide.[54] The structural imbalance of civil war-torn Lebanon increased the potential for radicalism and militancy, and provided the perfect conditions for a religious militia to emerge.[55] The Israeli invasion in 1982 served as a crisis catalyst in that it provided the impetus for the emergence of a radical militant organisation.[56] Initially, many Shia tacitly allowed the Israelis to expel the Palestine Liberation Organisation (PLO), a QSE that had effectively created a 'state within a state' in Southern Lebanon.[57] Yet, ongoing Israeli domination created an environment in which Hezbollah could flourish. Or, as Ehud Barak told *Newsweek* in 2006: 'When we entered Lebanon [...] there was no Hezbollah. We were accepted with perfumed rice and flowers by the Shia in the south. It was our presence there that created Hezbollah'.[58]

Hezbollah gained notoriety with a series of high-profile attacks. In November 1982, a car filled with explosives drove into the Israel Defense Forces (IDF) headquarters in Tyre, killing 141 people. The attack set a lethal trend and between 1982 and 1985 there were at least 30 similar attacks against Israeli and Western targets,[59] most notably the US embassy bombing in April 1983, and the attacks on the US marine barracks and the French forces in October 1983, the latter killing almost 300 people, including 241 US marines.[60] Because Hezbollah did not yet formally exist it is hard to determine which of those early actions can be attributed to the organisation, and Hezbollah leaders later made ambiguous statements regarding the attacks.[61] Yet, the United States concluded that Hezbollah was behind the bombings, and that Syria and Iran must have operated behind the scenes, as Hezbollah was not in a position to plan and execute such operations alone.[62]

The open letter to the 'Downtrodden in Lebanon and the World', by which Hezbollah declared its existence, and the formation of the 'Islamic Resistance', in February 1985, added to its radical image. The writers of the letter identified themselves as 'the sons of Hezbollah's *umma* (community of Muslims), whose vanguard God has given victory in Iran'.[63] They committed to abiding by the orders of the *Wali al-Faqih*, the jurisprudent (Ayatollah Khomeini).[64] They stated that 'each of us is a soldier when the call of *Jihad* demands it', and listed their bare minimum of aspirations as saving Lebanon from 'its dependence upon East and West, ending foreign occupation, and adopting a regime freely wanted by the people of Lebanon'.[65] Yet, despite the deeply religious rhetoric of the manifest, it called for the implementation of an 'Islamic order on the basis of direct and free choice [...] not on the basis of force'.[66]

Building a state within a state

Hezbollah's grass-roots organisation, and ability to operate as a successful QSE providing state function, grew the longer the Israeli occupation lasted. At the same time, attacks on the IDF intensified. By 1984, Shia insurgents were killing an Israeli soldier every three days.[67] In 1985, Israel pulled back to the 'security zone', an area comprising around 10 per cent of Lebanon's territory that proved to be a magnet for attacks on the IDF.[68] But, the poverty and misery of the Shia not only fuelled radicalism and militancy, they also gave Hezbollah's leadership no other option than to tackle some of the socio-economic problems within the Shia community in order to maintain support from the communities they fought among – and from which its fighters came. By providing aid to the families of killed militants and people who suffered from the Israeli attacks, and by creating crisis teams to rebuild houses, Hezbollah took the first steps towards what later would become its social organisation, providing public goods and exercising functions of state. In the late 1980s, Jihad al-Binaa – Hezbollah's construction organisation – the Islamic Health Committee (IHC) and the Relief Committee were officially recognised by the Ministry of Internal Affairs. They marked Hezbollah's first official ventures outside the secrecy of its militia. Over several decades, Hezbollah's social organisation professionalised and grew spectacularly. The organisation started to provide more and more 'government services' throughout the *Dahiya*, the Bekaa Valley and southern Lebanon, from water supply to education, and from garbage collection to electricity.[69] By 2013, Hezbollah managed to provide social welfare to the poorest families, run cooperative supermarkets and firms and operate a network of schools, hospitals and orphanages.[70]

Hezbollah as a political party

Hezbollah's leadership initially expressed doubts over whether participation in Lebanon's first post-civil war elections, in 1992, and in a 'non-Islamic' government, would be legitimate.[71] Yet, in 1991, Abbas al-Musawi replaced hardliner al-Tufayli as secretary general and started to shift the focus on political participation. This decision was widely popular among the politically disenfranchised Shia, and gave Hezbollah the chance to shape political dialogue and resist political initiatives.[72] Al-Musawi facilitated the release of the last hostages held in Lebanon. Most Lebanese resented the taking of hostages and the costs of losing popular support proved to be too high.[73] The end of the Lebanese Civil War and the Iran–Iraq War marked a period of change for Hezbollah. The Taif Agreement reinforced the power-sharing agreement of the National Pact, but also stipulated the disbanding of all militias.[74] Although Hezbollah signed the Agreement, with the consent of Iran, it justified keeping its forces armed as a resistance force aimed at ending the Israeli occupation.[75]

Al-Musawi reinvigorated the fighting against Israel but his term was cut short when, in February 1992, he and his family were killed by an IDF helicopter strike.[76] Hassan Nasrallah was quickly appointed as secretary general to oversee Hezbollah's participation in the 1992 elections. Internally, the organisation maintained a governing structure revolving around the personal appeal of its religious leaders and Islamic doctrine to keep party members in line. But, unlike other parties, it also presented a coherent political and social programme that emphasised non-religious themes, such as economic exploitation, corruption, inequality and security.[77]

The 'resistance' and its adversary, the IDF

While Hezbollah's military capabilities continued to grow, with the help of Iran and Syria, its exceedingly effective guerrilla army showed that it was willing to adhere to some rules. A *modus vivendi* arose that stipulated that the IDF would not attack civilians, and Hezbollah in turn would focus on military targets in the security zone.[78] In 1993, this understanding was clearly articulated after 'Operation Accountability', during which Israel bombed 50 villages and killed more than 130 civilians in response to Hezbollah's killing of eight IDF soldiers.[79] Despite continuing Hezbollah attacks on IDF targets, the 'rules of the game' led to relatively quiet years until 1996, when Israel launched 'Operation Grapes of Wrath' to undermine popular support for Hezbollah and force the Lebanese government to disarm the Islamic Resistance.[80] The contrary happened when Israeli shelling of the UNIFIL base at Qana killed 109 civilians who had taken refuge there. This only strengthened many Lebanese in their opinion that Hezbollah's military actions should continue. Rafik Hariri, at that time nearing the end of his first term as prime minister, stated that the Lebanese people had 'a legitimate right and duty to resist', until Israel abided by Security Council Resolution 425.[81]

Hezbollah's superior ability as a guerrilla organisation to manoeuvre effectively within the rules, eventually led to the withdrawal of Israel, in 2000. Largely deprived of the justification for their arms and actions against the IDF, Hezbollah used the Lebanese claim to the Shebaa Farms as a pretext to continue military operations, despite the UN Security Council conclusion that Israel had withdrawn its forces, in accordance with Resolution 425.[82] However, Hezbollah's military success against the IDF, in combination with its successful running of many state-like institutions in Shia-dominated areas, also meant that the government of Rafik Hariri was unable to disarm Hezbollah. The government therefore maintained the 'resistance' point of view, even after Security Council Resolution 1559 of 2 September 2004 again called for the disarmament of all militias.

The 2006 War

The assassination of Hariri in February 2005, and the subsequent establishment of the STL, changed the political environment in Lebanon drastically. However, as Sunni–Shia tensions increased concerning Syrian influence over Lebanon, the STL, and Hezbollah's weapons, the organisation managed to strengthen its position as the first and foremost protector of Shia interests in Lebanon. Moreover, it remained a staunch supporter of Syria and made clear it would protect Assad's interests in Lebanon. It became the leading party in the pro-Syrian 'March 8' alliance and relentlessly opposed the STL, at the time that Syria was the main suspect in the murder of Hariri. As a political party, Hezbollah consistently received a large part of the Shia vote,[83] yet it was only after Syrian military withdrawal that it was forced to join the government to protect its interests.[84] As part of the coalition government, a situation arose in which Hezbollah, in parallel, was a QSE retaining the means to fight, or threaten, the state in order to change it. However, the 'national unity' cabinet, of which Hezbollah became part, reached a stalemate soon after the 2005 elections. Hezbollah ministers refused to take part in cabinet meetings after it had voted in favour of an international tribunal, only to return to government after Prime Minister Siniora acknowledged Hezbollah's role as a national resistance movement.[85] With Syria out of Lebanon, and relative calm on the border with Israel, increasing numbers of Lebanese started to demand the disarmament of Hezbollah. In an attempt to silence the proponents of disarmament by military success, Hezbollah tried to capture five IDF soldiers. Although actions against military targets fell within the 'rules of the game', this time it pushed Israel to start a 34-day-long war in July 2006. Israel launched massive air strikes and artillery fire, an air and naval blockade and a ground invasion of southern Lebanon, while Hezbollah launched more than 4000 rockets into northern Israel and engaged the IDF in guerrilla warfare. The war came at great cost for both countries (an estimated US$2 billion for Israel and US$5 billion for Lebanon): large parts of the Lebanese civilian infrastructure were destroyed, including Beirut's international airport; almost every city in Lebanon was bombed; and large parts of Beirut were left in rubble.[86] The intensity of the bombing that took place just before the ceasefire agreement came into effect supports the accusation that Israel deliberately attacked and destroyed civilian infrastructure.[87] The conflict displaced approximately one million Lebanese civilians, and at least 1191 Lebanese and 44 Israeli civilians were killed, as well as 119 IDF soldiers and at least 250 Hezbollah fighters (the IDF claimed the number was over 600).[88]

For Israel, the war ended disastrously. As Hezbollah held out longer than Israel could withstand international pressure for a ceasefire, and by failing to come even close to destroying Hezbollah, the strength of the skilled and highly motivated militia against a regular army was again demonstrated.[89] Nasrallah claimed a 'divine victory' but, if anything, it was a pyrrhic victory; UNSC Resolution 1701, again called for Hezbollah's disarmament, and for the deployment of Lebanese soldiers and an enlarged UNIFIL force in southern Lebanon.[90] More important, the whole Lebanese population had suffered as a result of Hezbollah's actions. After the war, Hezbollah demanded a veto within the national unity government, but when the Hezbollah and Amal ministers resigned from the cabinet after Siniora had pushed for the STL its Shia constituencies were left without government representation. From then onwards, Hezbollah deemed Siniora's cabinet 'illegitimate', as did President Lahoud, and both continued to oppose the government's decision to work with the UN towards establishing the STL.

Hezbollah turns its weapons towards Beirut

When, in December 2006, Hezbollah protests against the government became more ferocious and the organisation blocked the streets of Beirut, the whole of Lebanon feared another round of sectarian violence. Although Nasrallah ended the protests in January 2007, it was a reminder that the fate of Lebanon was in the hands of Hezbollah's leaders.[91] The political deadlock over the Tribunal lasted until May 2008, when it escalated after the government moved to dissolve Hezbollah's parallel communications network and to remove the head of airport security over his alleged ties to Hezbollah.[92] Militants blocked the airport, as well as the main city streets, paralysing Beirut; gun battles erupted between Hezbollah supporters and pro-government loyalists; and Nasrallah called the government's decision 'a declaration of war'.[93] Deploying its militia on the streets of Beirut reminded the Lebanese that, despite Hezbollah's assurances that its weapons would always remain aiming south, they could also be used internally. After a week, the 'March 14' majority and 'March 8' opposition signed the Doha Agreement that ended the period of crisis that resulted in 14 assassinations of political leaders.[94]

Hezbollah came out of the crisis apparently more powerful than ever. It kept its communications network, the head of airport security was reinstated and its arsenal had been greatly enhanced by Iran.[95] General Suleiman, hailed for keeping the army on the sidelines during the crisis, became president. A national unity government was formed in which Hezbollah controlled 11 of the 30 ministerial posts and was effectively given veto power over government decisions. Yet the relationship between 'March 14' and 'March 8', and between Lebanon's Sunni and Shia, also further polarised. Moreover, it seemed Hezbollah was having trouble balancing the perceptions of its identity as a QSE, operating many state-like institutions, and a militia that denied the Lebanese state a legitimate monopoly on violence, and used force and the threat of force to change the system of the state. It was against this background that Hezbollah was confronted with an article in *Der Spiegel* that suggested that the STL was about to indict members of Hezbollah. The leaks pushed Hezbollah into a dangerous corner, forcing it to change its narratives and installing fear among Lebanese of a repetition of the crisis of 2008, or worse. Hezbollah's legitimacy, outside its core Shia constituencies, had been feeble at the best of times. Now, as its members were implicated in the murder of Hariri, it had to deal with legitimacy crises in various constituencies. It was to be the beginning of a series of legitimacy crises Hezbollah had to deal with as a result of the indictments and investigations of the STL and the revelations of Hezbollah's involvement in the assassination of Hariri.

The assassination of Rafik Hariri and the end of 'Pax Syriana'

To understand the impact of the murder of Hariri and the STL on Lebanon and Hezbollah, the key lies not in Beirut, but 55 miles to the east, in Damascus. By 2005, Syria had maintained a military presence in Lebanon for almost 29 years.[96] Contrary to the Taif Agreement, Syrian influence in Lebanon significantly increased after the civil war.[97] It was only after the withdrawal of Israeli forces from South Lebanon in 2000 that Syrian suzerainty started to be seriously challenged. Initially, Prime Minister Hariri, who had started his second term shortly after Israel's withdrawal and the death of Syrian President Hafez al-Assad, steered clear of taking a position in this debate, yet it was public knowledge that his relationship with President Lahoud – described either as a staunch ally of Syria or as a puppet of Assad – was severely strained, often to a point where it paralysed the government.[98]

As the presidency of Lahoud was due to reach its constitutional six-year limit in November 2004, (Maronite) presidential prospects started lining up. [99] Although Assad declared in public that the presidential election was an internal Lebanese affair, Damascus started to push for an extension of Lahoud's mandate, for which it needed Hariri's bloc in parliament to vote in favour of a constitutional amendment.[100] While he defended Assad in public, the discussion on constitutional amendments became part of the wider discussion about Syria's presence in Lebanon, and Hariri was warned by Assad not to oppose the extension.[101] According to Hariri, the Syrian president had threatened that he 'would rather break Lebanon over the heads of Hariri and [Druze leader] Jumblatt than see his word in Lebanon broken'.[102] With a large Syrian troop presence in Lebanon, Hariri deemed the risk of plunging the country into another round of political and sectarian violence to be too high, and told confidants that Assad had left him no choice but to support the extension.[103]

The 2004 constitutional crisis

As the relationship between Hariri's Western allies and Syria had deteriorated in the wake of the attacks of 11 September 2001, Hariri had found himself in an increasingly difficult position. On 2 September 2004, the UN Security Council adopted Resolution 1559, calling for the disarmament of all militias (including

Hezbollah), free and fair elections and the withdrawal of all remaining foreign troops from Lebanon.[104] The Resolution, pushed by France and the United States, did not mention Syria explicitly but contained an unequivocal message, addressed to the Assad government, to end the Syrian hold on Lebanon. Assad held Hariri personally responsible for the action of the Council but, even though a day after the Resolution passed Hariri reluctantly voted with the parliamentary majority in favour of extending the presidential term, he announced only days later that he would resign as prime minister. On 1 October, Druze politician Marwan Hamadeh, a Hariri ally, who had voted against the constitutional amendment, was severely injured when a bomb exploded next to his car. While tensions were rising in Lebanon, Lahoud accepted Hariri's resignation only for Hariri immediately to start negotiations with political leaders of other sects to form a broad anti-Syrian coalition for the upcoming elections.[105]

Mass protest and shifting legitimacy follow the killing of Hariri

It was against this background that Hariri was killed, on 14 February 2005. Although there was no direct evidence of Syrian involvement, it was clear in the minds of many Lebanese that the Assad regime had a motive to silence the anti-Syrian opposition. Moreover, few believed that such a sophisticated plot could be executed without prior knowledge of the head of Syrian intelligence in Lebanon, Rustum Ghazaleh. Almost instantly, Syria's presence in Lebanon was plunged into the downward spiral of a legitimacy crisis, which it was not to overcome. Hours after the attack, leading members of the opposition stated that they held 'the Lebanese authority and the Syrian authority, being the authority of tutelage in Lebanon, responsible for this crime'.[106] Most Western governments, although stopping short of accusing Syria of the bombing outright, also called for an immediate Syrian withdrawal.[107] On 21 February, French President Jacques Chirac and US President George W. Bush released a joint declaration calling on Syria to leave Lebanon.[108] Assad himself conveyed his 'sincerest condolences to the family of Mr Hariri', and said that Syria stood fraternally alongside Lebanon in difficult times,[109] yet the streets of Beirut filled with mourners who called for Assad to withdraw his troops. On 19 February, opposition leaders called for 'an intifada for independence', and daily mass protests against Syria on Beirut's Martyr Square forced pro-Syrian Prime Minister Omar Karami to resign on 28 February.[110] A week later, under pressure from the international community and mass protests in Lebanon, and after even Russia had urged its ally to withdraw its troops from Lebanon, Assad pledged the withdrawal of all Syrian troops from Lebanon.[111] However, on 8 March, a reported one million protesters, mainly Shia supporters of Hezbollah and Amal, came down to central Beirut in a counter demonstration organised by pro-Syrian parties.[112] They thanked Syria, protested against Resolution 1559 and denounced what Nasrallah called 'the interfering of the United States and Israel in Lebanon's internal affairs'.[113] On 14 March, an even larger crowd came to Martyr Square – by then the place of Hariri's tomb – demanding the immediate withdrawal of Syrian troops and the arrest of the chief of the security and intelligence services.[114] These mass demonstrations together drew half the Lebanese population to downtown Beirut. They also showed the deep divide within the country. From then onwards, 'March 8' and 'March 14' would be used to identify the pro- and anti-Syrian blocs in parliament, respectively. On 26 April 2005, Syria informed the UN that its 'forces stationed in Lebanon [...] have fully with- drawn all their military, security apparatus and assets to their positions in Syria'.[115] 'March 14', led by Rafik Hariri's son Saad, won the first Lebanese elections without a Syrian security presence in June 2005. The next month, Fouad Siniora became prime minister of a 'national unity' government that included members of Hezbollah.[116]

Leaks, rumours and indictments

One of the first acts of the STL after it opened, in March 2009, was to order the release of four Lebanese generals who had been detained by the Lebanese authorities in connection with the Hariri investigation. The pre-trial judge ruled that, on the basis of the information available to the Tribunal, there was no cause to hold Jamil El Sayed, Ali El Hajj, Raymond Azar and Mostafa Hamdan.[117] After his release, General El Sayed claimed that the evidence provided by what he called false witnesses, paid by Saad Hariri, had led to his detention and suspi- cion of Syria.[118] He filed an unsuccessful request to the president of the STL to disqualify the Lebanese judges, as well as an application requesting 'evidentiary material related to the crimes of libellous denunciations and arbitrary deten- tion'.[119] The generals had been held on the basis of investigations done by UNIIIC and, in particular, the statements of two self-proclaimed former Syrian intelligence officers. The STL later declared that these witnesses were not con- sidered to be reliable witnesses but the Tribunal had no jurisdiction to prosecute them for giving false statements to the UN investigation.[120] Despite the fact that the Tribunal was unable to do anything against 'false testimonies' and those that allegedly gave them, and did not rely on these witnesses, the generals' claim that 'false witnesses' had testified was used by opponents of the STL in their efforts to delegitimise the Tribunal. This became a frequent talking point in the criticisms of 'March 8' officials, directed at the Tribunal.[121] The pro-Syrian fac- tions, led by Hezbollah, managed to make it the primary focus of the public debate, overshadowing the work of the Tribunal and, at times, even the crime it was established to investigate.

The counter narratives, including 'false witnesses', aimed at discrediting the Tribunal, intensified when, in May 2009, German news magazine *Der Spiegel* published a report that the Tribunal was investigating members of Hezbollah in connection with the murder of Hariri. The author, Erich Follath, claimed that he 'learned from sources close to the tribunal and verified by examining internal documents' that '[i]ntensive investigations in Lebanon are all pointing to a new conclusion: that it was not the Syrians, but instead special forces of the Lebanese Shia organization Hezbollah [...] that planned and executed the diabolical attack'.[122] The article revealed how the phone data investigated by Captain Wissam Eid – who, by the time the article was published, had been assassinated himself – had identified circles of mobile phones used by those believed to be involved in the attack.[123] One of the phones had been linked to Abd al-Majid Ghamlush, a member of Hezbollah, after he used it to call his girlfriend.[124] Allegedly, this led the investigators to the masterminds of the attack, Salim Jamil Ayyash and Mustafa Amine Badreddine, known members of Hezbollah.[125]

Hezbollah reacted by saying that the article 'was an attempt to tarnish its image before parliamentary elections in Lebanon on June 7'.[126] In a speech, Nasrallah said that 'we see the *Der Spiegel* report as an Israeli accusation', and claimed that '*Der Spiegel* belongs to the Zionist lobby, which funds its operations'.[127] Yet, the general election that took place a week after the article in *Der Spiegel* remained peaceful and, in a speech on *al-Manar*, Nasrallah conceded the victory to 'March 14', and congratulated his opponents.[128] However, he also said that Hezbollah would only work within a national unity government if it retained its veto over cabinet decisions.[129]

The fear of plunging the country into a sectarian war meant that even Saad Hariri and his 'March 14' coalition decided to avoid rhetoric that could be interpreted as bellicose or supporting accusations that Hezbollah was involved in killing Hariri. Moreover, as no other sources had backed up the *Der Spiegel* story, by the beginning of 2010, it seemed that the Tribunal could be deterred from proceeding towards a meaningful prosecution.[130] While Nasrallah continued his rhetoric against the STL, condemning the investigation and claiming it to be an Israeli project to destabilise Lebanon and the unity government, the STL investigation – and the suggestion that Hezbollah might have been behind the attack on his father – put Saad Hariri in an increasingly difficult position.[131]

The situation became potentially explosive in summer 2010. Nasrallah announced that Saad Hariri shared the information with him that members of Hezbollah would be indicted by the STL. To defuse the situation Hariri had assured Nasrallah that those implicated by the STL were 'undisciplined' Hezbollah members, and that it was not the party itself that would be accused of murdering his father.[132] Hariri thereby provided Hezbollah with an opportunity to distance itself from the suspects, while he maintained the peace, stayed in power and continued to support the Tribunal. However, this strategy failed when Nasrallah vowed that he would resist even the arrest of 'half a member' of Hezbollah.[133] Tensions rose so high in late July that, amid fears a sectarian conflict would erupt, a delegation of Arab leaders consisting of Syrian President Bashar al-Assad, Saudi King Abdullah and Emir of Qatar Sheikh Hamad al-Thani visited Lebanon in an effort to calm the situation and to ensure the continued power sharing between their respective clients: Hezbollah and Saad Hariri.[134]

Paul Salem, the head of the Beirut-based Carnegie Middle East Centre, was quoted in relation to the alarming situation and 'worrisome position' of Hezbollah, in summer 2010:

If there is movement towards peace in the region, then Hezbollah has a problem. If there's movement toward war, Hezbollah has a problem. And now if the tribunal moves forward, they will also have a problem.[135]

This precarious situation gave Hezbollah all the more reason to continue its attacks on the Tribunal. In a speech on 8 August 2010, Nasrallah presented evidence that Israel was behind the killings.[136] Nasrallah urged all Lebanese to boycott the investigation, branding cooperation with the STL as an 'attack on the resistance'.[137] He said that Hezbollah would 'cut off the hand' of anyone who tried to arrest any of its members charged by the STL.[138] Meanwhile, Saad Hariri backtracked and declared that he had made a mistake by accusing Syria and that this had been a political accusation, though at the same time he assured that the Tribunal was not political and would 'only look at evidence'.[139]

The political crisis culminated in the collapse of the Hariri government in January 2011. Eleven Hezbollah ministers and their 'March 8' allies resigned from the national unity cabinet, as indications that Hezbollah members would be indicted became stronger and after Hariri had refused to call a cabinet meeting to discuss withdrawing Lebanon's cooperation with the STL.[140] Hariri would have been unable to end the cooperation with the STL, both in terms of losing support among his Sunni constituents and the international community, and in the light of international agreements and the UNSC resolution. The latter was confirmed by the fact that his successors as prime minister, the Hezbollah-backed Najib Mikati, and later independent 'consensus Prime Minister' Tammam Salam have never been able to end the cooperation with the STL either.

A week after the fall of the Hariri government, the first indictments were submitted to the pre-trial judge of the STL, the contents of which remained confidential, at that stage. When, in March 2011, an amended indictment was filed by the Prosecutor, this led to speculation that senior Hezbollah members would be indicted as well, but it took until 28 June 2011 for the Tribunal to issue sealed arrest warrants to the Prosecutor General of Lebanon.[141] Only a day later, the names of the suspects were leaked to the press: Salim Ayyash, Mustafa Badreddine, Hussein Anaissi and Assad Sabra, all four known to be Hezbollah members.[142] As a result of the leak, Hezbollah had had time to prepare when, on 28 July, the pre-trial judge ordered the lifting of confidentiality of personal details of the individuals named in the indictment.[143] Unsurprisingly, in August, the Lebanese authorities had to report back to the STL that it had not been able to apprehend the suspects. Although Nasrallah was given another chance to distance himself and Hezbollah from the accused, he again decided not to do so. Instead, he rejected the Tribunal as a foreign conspiracy against his organisation, and reiterated that the indicted individuals would not be arrested, under any circumstances.[144]

By the time the first trial started, in January 2014, the political situation in Lebanon had changed dramatically. First, the civil war in Syria led to the influx of more than a million Syrian refugees into Lebanon, representing more than 25 per cent of the country's population and putting enormous pressure on government and society.[145] Second, although Hezbollah supported Assad from the beginning of the conflict, from 2013 onwards Hezbollah deployed thousands of fighters in support of Syrian government forces.[146] It was in Syria that Mustafa Badreddine, one of the five standing trial by the STL for the assassination of Hariri, was killed in a major explosion in Damascus in May 2016. After his death it became clear that Badreddine had succeeded his cousin, Imad Mughniyeh, as Hezbollah's operations chief, after the latter had been assassinated in Damascus in 2008.[147] As long as Hezbollah's other sponsor, Iran, supported Assad, Nasrallah had little choice but to fight by the side of the Syrian government. It was against this background that the STL did its work. It opened four contempt cases, one of which was against pro-March 8 newspaper *Al Akhbar* that ended in a conviction for interfering with the administration of justice by publishing information on purported confidential witnesses.[148] More important, the trial against the five accused took place during this time. Between 16 January 2014 and July 2016, 201 witnesses testified before the Trial Chamber; the statements of 101 witnesses were admitted in writing; and 1378 exhibits were admitted into evidence.[149] It was during that period that the Prosecutor made his case and presented evidence, providing a narrative of what he contended happened in the run-up to, and on, 14 February 2005.

The impact of the STL on Hezbollah: a quasi-state entity-cum-political party

The ability of Hezbollah to maintain legitimacy in various constituencies over time, and how and to what extent the indictment by the STL of five of its members for the assassination of Hariri impacted on that ability, is not always easy to see at first glance.[150] Even if there had been comprehensive polling data available that measured the opinions held about Hezbollah and its actions among different constituencies and at different moments, one would still not know on what beliefs those opinions were based. Yet, by looking at legitimacy crises and changing narratives, especially those under pressure by the STL investigation, and by looking at the bases, performance and support that in congruence constitute legitimacy in different constituencies, one can discern how the organisation claims legitimacy and where and when these claims are accepted.

By assessing the legitimacy crises the organisation overcame over the course of its existence, it becomes clear that the leadership of Hezbollah demonstrated an understanding that legitimacy was a prerequisite for its success. Moreover, throughout its existence, Hezbollah has gained experience in dealing with constituencies whose interests do not always converge, and whose beliefs differ widely. Legitimacy constantly changes and, in the case of Hezbollah, was sometimes ephemeral, when the support, based on its military performance, which strengthened the bases of its legitimacy, came and went. By its members joining the cabinet the organisation became part of the government; Hezbollah formally became part of the same entity it was competing against over statehood. Operating as a QSE and a political party, at the same time, in a country that is deeply divided along sectarian lines, Hezbollah had to seek legitimacy in multiple 'home' constituencies simultaneously. Moreover, it had to influence the triangle of political leaders, armed forces and the people of its arch-foe, Israel, as well as the multiple global audiences that affected the environment in which it operates. Creating and maintaining legitimacy, even among its core constituencies, at times, led to a complicated balancing act, as the perceived interests of the Lebanese Shia, and its main sponsors Iran and Syria, did not always align.

Legitimacy in Hezbollah's core Shia constituencies

When looking at Hezbollah, in light of the three types of legitimising authority Weber describes, its legitimacy within the Shia community was firmly based on traditional grounds.[151] The all-encompassing life system of Islam includes religion, state and law, and provides a framework of identity. The claims to legitimacy of Hezbollah were, and still are, primarily based on Islamic doctrine, religious symbolism and, to a lesser extent, charismatic grounds.[152] This basis was strengthened by the success of the 'Islamic Resistance' in forcing the Israeli withdrawal from most of Lebanon's territory in 1985 and, during Israel's 18-year occupation of southern Lebanon, Hezbollah's success in fighting the IDF rendered its ideology and actions more persuasive to many Shia. Hezbollah proved successful in convincing people not to take refuge in the north and in preventing the population from turning against the organisation by swiftly responding to destruction caused by Israeli retaliations, and by rebuilding houses and providing aid for the families of militants. Not only the success of the 'Islamic Resistance', fighting among the people, depended on the support, cooperation and hospitality of the civilian population; the social organisation that was vital to ensuring this success, today, touches on almost every aspect of Shia life in Lebanon. It remains essential for Hezbollah's existence, and generates an unrivalled grass-roots support that strengthens the basis of legitimacy.[153] Before they could become politically active, the living conditions of the impoverished Shia masses had to improve. But when they did, Hezbollah's participation in the elections was very popular among the politically disenfranchised Shia, and they formed the basis of its political success.

Legitimacy (crises) in a multi-confessional state

Participating in the democratic process was also an attempt to create legitimacy, in the eyes of the various non-Shia constituencies, in Lebanon. Among many Shia, beliefs about what Hezbollah, and what it should be doing, are mainly based on religious authority, but it lacks such basis among the members of other sects in Lebanon. Hezbollah leader Hassan Nasrallah is widely regarded as charismatic but, as a Shia cleric, the norms he sets and the statements he makes do not have the same effect on non-Shia, and at times even alienate them. Where the bases of legitimacy are weak, the success and support elements become more important to claims to legitimacy. As a QSE, Hezbollah was not backed up by regime legitimacy, and only had limited symbolic functions for Lebanese nationalism that might contribute to its legitimacy.[154] So the main function of Hezbollah's military efforts contributing to legitimacy among the members of the various non-Shia sects was that it was fighting a common enemy shared by the vast majority of Lebanese. As Hezbollah took it upon itself to provide security against Israel, doing so effectively was an imperative for legitimacy. It is clear that the environmental support and the effectiveness of Hezbollah at some point compensated for weaker bases among non-Shia, and its military organisation could count on considerable support. But that support relied heavily on its military performance, and different legitimacy crises proved it to be somewhat unstable. Most notably, after Israel withdrew, it constantly had to prove its weapons were only aimed at Israel and when, by 2005, the euphoria of the Israeli withdrawal had faded, Hezbollah faced another legitimacy crisis. In the 2006 War, Hezbollah proved to be an effective military organisation. The indiscriminate violence Israel used in the war and the excessive damage caused by IDF bombing strengthened the conviction of many Lebanese that an armed Hezbollah was indispensable to protect the country against Israel. Yet, at the same time, actions leading to the war could count on a lot of criticism, especially from non-Shia. This was not because of the actions, per se, but because the motivation behind them was believed to serve the interests of Hezbollah alone and because of the suffering of the Lebanese during the war.

Hezbollah's opponents always feared that the party was only feigning attachment to Lebanon as a pluralist society and that its ultimate aim was to transform it into an Islamic state. This was despite Hezbollah's repeated statements that the conditions for establishing an Islamic regime would probably never exist in Lebanon and demonstrations of pragmatism as a political party. As the relationship between 'March 8' and 'March 14' hardened, these fears increased. In the aftermath of the 2006 War, the political stalemate over the STL and Hezbollah's demonstrations of military power to enforce political demands reinvigorated a feeling of discomfort about Hezbollah's weapons among non-Shia. Yet it was with the 2008 blockade of Beirut that the 'veneer of its domestic neutrality vanished, greatly reducing its legitimacy as a popular resistance movement and heightening opposition to its armed status'.[155] The message to Shia was that it was Hezbollah that safeguarded Shia political interests, but this was interpreted by many non-Shia as meaning that Hezbollah was willing to put Shia (and Syrian) interests before the stability of Lebanon. Hezbollah had to negotiate this crisis successfully to re-legitimise itself, especially its military apparatus, among non-Shia.

Impacting on the legitimacy of its opponents

Unlike most other QSEs, besides operating state functions within the state it aimed to transform, Hezbollah also claimed legitimacy for its military organisation's fighting a war against another state, and for a conventional political party. Hezbollah never claimed legitimacy for its organisation and actions in the eyes of the Israeli trinity of public, government and armed forces. But contemporary armed conflict is also a battle for wills, or multiple wills, in which diminishing the legitimacy of the opponent and its actions are objectives. Israel's objective, in the 1980s, besides ending the PLO presence in Lebanon, was to create an environment in which a friendly regime in Lebanon would guarantee a peaceful northern border. It emerged that military superiority and taking hold of territory was not sufficient, in a war that was fought among the people, for the will of the people, and upon occupation Israel lost the initiative to the occupied. Israel learned that its 'soft' objectives would not be reached quickly and that, fighting an enemy like Hezbollah – which did not present a target and avoided confrontation on Israeli terms – would take a long time. Hezbollah, on the other hand, proved to be superior in fighting such a war and, over the years, learned how to make effective use of every available network to fight Israel. The success of the attacks on the IDF in the security zone led to a rising belief among Israelis that the government should discontinue the occupation of southern Lebanon. In the long run, Hezbollah, as a guerrilla force, was better able to inflict damage while manoeuvring within 'the rules of the game' than the IDF. Additionally, Israel's political situation prevented it from using all its force to achieve its aims at all costs, especially in the final stages of the occupation and when forced by the international community to accept a ceasefire in 2006. Moreover, its ineffectiveness against the small targets Hezbollah militants presented created a lot of frustration within the IDF.[156] In highly militarised Israel, the domestic belief that what the IDF was doing was right and justified was highly important to military leaders.[157] By influencing the will of the Israelis – in that the costs were perceived to be higher than the benefits – Hezbollah gained relative strength over the IDF.[158] In 2000, Israel withdrew after 18 years, without reaching its goal, and in the years that followed, most notably in the 2006 War, Israel proved unable to break the will or strength of Hezbollah.

The multiple constituencies that form the international community

Throughout the Sunni-dominated Arab and Muslim world, the fact that Hezbollah was the only force successfully fighting the IDF provided it with bases for legitimacy that no other Shia organisation could claim among those constituencies. It was generally seen as a legitimate resistance movement among Arab populations. This image continued after the Israeli withdrawal in 2000 and the July War in 2006. Hezbollah fought on the side of the PLO in the War of the Camps in the late 1980s, and it served as an inspiration for other militant organisations, most notably Hamas. However, its stance against any (implied) recognition of Israeli statehood and its condemnation of every Arab state and organisation that engaged in talks with Israel deteriorated its relations with the PLO and led to decreasing legitimacy for Hezbollah's military actions in the eyes of many Sunni governments. In 2006, for instance, key Arab states were quick to voice their disapproval of Hezbollah's action; Saudi Arabia criticised what it labelled 'uncalculated adventures' and Jordan, Egypt and the United

Arab Emirates followed suit.[159] But, at the same time, its success against Israel (temporarily) inflated Hezbollah's popularity across Arab populations[160] as neighbouring countries were also marked by deepened animosity between the two main sects in Islam in the years that followed and, as Hezbollah made very clear that first and foremost, it represented Shia interests, more criticism of the Hezbollah could be heard in various (Sunni) Arab constituencies.

Originally founded with Iranian and Syrian aid, Hezbollah relied heavily on their (financial) support. Both regimes repeatedly expressed their belief in the legitimacy of Hezbollah's military activities and remained close to the organisation. However, Syria always applied 'divide and rule' tactics to keep control over Lebanese politics – tactics of which Hezbollah was victim, at times, when the Assad regime deemed it to be too powerful. Nevertheless, Hezbollah remained close to the Assad regime, as proved by its staunch support after the assassination of Hariri and, more recently, sending its fighters to support government forces in the Syrian Civil War; Hezbollah relied heavily on Iran for its weapons, but had to balance its tone to secure domestic legitimacy with the 'Islamic Republic' rhetoric of its Iranian sponsor. In combination with Supreme Leader Khamenei not being as highly regarded by Hezbollah's leadership as Khomeini was, it became increasingly financially and doctrinally independent from Iran.[161]

Hezbollah's radical origin, its manifesto and its actions against Western targets in the 1980s made it notorious among Western publics and governments alike. Whether it really was behind attacks on Western targets, such as the US marine barracks, or not, was irrelevant as the organisation was widely believed to be responsible. This radical image was enhanced by Israel's ability to provide a narrative that was easier to understand and fitted into pre-existing ideas in the West about Hezbollah and terrorism. This illustrates one of the problems for Hezbollah in dealing with multiple constituencies: its inability to find effective means to change its image in the West. Since its transformation in the early 1990s, Hezbollah made considerable efforts to play by the rules in its conflicts with Israel; it made an effort to spare civilian lives and it generally attacked military targets. Unlike other 'terrorist' organisations, it never targeted the United States, nor did it attack US citizens, after the end of the civil war.[162] Nevertheless, Hezbollah was largely unable to convince the West that it was not a terrorist organisation. Its past deeds and other actions – rightfully or wrongfully – attributed to Hezbollah, played a major part in this. So did its reluctance to distance itself from those actions and its radical Islamic rhetoric. In the wake of 9/11, for instance, Israeli officials were quick to assert the 'common struggle' faced by Israel and the United States in the declared 'war on terrorism'.[163] During those years, the Israeli government proved to be successful in disassociating the violence of Hezbollah from Israeli policy towards Lebanon and the occupied territories. It even managed to associate the violence Hezbollah employed with that of al-Qa'ida, notwithstanding the fact the latter is a radical Sunni organisation that considers Hezbollah's Shias heretics and its natural enemy. Yet, Israel thereby successfully continued to legitimise the violence it used and delegitimise Hezbollah and its actions in most 'Western' constituencies. Hezbollah proved unable to convey successfully a counter message that fitted in with most international constituencies. The news media provided images that were the 'most salient instruments' with regard to multiple constituencies and determining the balance of legitimacy in contemporary warfare.[164] Although Hezbollah's operating of *al-Manar* suggests that the organisation understood the importance of moving images, the international satellite networks were the providers of images for broadcasters around the world, not *al-Manar*. Hezbollah failed to provide the moving images and the narratives to shape attitudes. After 9/11, the American news media engaged in reductive polarisation into pro- and anti-Western forces, along the lines of George W. Bush's false dichotomy 'either you are with us or you are with the terrorists'.[165] Hezbollah was often mentioned in the same breath as al-Qa'ida and Hamas. This portrayal denied the grass-roots support and the considerable level of domestic legitimacy Hezbollah enjoyed at the time.[166] Additionally, Western media used 'terrorism' and 'murder' for acts by Hezbollah and 'strikes' and 'incursions' for those by the IDF. The image of a bearded cleric denouncing the West and calling for jihad fitted existing societal concepts, values and knowledge, and put it into a context that the audience could understand – that is, the prevailing mainstream narrative. There were images available of Nasrallah as an eloquent leader, almost serenely explaining his party's motivation and policies, but the radical images were shown. However, Hezbollah continued to provide those images by addressing its domestic public with anti-Israel/America rhetoric, in a world in which every image was almost instantly spread around the world, and both its intended and unintended message reached different constituencies.

Hezbollah was added to the US list of terrorist organisations with a 'global reach', in 2001. Hezbollah's participation in elections did not change US government ideas about its legitimacy. Neither did Nasrallah's condemnation of the 11 September 2001 attacks on the World Trade Center.[167] Washington had traditionally boycotted any action that would lead to the reinforcement of Hezbollah's position; it supported Israel in the 2006 War. Most European countries differentiated between Hezbollah's militia and its social/political organisation, an artificial differentiation, as it was one organisation in both practice, leadership and in the eyes of Hezbollah leaders. Yet, some European governments established contacts with the movement's political wing, while condemning the same Hezbollah for being a militia. Former EU High Representative Javier Solana acknowledged that the movement was 'part of political life in Lebanon and is represented in the Lebanese parliament'.[168] Its democratic credentials meant that the EU resisted Israeli and US pressure to add Hezbollah to the official list of terrorist organisations until 2013.

Shifting narratives ad the impact of the STL

In the changing narratives and counter narratives aimed at the STL, the impact of international criminal justice on the legitimacy of Hezbollah could be observed long before the indictment. The establishment of the Tribunal, leaks at

UNIIIC, investigations into the murder of Hariri, alleged leaks at the Tribunal and speculation concerning who would be indicted for the murder of Hariri, all forced the organisation to change its narratives. Yet the outstretched process of ongoing investigation by the STL, its closed indictments, published indictments and, eventually, arrest warrants, and more important the leaking information along the way, gave rise to one commentator calling it: ' "The Indictment": A Thriller lacking in action'.[169] The amount of time that the STL gave Hezbollah to prepare for what was coming and develop counter narratives might have reduced the impact the indictments could have had.

While Hezbollah could still dismiss the leaks in *Der Spiegel*, in 2009, especially as there were no other sources to back up the story, this was no longer possible by the time Saad Hariri informed Hezbollah about the imminent indictment of its members, in summer 2010. By then, however, Hezbollah and other pro-Syrian factions had opposed the STL since its inception, had criticised it since it had opened and the strategy of focusing on allegedly false testimonies seemed to have worked, to a certain degree. Hezbollah had chosen an offensive defence, after *Der Spiegel*'s revelation, and had stepped up its efforts against the STL. It gratefully used the 'false witnesses' narrative, claimed that Saad Hariri had paid them and that the STL refused to deal with them, disregarding the fact that the Tribunal lacked any jurisdiction to prosecute these witnesses for perjury, or contempt of court, as these individuals had given their statements to UNIIIC. Hezbollah claimed that the investigation was one-sided and single-minded about implicating Syria. Nasrallah clearly hoped to undercut any indictment, not only by breaking the news himself in advance, but also by invoking Saad Hariri, who has long been the Tribunal's chief supporter. Nevertheless, the narrative Nasrallah chose showed that Hezbollah had to make a choice. By not taking the way out provided by Hariri – to declare the suspects 'rogue members'– and instead declaring that it would never allow the arrest of any of its members, it chose to strengthen its legitimacy in its core Shia constituency.

Critical legitimacy moments and prioritising core support

By 2010, this choice to strengthen legitimacy in its core constituencies had possibly already been made, to a point of no return. While Hezbollah's first participation in elections had given hope to some that it would eventually transform into a conventional political party by integrating its militia into the army and its social organisation into government institutions, it had been clear for a long time that Hezbollah had decided against giving up its quasi-state qualities. The reaction of Hezbollah to the indictment should also be seen in the light of legitimacy crises Hezbollah had to deal with that were not direct results of the Tribunal's actions, although many of them were closely connected with the STL. The assassination of Hariri itself, in 2005, would prove to be the catalyst for a popular revolution that ended the 'Pax Syriana'. In the years that followed, the divide between pro- and anti-Syrian parties was deepened, both over discussions about Hezbollah's arms and about the STL (when it was still believed it would hold

Syria responsible for the murder of Hariri). Moreover, by the time the notion that Hezbollah members would be indicted by the STL took hold, the Sunni–Shia schism had already replaced the Christian–Muslim schism in Lebanon. Part of Lebanon's Christians and, at times, the Druze – largely united under the banner of Walid Jumblatt's PSP – had decided that their interests would be best served by siding with the pro-Syrian 'March 8' alliance. As a result, Hezbollah could claim more political power in the Lebanese power-sharing system. Hezbollah also strengthened its support base among the Shia population. Hezbollah's core constituency no longer only consisted of the 'downtrodden of the world', the disenfranchised Shia, susceptible to radicalisation, but also of more moderate Shia.

The 2008 blockade of Beirut had clearly revealed a critical legitimacy moment in Sunni (and other non-Shia) constituencies over the arms of Hezbollah. Hezbollah's ability to claim legitimacy for its actions and institutions in the Sunni constituency was being lost, but although the murder of Hariri, his legacy, and sectarian tension had united more Lebanese Sunni in Saad Hariri's Future Movement, the 'March 14' coalition he led was not very stable. Moreover, the pro-Syrian 'March 8' opposition had weakened the government further, hammering on about 'false witnesses', as had the self-imposed paralyses of the government, over the STL. It was clear that Saad Hariri and his government would try to avoid escalation into sectarian war at almost any cost.

A (successful) strategy of counter narratives

Being implicated in the murder of Hariri by the STL indictment both accelerated this process of legitimacy loss, and influenced Hezbollah's reaction to it. Hezbollah focused on the constituency that it needed most, and in which its bases were the strongest. It also provided narratives that appealed to these constituencies, i.e. Israel killed Hariri, and Hezbollah will never hand over a member. These narratives Hezbollah used in their attempts both to delegitimise the investigation into the murder and STL were aided by the fact that the Tribunal at times seemed to be as leaky as a sieve. Although the *Der Spiegel* leak most likely originated from within the UN investigation, later leaks came from within the Tribunal, or the UN.[170]

This gave the organisation the chance to prepare for what was coming. Hezbollah used the time it had before the indictments and arrest warrants were publicised to provide 'evidence' that Israel was behind the bombing of the former prime minister and that the STL was a Zionist conspiracy. The evidence, presented by Nasrallah, among other documents, consisted of statements made by agents of Israel arrested in Lebanon, a demonstration of Hezbollah's ability to capture images from Israeli drones and 'prove' that the Lebanese telecoms' infrastructure was infiltrated by Israel. Although it may not have been 'evidence' in the sense that it would have exonerated Hezbollah in a court of law, it was not meant to be.[171] It was effective rhetoric. Nevertheless, it was the first time that Hezbollah came with an alternative story about the murder of Hariri, instead of focusing on the argument that the STL was a political court.[172]

When, in June 2011, the STL finally issued arrest warrants based on the indictments for the murder of Hariri and, a month later, the Tribunal officially named four individuals known to be members of Hezbollah, the organisation had had time to brace for the impact and came prepared. In the same way that Saad Hariri had tried to avoid an escalation in the months before the indictment, newly installed Prime Minister Mikati now had to walk a tightrope of ambiguous statements between Hezbollah and its allies on one side, and the international community and 'March 14'on the other. Yet the indictments did not 'provoke a political earthquake against Hezbollah, as many were hoping'.[173] The absence of this 'earthquake' did not mean that the indictments, or the STL in general, did not change the landscape. The impact the establishment of the STL had on the Lebanese political landscape as a whole, is hard to underestimate. However, the indictments did not provide a strong compelling narrative of how exactly the accused assassinated Hariri, why Hezbollah members did so and who ordered it. Naming the accused and citing Call Data Records of groups of mobile phones connected to the accused, the crime scene and previous monitoring of Hariri's movements, and the false claim to *Al Jazeera*, might be sufficient evidence in court, but was very technical. The leaks meant that instead of one critical legitimacy moment, or crisis, Hezbollah made sure that the revelations that its members would be implicated in the murder of Hariri became a rather muddled string of critical legitimacy moments with, at times very effective, counter narratives in between.[174] Moreover, at times the political tensions in Lebanon prevented its opponents from using the indictment and international criminal justice narratives to the fullest in attempts to delegitimise the organisation and its actions. Shortly before the indictment came out, protests had started against the Assad regime in Syria. Soon after the indictment, the Syrian Civil War broke out. Although all relevant parties in Lebanon showed a strong will not to let the war in Syria spark a sectarian war in Lebanon, the decision of Hezbollah in May 2013 to enter the Syrian Civil War on the side of the Syrian regime added to the existing tensions. According to Geneive Abdo Nasrallah, 'once a leader who had support among the Sunni for defeating Israel [...] in fighting for Assad, has transformed himself and his movement into a strictly Shia paramilitary force'[175]

The establishment of the STL had led to political stalemate in Lebanon, and the indictment, in phases because of leaks, had led to critical legitimacy moments for Hezbollah. Yet, by the time the trial took place, Hezbollah had already been forced by legitimacy crises to make decisions, and it had chosen to aim its legitimating narratives at its core Shia constituents. Moreover, it had chosen to remain loyal to Assad, and by doing so not only lost its capacity to successfully claim legitimacy in various Lebanese constituencies, but diminished its ability to do so in many of the large number of constituencies that together make up the international community, most notably both in the Arab world and in the West. By tying up its fighters in a war in Syria it also minimised its capacity to be an effective force against the IDF, further diminishing its chances to gain legitimacy through military success. As a result, the trial that took place in Leidschendam from January 2014 was constantly overshadowed by the war in Syria. Even though the Prosecutor provided a much clearer and compelling narrative in it of how the five accused (proceedings against Badreddine were terminated when sufficient evidence of his death had been presented to the Court in July 2011) co-conspired to bomb Hariri's convoy. Moreover, as the trial continued, it became even clearer just how unlikely it was that any of the suspects would, when convicted, ever serve their sentence. Badreddine was the highest-ranking member of Hezbollah killed in action in Syria while fighting the Syrian opposition and was buried in Beirut with 'full military honours and a marching band'.[176] Furthermore, Hezbollah vowed to prevent the arrest of the other four accused.

Yet, despite many circumstances mitigating the effect of the STL, the establishment of the Tribunal, its investigations, proceedings and especially when it became clear that Hezbollah members would be implicated in the murder of Hariri, all clearly had an impact on Hezbollah's legitimacy. Clearly, something had changed. The relentless attacks of Hezbollah on the STL and the investigation into the murder of Hariri not only reveal that the STL impacted on Hezbollah's ability to create and maintain legitimacy in various constituencies, but Hezbollah's efforts to prevent the STL from continuing to operate also show that the only way for Hezbollah to really mitigate the threat to its legitimacy stemming from the STL would be to stop its operating, or at least to stop it from reaching a verdict, something it did not manage to do. Thus far, the STL did not have the earthquake effect on Hezbollah's legitimacy that some anticipated, mainly because other events did so first. However, if a verdict by the Court leads to the conviction of its members, and if combined with a credible narrative of the events, this might have the critical legitimacy impact some anticipated. However, this would be a conviction that has come about despite all the counter narratives provided by Hezbollah.

Notes

1 A. Knudsen, and M. Kerr, 'Introduction: The Cedar Revolution and Beyond', in: A. Knudsen, and M. Kerr, (eds), *Lebanon: After the Cedar Revolution*, London: Hurst and Co., 2012, pp. 3–23 at p. 5–6.

2 Knudsen and Kerr, 'Introduction: The Cedar Revolution and Beyond', p. 5.

3 UN Security Council Resolution 520 of 17 September 1982.

4 United Nations Security Council 5122nd meeting, New York, 15 February 2005, S/PV.5122, p. 2.

5 Report of the International Independent Investigation Commission established pursuant to Security Council Resolution 1595 (2005), 20 October 2005, S/2005/662, § 38 (also known as the 'Fitzgerald Report').

6 N. Assaf, 'Hariri assassins not Australian suspects', *Daily Star*, 19 February 2005.

7 Report of the Fact-finding Mission to Lebanon, p. 2.

8 UN Security Council Resolution 1595, 7 April 2005.

9 '*la ghalib la mahlub*' A. Knudsen, and M. Kerr, 'Introduction: The Cedar Revolution and Beyond', in: A. Knudsen, and M. Kerr, (eds), *Lebanon: After the Cedar Revolution*, London: Hurst and Co., 2012, pp. 3–23, p. 5.

10 Knudsen and Kerr, 'Introduction: The Cedar Revolution and Beyond', p. 13. A. Knudsen, 'Special Tribunal for Lebanon: Homage to Hariri?' in: Knudsen and Kerr, *Lebanon: After the Cedar Revolution*, pp. 219–233, p. 220.

11　Ibid.
12　Ibid., p. 221.
13　Ibid. A. Knudsen, 'The Law, the Loss and the Lives of Palestinian Refugees in Lebanon', *CMI Working Paper*, 2007, no. 1, p. 6.
14　Samir Geagea, the leader of the Lebanese Forces militia, was the only warlord convicted for crimes committed during the civil war. In 1994 he was found guilty of ordering four political assassinations, including the murder of Prime Minister Karami, and sentenced to four death sentences that were commuted to life imprisonment. Shortly after the 2005 elections, in which the 'March 14' coalition won a majority, parliament approved an amnesty for Geagea. 'Amnesty for Lebanese ex-warlord' *BBC News*, 18 July, 2005.
15　Knudsen, 'Special Tribunal for Lebanon: Homage to Hariri?' p. 221.
16　UN Security Council Resolution 1644, 15 December 2005. About the STL, www.stl-tsl.org/en/about-the-stl/creation-of-the-stl (accessed 14 May 2013).
17　'Hezbollah ministers quit cabinet', *BBC News*, 12 November 2006.
18　Knudsen and Kerr, 'Introduction: The Cedar Revolution and Beyond', p. 10.
19　UN Security Council Resolution 1757, 30 May 2007.
20　Knudsen, 'Special Tribunal for Lebanon: Homage to Hariri?' p. 221.
21　Knudsen, 'Special Tribunal for Lebanon', p. 227
22　Statute of the STL, Article 2.3.
23　STL Seventh Annual Report (2015–2016).
24　J. Neumann, 'Hariri Assassination Still Clouds Lebanese Politics', *Voice of America News*, 25 October 2011.
25　Statute of the STL, Article 1.
26　Ibid.
27　'Hundreds mourn Beirut journalist', *BBC News*, 4 June 2005. 'Anti-Syrian Politician Killed in Lebanon', *Washington Post*, 22 June 2005. 'May Chidiac, Lebanese Broadcasting Corporation Attacked', *Committee to Protect Journalists*, 25 September 2005. 'Beirut bomb targets top minister', *BBC News*, 12 July 2005.
28　Order Directing the Lebanese Judicial Authority Seized with the Case Concerning the Attack Perpetrated against Mr Elias El-Murr on 12 July 2005 to Defer to the Special Tribunal for Lebanon, 19 August 2011, STL-11-02/D/PTJ.
29　*The Prosecutor v. Salim Jamil Ayyash, Mustafa Amine Badreddine, Hussein Hassan Oneissi, and Assad Hassan Sabra*, Public Redacted Amended Indictment, 6 February 2013, STL-II-OIIPTIPTJ, F08601 AOIIPRV/201305281R 143331-R I 43372/EN/nc.
30　Statute of the STL, Article 1.
31　J. Yun, 'Special Tribunal for Lebanon: A Tribunal of an International Character Devoid of International Law', *Santa Clara Journal of International Law*, vol. 7, no. 2, 2010, pp. 181–196, p. 182. M. Milanovic, 'An Odd Couple: Domestic Crimes and International Responsibility in the Special Tribunal for Lebanon', *Journal of International Criminal Justice*, vol. 5, 2007, pp. 1139–1152, p. 1139.
32　Statute of the STL, Articles 3(1)(b) and 3(2). B. Elberling, 'The Next Step in HistoryWriting through Criminal Law: Exactly How TailorMade is the Special Tribunal for Lebanon?' *Leiden Journal of International Law*, vol. 21, 2008, pp. 529–538, p. 534. Milanovic, 'An Odd Couple', p. 1140.
33　For a more detailed discussion on Article 3 of the Statute, see: Milanovic, 'An Odd Couple' and Elberling, 'The Next Step in HistoryWriting through Criminal Law'.
34　Interlocutory Decision on the Applicable Law: Terrorism, Conspiracy, Homicide, Perpetration, Cumulative Charging, Case No. STL-11-01/I (16 February 2011) § II A.
35　Ibid., § II B.
36　§§ 83–85.
37　K. Ambos, 'Judicial Creativity at the Special Tribunal for Lebanon: Is There a Crime of Terrorism under International Law?' *Leiden Journal of International Law*, vol.

24, no. 3, 2001, pp. 655–675. M.P. Scharf, 'Special Tribunal for Lebanon Issues Landmark Ruling on Definition of Terrorism and Modes of Participation', *ASIL Insights*, vol. 15, no. 6, 4 March 2011. M.J. Ventura, 'Terrorism According to the STL's Interlocutory Decision on the Applicable Law: A Defining Moment or a Moment of Defining?' *Journal of International Criminal Justice*, 2011, pp. 1–22, p. 8, p. 21.

38 Ventura, 'Terrorism According to the STL's Interlocutory Decision on the Applicable Law', p. 5.

39 Statute of the STL, Art. 22. Elberling, 'The Next Step in History Writing through Criminal Law', p. 537.

40 *The Prosecutor v. Salim Jamil Ayyash, Mustafa Amine Badreddine, Hussein Hassan Oneissi and Assad Hassan Sabra*, Decision to Hold Trial in Absentia, STL-ll-OI/I/ TC FO112/201202011RI09799-RI09846nEN/pvk.

41 P. Gaeta, 'To Be (Present) or Not To Be (Present): Trials In Absentia before the Special Tribunal for Lebanon', *Journal of International Criminal Justice*, vol. 5, 2007, pp. 1165–1174, p. 1173. N. Pons, 'Some Remarks on in Absentia Proceedings before the Special Tribunal for Lebanon in Case of a State's Failure or Refusal to Hand over the Accused', *Journal of International Criminal Justice*, vol. 8, 2010, pp. 1307–1321, p. 1319.

42 C. Jenks, 'Notice Otherwise Given: Will In Absentia Trials at the Special Tribunal for Lebanon Violate Human Rights?' *ExpressO*, 2009. W. Jordash and T. Parker, 'Incompatibility with International Human Rights Law', *Journal of International Criminal Justice*, vol. 8, 2010, pp. 487–509, p. 487.

43 Knudsen and Kerr, 'Introduction: The Cedar Revolution and Beyond', p. 14.

44 Elberling 'The Next Step in History Writing through Criminal Law', p. 531.

45 F. Mégret, 'A Special Tribunal for Lebanon: The UN Security Council and the Emancipation of International Criminal Justice', *Leiden Journal of International Law*, vol. 21, 2008, pp. 485–512, p. 485.

46 Mégret, 'A Special Tribunal for Lebanon', p. 486.

47 B. Fassbender, 'Reflections on the International Legality of the Special Tribunal for Lebanon' *Journal of International Criminal Justice*, vol. 5, 2007, pp. 1091–1105.

48 Elberling 'The Next Step in History Writing through Criminal Law', p. 529.

49 Ibid., p. 538.

50 STL Press Release, 22 January 2013, 'STL Condemns Media Reports on Alleged Witness Identities'. STL Press Release, 2 July 2013, 'STL Appoints Investigator to Probe Unauthorised Disclosures'.

51 Knudsen, 'Special Tribunal for Lebanon: Homage to Hariri?' p. 228.

52 A.R. Norton, *Hezbollah: A Short History*, Princeton: Princeton University Press, 2007, p. 34.

53 H. Jaber, *Hezbollah: Born with a Vengeance*, New York: Columbia University Press, 1997, p. 10. J. Palmer Harik, *Hezbollah: The Changing Face of Terrorism* (2nd edn. 2006) London: I.B.Taurus, 2004, p. 18.

54 J.E. Alagha, *The Shifts in Hizbullah's Ideology: Religious Ideology, Political Ideology and Political Program*, Amsterdam: Amsterdam University Press, 2006, pp. 26–29. Hamzeh, *In the Path of Hizbullah*, pp. 17–20. Jaber, *Hezbollah: Born with a Vengeance*, p. 12.

55 Hamzeh, *In the Path of Hizbullah*, p. 15. Norton, *Hezbollah: A Short History*, p. 97. P. Waldmann, *The Radical Community: A Comparative Analysis of the Social Background of ETA, IRA, and Hezbollah*, Amsterdam: IOS, 2006, p. 9, 11–12, 134.

56 Jaber, *Hezbollah: Born with a Vengeance*, p. 14. A.N. Hamzeh, *In the Path of Hizbullah*, Syracuse, New York: Syracuse University Press, 2004, p. 22. A. Bregman, *Israel's Wars: A History Since 1947* (Second edition 2002), Abington: Routledge, 2000, p. 146. J.I. Victoroff (ed.), *Tangled Roots: Social and Psychological Factors in the Genesis of Terrorism*, Amsterdam: IOS Press, 2006, p. 134.

57 Hamzeh, *In the Path of Hizbullah*, p. 17, Victoroff, *Tangled Roots*, p. 135. Norton, *Hezbollah: A Short History*, p. 34.
58 Newsweek, 18 July 2006 quoted in: Norton, *Hezbollah: A Short History*, p. 34.
59 Hamzeh, *In the Path of Hizbullah*, p. 83. R. Pape, *Dying To Win: The Strategic Logic of Suicide Terrorism*. New York: Random House, 2005, Appendix 1, 'Suicide Terrorist Campaigns, 1980–2003'.
60 Jaber, *Hezbollah: Born with a Vengeance*, p. 77.
61 Ibid., p. 80.
62 Ibid., pp. 75, 80–81, and 113. Hamzeh, *In the Path of Hizbullah*, p. 82. A.R. Norton, *Hizballah of Lebanon: Extremist Ideals v. Mundane Politics*, New York: Council on Foreign Relations, 1999, pp. 10–11.
63 English translation of 'The Open Letter' in: Alagha, *The Shifts in Hizbullah's Ideology*, pp. 223–238.
64 Ibid.
65 Hamzeh, *In the Path of Hizbullah*, p. 26. Norton, *Hezbollah: A Short History*, pp. 34–35. English translation of 'The Open Letter' in: Alagha, *The Shifts in Hizbullah's Ideology*, pp. 223–238.
66 English translation of 'The Open Letter' in: Alagha, *The Shifts in Hizbullah's Ideology*, pp. 223–238.
67 Norton, *Hezbollah: A Short History*, p. 81.
68 Ibid., p. 80.
69 Jaber, *Hezbollah: Born with a Vengeance*, pp. 146–155.
70 Ibid.
71 Norton, *Hizballah of Lebanon*, pp. 2, 99.
72 Norton, *Hezbollah: A Short History*, p. 100.
73 Lebanon was tormented by a hostage crisis in which, from 1982 till 1992, at least 87 foreigners were kidnapped. Jaber, *Hezbollah: Born with a Vengeance*, p. 124). Palmer Harik, *Hezbollah: The Changing Face of Terrorism*, pp. 193–194.
74 The 1943 National Pact – an unwritten agreement between the Maronite and Sunnite leadership – laid the foundation of Lebanon as a multi-confessional state, and allocated political power along confessional lines on the basis of the 1932 census. It stipulated that the president had to be a Maronite, the prime minister a Sunni and the speaker of parliament a Shia.
75 M. Ranstorp, *Hizb'allah in Lebanon: The Politics of the Western Hostage Crisis*, New York: St Martin's Press, 1997, p. 105. Palmer Harik, *Hezbollah: The Changing Face of Terrorism*, p. 45.
76 N. Qassem, *Hizbullah: The Story from Within*, London: Saqi, 2005, p. 108.
77 Jaber, *Hezbollah: Born with a Vengeance*, p. 64. Qassem, *Hizbullah: The Story from Within*, p. 192.
78 Norton, *Hizballah of Lebanon*, pp. 83–84.
79 Jaber, *Hezbollah: Born with a Vengeance*, pp. 171–172.
80 Norton, *Hezbollah: A Short History*, p. 84. Jaber, *Hezbollah: Born with a Vengeance*, p. 170. Amnesty International, 'Israel/Lebanon: Deliberate Destruction or "Collateral Damage"? Israeli Attacks on Civilian Infrastructure', August 2006, p. 15.
81 Jaber, *Hezbollah: Born with a Vengeance*, p. 181. Although fighting continued – and both parties sometimes disregarded the immunity of non-combatants – US Secretary of State Warren Christopher managed to persuade both parties to return to the rules not to attack civilians, and they usually apologised afterwards for attacks on civilians. (Norton, *Hezbollah: A Short History*, p. 86.)
82 The Shebaa Farms area is a small disputed territory. Israel claims it is part of the Golan Heights it occupied. Lebanon's claim to the farms provides Hezbollah with a justification to keep fighting Israel. 'Security Council Endorses Secretary-General's Conclusion on Israeli Withdrawal from Lebanon as of 16 June', Press Release SC/6878, 18 June 2000.

83 In the 1992 elections, Hezbollah won 12 seats, 8 of the 27 seats reserved for Shia and 4 seats that went to non-Shia electoral allies. (Hamzeh, *In the Path of Hizbullah*, p. 129) In the following election, in 1996, Hezbollah lost some of its 12 seats, but in the 2000 elections, shortly after the withdrawal of Israel, the party was so popular that it could have won a large majority of the Shia vote. However, Syria was heavily involved in all of Lebanon's elections from 1992 until 2005, and managed to draw electoral districts in its typical 'divide and conquer' manner, which prevented parties from becoming too powerful. As the number of Hezbollah candidates in that year's election was limited, Hezbollah formed an alliance with its former foe, AMAL, that won more than a quarter of all seats in parliament. (A.R. Norton, 'The Role of Hezbollah in Lebanese Domestic Politics', *The International Spectator*, vol. 42, no. 4, 2007, pp. 475–491, at p. 482.)

84 Knudsen and Kerr, 'Introduction: The Cedar Revolution and Beyond', p. 6

85 'Lebanon Shia ministers end boycott', *Al Jazeera*, 2 February 2006. Hezbollah won 14 of the 128 Parliamentary seats in 2005, but the elections were won by the anti-Syrian coalition.

86 Human Rights Watch, *Fatal Strikes: Israel's Indiscriminate Attacks Against Civilians in Lebanon*, vol. 18, no. 3 August 2006, p. 6.

87 Amnesty International, 'Israel/Lebanon: Deliberate destruction or "collateral damage"?' p. 6.

88 United Nations General Assembly. 23 November 2006. Report of the Commission of Inquiry on Lebanon pursuant to Human Rights, Council Resolution S-2/1, 26. A.H. Cordesman, G. Sullivan and W.D. Sullivan, *Lessons of the 2006 Israeli-Hezbollah War*, Washington DC: CSIS Press, 2007, p. 16.

89 M. Kerr, 'Before the Revolution', in: Knudsen and Kerr, (eds), *Lebanon: After the Cedar Revolution*, pp. 23–38 at p. 28. On 11 August 2006, the UN Security Council unanimously approved Resolution 1701 in an effort to end the hostilities. UN Security Council Resolution 1701, 11 August 2007.

90 UN Security Council Resolution 1701, 11 August 2007.

91 Nasrallah appeared on al-Manar and declared that 'anyone using a firearm against a Lebanese brother is working for Israel'.

92 Blanford, *Warriors of God*, p. 448.

93 N. Ladki, 'Hezbollah says Beirut government declares war', *Reuters*, 8 May 2008.

94 J. Muir, 'Deep divisions haunt Lebanese politics', *BBC News*, 22 September 2010.

95 Knudsen and Kerr, 'The Cedar Revolution and Beyond', p. 7.

96 Although Syrian troops became part of the Arab Deterrence Force (ADF), established in October 1976, it legally became an occupation force when the ADF mandate ended in 1982. G. von Glahn, *Law Among Nations: An Introduction to Public International Law*, New York: Macmillan, 1992, pp. 687–688. J. Yun, 'Special Tribunal for Lebanon: A Tribunal of an International Character Devoid of International Law', *Santa Clara Journal of International Law*, vol. 7, no. 2, 2010, pp. 181–196, 184.

97 United Nations Security Council Report of the Fact-finding Mission to Lebanon inquiring into the causes, circumstances and consequences of the assassination of former Prime Minister Rafik Hariri, S/2005/203, 24 March 2005, (Hereinafter 'Report of the Fact-finding Mission to Lebanon') p. 5.

98 'Lebanese president gives full backing to Hezbollah' *CBC News*, 31 July 2006. Report of the Fact-finding Mission to Lebanon, p. 5.

99 The Lebanese Constitution, 23 May 1926, Article 49 (2). Blanford, *Killing Mr Lebanon*, p. 99.

100 P. Seeberg, 'Fragmented loyalties: Nation and Democracy in Lebanon after the Cedar Revolution', *Centre for Contemporary Middle East Studies University of Southern Denmark: Working Paper Series*, No. 8, February 2007, p. 11.

101   Blanford, *Killing Mr Lebanon*, pp. 99–101. Report of the International Independent Investigation Commission established pursuant to Security Council Resolution 1595 (2005), 20 October 2005, S/2005/662, (Hereinafter: Report of the International Independent Investigation Commission) § 26. A. Knudsen and M. Kerr, 'Introduction: The Cedar Revolution and Beyond', in: A. Knudsen, and M. Kerr, (eds), *Lebanon: After the Cedar Revolution*, London: Hurst and Co., 2012, pp. 3–23 at p. 3.

102   Report of the Fact-finding Mission to Lebanon, p. 6. Report of the International Independent Investigation Commission, § 26. J. Chirac, *Mémoires.*

103   Blanford, *Killing Mr Lebanon*, pp. 100–103.

104   UN Security Council Resolution1559, 2 September 2004.

105   Report of the Fact-finding Mission to Lebanon, p. 6.

106   'Explosion kills former Lebanon PM', *BBC News*, 14 February 2005.

107   'US warns Syria over Lebanon role', *BBC News*, 14 February 2005.

108   In his memoirs, Jacques Chirac recounts how he told President Bush, during a meeting in Brussels, that for those who knew the workings of the system in Damascus, there was no other hypothesis possible but the one in which Assad had taken the decision [to assassinate Hariri]. (Chirac, *Mémoires*). W. Vloeberghs, 'The Making of a Martyr: Forging Rafik Hariri's Symbolic Legacy'. In: A. Knudsen and M. Kerr, *Lebanon After the Cedar Revolution*, London, Hurst and Co., 2012. pp. 163–184 at p. 165).

109   'In quotes: World reacts to Hariri death', *BBC News*, 14 February 2005.

110   That the protests became known as the 'Cedar Revolution', outside Lebanon, was the doing of US Undersecretary of State Paula Dobriansky, who coined the phrase in a press conference on 28 February. 'Intifada', in Arabic, literally means 'shaking off' but, due to association with the Palestinian Intifadas, the Bush administration preferred to support a 'revolution'. J. Morley, 'The Branding of Lebanon's "Revolution"', *Washington Post*, 3 March 2005. N. Raad, 'Opposition demands "intifada for independence"', *Daily Star*, 19 February 2005.

111   'Syria looks to Riyadh for support', *BBC News*, 3 March 2005. 'Assad pledges Lebanon withdrawal', *BBC News*, 2 March 2005.

112   N. Noe, *Voice of Hezbollah: The Statements of Sayed Hassan Nasrallah*, London: Verso, 2007, pp. 319–320.

113   Hassan Nasrallah, 'You will today decide the fate of your nation and country', speech given on 8 March 2005 in Beirut. In Noe, *Voice of Hezbollah*, p. 326.

114   Report of the International Independent Investigation Commission, p. 7.

115   'Syrian troops leave Lebanese soil', *BBC News*, 26 April 2005.

116   'Lebanese leaders agree on cabinet', *BBC News*, 19 July 2005.

117   'Timeline Jamil El Sayed', Press Release of the STL, 12 May 2011. In September 2010 the pre-trial judge ruled that the Tribunal has jurisdiction over this matter, but not all evidence could be handed over to El Sayed.

118   'Lebanon summons general on comments', *Al Jazeera*, 16 September 2010.

119   'Timeline Jamil El Sayed', Press Release of the STL, 12 May 2011.

120   P. Galey, 'STL not investigating false witnesses, says tribunal's registrar on Twitter', *Daily Star*, 8 December 2011.

121   Ibid.

122   E. Follath, 'Breakthrough in Tribunal Investigation: New Evidence Points to Hezbollah in Hariri Murder', *SPIEGEL ONLINE*, 23 May 2009.

123   Ibid.

124   Ibid.

125   Ibid.

126   H. Dakroub, 'Hezbollah denies report about Hariri assassination', *The Guardian*, 24 May 2009.

127   'The Victory of May' speech by Hassan Nasrallah, *ShiaTV*, 25 May 2009 at 7 minutes and from 63 minutes onwards.

128   'Nasrallah concedes election defeat' *Al Jazeera*, 9 June 2009.

129 Ibid.
130 Knudsen, 'Special Tribunal for Lebanon: Homage to Hariri?' p. 229.
131 L. Andoni, 'Border skirmish a "fire douser"', *Al Jazeera*, 4 August 2010.
132 R.F. Worth, 'Hezbollah looks for shield from indictments' sting', *New York Times*, 24 July 2010.
133 M. Karouny, 'Hariri tribunal to accuse Hezbollah members: Nasrallah', *Reuters*, 22 July 2010.
134 N. Yazbeck, 'Lebanon on edge after Hezbollah revelation', *AFP*, 23 July 2010. For Assad it was the first time he visited Lebanon after the assassination of Rafik Hariri.
135 N. Yazbeck, 'Lebanon on edge after Hezbollah revelation'.
136 Nasrallah's evidence included Israeli drone surveillance of the route Hariri took on 14 February 2005; Hezbollah had the technology to intercept the video streams of Israeli surveillance drones for years without the Israeli's knowing, and the revelation ended a 15-year search of the IDF for a leak in its organisation. Blanford, *Warriors of God*, pp. 93–94. 'Nasrallah unveils "Hariri proof"', *Al Jazeera*, 10 August 2010. Knudsen, 'Special Tribunal for Lebanon: Homage to Hariri?' p. 230.
137 'Hezbollah urges Hariri case boycott', *Al Jazeera*, 28 October 2010.
138 E. Sakr, 'Nasrallah: We will not allow arrest of fighters', *Daily Star*, 12 November 2010.
139 'Hariri says was wrong to accuse Syria over killing', *Reuters*, 6 September 2010.
140 'Hezbollah and allies topple Lebanese unity government', *BBC News*, 12 January 2011.
141 Warrant to Arrest Mr Salim Jamil Ayyash Including Transfer and Detention Order, 28 June 2011, STL-11-01/I/PTJ/F0013/Cor/20110816/R091919-R091925/FR-EN/pvk. Warrant to Arrest Mr Mustafa Amine Badreddine Including Transfer and Detention Order, 28 June 2011, STL-11-01/I/PTJ/F0014/Cor/20110816/R091931-R091937/FR-EN/pvk. Warrant to Arrest Mr Hussein Hassan Oneissi Including Transfer and Detention Order, 28 June 2011, STL-11-01/I/PTJ/F0015/Cor/20110816/R091944-R091950/FR-EN/pvk. Warrant to Arrest Mr Assad Hassan Sabra Including Transfer and Detention Order, 28 June 2011, STL-11-01/I/PTJ/F0016/Cor/20110816/R091956-R091962/FR-EN/pvk.
142 'Hezbollah leader Nasrallah rejects Hariri indictments', *BBC News*, 3 July 2011.
143 Order on the Prosecutor's Motion for Variation of the Order for Non-disclosure of the Indictment, 28 July 2011, STL-11-01/I/PTJ/F0026/20110728/R091381-R091384/EN/pvk.
144 'Hezbollah leader Nasrallah rejects Hariri indictments', *BBC News*, 3 July 2011. 'Nasrallah implies Israel behind Hariri murder', *Al Jazeera*, 2 July 2011.
145 UNHCR Inter-Agency Information Sharing Portal (2016) *UNHCR Syria regional refugee response*. Available at: http://data.unhcr.org/syrianrefugees/country.php?id=122 (Accessed: 16 August 2016).
146 The Economist (2015) *Hizbullah's Learning Curve: Deadly Experience*. Available at: www.economist.com/news/middle-east-and-africa/21661826-costly-valuable-lessons-guerrilla-army-once-fought (Accessed: 16 August 2016).
147 The Economist (2016) *Hizbullah's Military Commander Is Killed*. Available at: www.economist.com/news/middle-east-and-africa/21698768-israel-usual-suspectbut-may-not-have-been-responsible-time-hizbullahs (Accessed: 16 August 2016).
148 *Prosecutor vs Ibrahim Al Amin and Akhbar Beirut S.A.L* [2016] Contempt Judge STL Judgement 06/T/CJ/F0262/PRV/20160715/R007725-R007795/EN/af.
149 STL (no date) *About the Ayyash et al. Trial*. Available at: www.stl-tsl.org/en/the-cases/about-the-trial (Accessed: 16 August 2016).
150 In October 2013, the indictment of a fifth individual, Hassan Habib Merhi, for the 14 February 2005 Beirut attack was made public by the STL. Merhi was also identified by the Tribunal as a 'Hezbollah supporter'. *The Prosecutor v. Hassan Habib Merhi*, Public Redacted Indictment, 5 June 2013, STL-13-04.

151 M. Weber, *The Theory of Social and Economic Organization*, New York: Free Press, 1947, p. 78. Weber argues that, in the West, the emergence of modernity progressively replaced traditional and charismatic authority by rational-legal authority. Hezbollah's later actions suggest that it also attempted to base its legitimacy, increasingly, on rational-legal authority to strengthen its base in other constituencies.

152 The latter, for instance by means of banners with portraits of Musa al-Sadr, Khomeini, Nasrallah and Hezbollah martyrs, and can be seen throughout Hezbollah territory. Noe, *Voice of Hezbollah*, p. 234.

153 Norton, 'The Role of Hezbollah in Lebanese Domestic Politics', p. 486.

154 Gow, *Legitimacy and the Military*, pp. 27–30.

155 Knudsen and Kerr, 'Introduction: The Cedar Revolution and Beyond', p. 8.

156 Jaber, *Hezbollah: Born with a Vengeance*, p. 178.

157 'Why They Died: Civilian Casualties in Lebanon during the 2006 War', *Human Rights Watch*, vol. 19, no. 5(E) September 2007.

158 R. Smith, *The Utility of Force: The Art of War in the Modern World*, London: Penguin Books, 2005, p. 242.

159 Norton, 'The Role of Hezbollah in Lebanese Domestic Politics', p. 484.

160 Knudsen and Kerr, 'Introduction: The Cedar Revolution and Beyond', p. 8.

161 Blanford, *Warriors of God*, pp. 482–483. Hamzeh, *In the path of Hezbollah*, pp. 32–34.

162 T. Dunning, '"Mind Forged Manacles": Hamas, Hezbollah and Orientalist Discourse', *Refereed paper delivered at Australian Political Studies Association Conference*, 6–9 July 2008, Hilton Hotel, Brisbane Australia, p. 7.

163 R. Fisk, *Pity the Nation: The Abduction of Lebanon*, 4th edn, New York: Thunder's Mouth Press, p. xii.

164 M. Michalski and J. Gow, *War, Image and Legitimacy: Viewing Contemporary Conflict*, Abington: Routledge, 2007, p. 197 and p. 205.

165 President Bush's address to a joint session of Congress on Thursday 20 September 2001.

166 Dunning, '"Mind Forged Manacles": Hamas, Hezbollah and Orientalist Discourse', p. 5.

167 R. Wright, 'Inside the mind of Hezbollah', *Washington Post*, 16 July 2006, p. B01.

168 'EU's Solana meets Hezbollah in Beirut', *BBC News*, 13 June 2009.

169 K. Sharro, '"The Indictment": A Thriller lacking in action. The STL Predicament', *Karl ReMarks*, 30 June 2011.

170 J. Muir, 'Lebanon tense as fingers point over Hariri killing', *BBC News*, 25 November 2010.

171 K. Sharro, 'The Forensic Alternative to the Truth: Thoughts on the Nasrallah Speech and the Difficulty of Writing History in Lebanon', *Karl ReMarks*, 9 August 2010.

172 Ibid.

173 B. Berti, 'Middle East Media Monitor Hezbollah On Trial: Lebanese Reactions to the UN Special Tribunal's Indictments', *Foreign Policy Research Institute*, August 2011.

174 When the indictments came out, Paul Salem, the director of the Carnegie Middle East Center, said: 'Names without a story doesn't have much impact. If the public comes to see there's massive evidence of a terrible story, that will have a big public impact by itself, but that hasn't happened yet'. N. Bakri, 'Tribunal names 4 in '05 killing of Lebanese leader', *New York Times*, 30 June 2011.

175 Abdo, G. (2013) *Why Sunni–Shia conflict is worsening*. Available at: http://edition.cnn.com/2013/06/07/opinion/abdo-shia-sunni-tension/index.html (Accessed: 16 August 2016).

176 Chulov, M., Shaheen, K. and Beaumont, P. (2016) *Thousands gather for funeral of Hezbollah's Mustafa Badreddine*. Available at: https://www.theguardian.com/world/2016/may/13/thousands-gather-for-funeral-of-hezbollahs-mustafa-badreddine (Accessed: 17 August 2016).

Bibliography

Abdo, G. (2013) *Why Sunni–Shia conflict is worsening*. Available at: http://edition.cnn. com/2013/06/07/opinion/abdo-shia-sunni-tension/index.html (Accessed: 16 August 2016).

Al Jazeera (2006) *Lebanon Shia ministers end boycott*. Available at: www.aljazeera.com/arc hive/2006/02/200841012161236825.html (Accessed: 17 August 2016).

Al Jazeera (2009) *Nasrallah concedes election defeat*. Available at: www.aljazeera.com/ news/middleeast/2009/06/2009681835910848.html (Accessed: 17 August 2016).

Al Jazeera (2010a) *Hezbollah urges Hariri case boycott*. Available at: www.aljazeera.com/ news/middleeast/2010/10/2010102819122690558.html (Accessed: 17 August 2016).

Al Jazeera (2010b) *Lebanon summons general on comments*. Available at: www. aljazeera.com/news/middleeast/2010/09/2010916145846926793.html (Accessed: 17 August 2016).

Al Jazeera (2010c) *Nasrallah unveils 'Hariri proof'*. Available at: www.aljazeera.com/ news/middleeast/2010/08/2010891991920480.html (Accessed: 17 August 2016).

Al Jazeera (2016) *Nasrallah implies Israel behind Hariri murder*. Available at: www. aljazeera.com/news/middleeast/2011/07/201172183540290278.html (Accessed: 18 August 2016).

Al Jazeera and Yazbeck, N. (2011) *Views on Lebanon political crisis*. Available at: www.aljazeera.com/news/middleeast/2011/01/20111138579772871.html (Accessed: 18 August 2016).

Alagha, J. (2007) *The Shifts in Hizbullah's Ideology: Religious Ideology, Political Ideology, and Political Program*. Leiden: Amsterdam University Press.

Ambos, K. (2001) 'Judicial Creativity at the Special Tribunal for Lebanon: Is There a Crime of Terrorism under International Law?' *Leiden Journal of International Law*, 24(03), pp. 655–675. doi: 10.1017/s0922156511000215.

Amnesty International (2006) *Israel/Lebanon: Deliberate Destruction or 'collateral damage'? Israeli attacks on civilian infrastructure*.

Andoni, L. (2016) *Border skirmish a 'fire douser'*. Available at: www.aljazeera.com/focu s/2010/08/20108414293958951.html (Accessed: 18 August 2016). Al Jazeera.

Bakri, N. (2014) *4 indicted in killing of Rafik Hariri, ex-leader of Lebanon*. Available at: www.nytimes.com/2011/07/01/world/middleeast/01lebanon.html?pagewanted=all&_ r=0 (Accessed: 18 August 2016).

BBC (2005a) *Amnesty for Lebanese ex-warlord*. Available at: http://news.bbc.co.uk/1/hi/ world/middle_east/4693091.stm (Accessed: 17 August 2016).

BBC (2005b) *Assad pledges Lebanon withdrawal*. Available at: http://news.bbc.co.uk/1/ hi/world/middle_east/4310699.stm (Accessed: 17 August 2016).

BBC (2005c) *Beirut bomb targets top minister*. Available at: http://news.bbc.co.uk/1/hi/ world/middle_east/4674441.stm (Accessed: 17 August 2016).

BBC (2005d) *Explosion kills former Lebanon PM*. Available at: http://news.bbc.co.uk/1/ hi/world/middle_east/4263893.stm (Accessed: 18 August 2016).

BBC (2005e) *Hundreds mourn Beirut journalist*. Available at: http://news.bbc.co.uk/1/hi/ world/middle_east/4609329.stm (Accessed: 17 August 2016).

BBC (2005f) *In quotes: World reacts to Hariri death*. Available at: http://news.bbc.co. uk/1/hi/world/middle_east/4264975.stm (Accessed: 17 August 2016).

BBC (2005g) *Lebanese leaders agree on cabinet*. Available at: http://news.bbc.co.uk/1/ hi/world/middle_east/4697587.stm (Accessed: 17 August 2016).

BBC (2005h) *Syria looks to Riyadh for support*. Available at: http://news.bbc.co.uk/1/hi/ world/middle_east/4315107.stm (Accessed: 18 August 2016).

BBC (2005i) *Syrian troops leave Lebanese soil.* Available at: http://news.bbc.co.uk/1/hi/world/middle_east/4484325.stm (Accessed: 18 August 2016).

BBC (2005j) *US warns Syria over Lebanon role.* Available at: http://news.bbc.co.uk/1/hi/world/middle_east/4269351.stm (Accessed: 18 August 2016).

BBC (2006) *Hezbollah ministers quit cabinet.* Available at: http://news.bbc.co.uk/1/hi/world/middle_east/6139730.stm (Accessed: 17 August 2016).

BBC (2009) *EU's Solana meets Hezbollah in Beirut.* Available at: http://news.bbc.co.uk/1/hi/8099074.stm (Accessed: 17 August 2016).

BBC (2011a) *Hezbollah and allies topple Lebanese unity government.* Available at: www.bbc.co.uk/news/world-middle-east-12170608 (Accessed: 17 August 2016).

BBC (2011b) *Hezbollah leader Nasrallah rejects Hariri indictments.* Available at: www.bbc.co.uk/news/world-middle-east-14004096 (Accessed: 17 August 2016).

Berti, B. (2011) Middle East Media Monitor, *Hezbollah On Trial: Lebanese Reactions to the UN Special Tribunal's Indictments.* Foreign Policy Research Institute.

Bregman, A. (2000) *Israel's Wars: A History since 1947.* Abingdon: Routledge.

Bush, G.W. (2001) *President Bush's address to a joint session of Congress on Thursday 20 September 2001.*

CBS News (2006) *Lebanese president gives full backing to Hezbollah.* Available at: www.cbc.ca/news/world/story/2006/07/28/lahoud-interview.html (Accessed: 17 August 2016).

Committee to Protect Journalists (2005) *May Chidiac, Lebanese Broadcasting Corporation Attacked.* Available at: http://cpj.org/2005/09/lebanon-1.php (Accessed: 17 August 2016).

Cordesman, A.H., Sullivan, G. and Sullivan, W.D. (2007) *Lessons of the 2006 Israeli-Hezbollah War.* Washington DC: Center for Strategic and International Studies.

Elberling, B. (2008) 'The Next Step in History-Writing through Criminal Law: Exactly How Tailor-Made Is the Special Tribunal for Lebanon?' *Leiden Journal of International Law*, 21(02). doi: 10.1017/s0922156508005086.

Fassbender, B. (2007) 'Reflections on the International Legality of the Special Tribunal for Lebanon', *Journal of International Criminal Justice*, 5(5), pp. 1091–1105. doi: 10.1093/jicj/mqm070.

Fisk, R. (2002) *Pity the Nation: The Abduction of Lebanon*, 4th edn. New York: Thunder's Mouth Press/Nation Books.

Fitzpatrick, J. (2002) 'Jurisdiction of Military Commissions and the Ambiguous War on Terrorism', *American Journal of International Law*, 96(2), pp. 345–354. doi: 10.2307/2693929.

Fleming, C.M. (2009) 'New or old wars? Debating a Clausewitzian Future', *Journal of Strategic Studies*, 32(2), pp. 213–241. doi: 10.1080/01402390902743175.

Follath, E. (2009) *Breakthrough in tribunal investigation: New evidence points to Hezbollah in Hariri murder – SPIEGEL ONLINE.* Available at: www.spiegel.de/international/world/breakthrough-in-tribunal-investigation-new-evidence-points-to-hezbollah-in-hariri-murder-a-626412.html (Accessed: 18 August 2016). SPIEGEL ONLINE.

Gaeta, P. (2007) 'To Be (Present) or Not To Be (Present): Trials In Absentia before the Special Tribunal for Lebanon'. *Journal of International Criminal Justice*, 5, pp. 1165–1174.

Galey, P. and the *Daily Star* (2011) *STL not investigating false witnesses, says tribunal's registrar on Twitter.* Available at: www.dailystar.com.lb/News/Politics/2011/Dec-08/156295-stl-not-investigating-false-witnesses-says-tribunals-registrar-on-twitter.ashx#ixzz2WtgCmi8I (Accessed: 18 August 2016).

Hamzeh, A.N. (2004) *In the Path of Hizbullah.* Syracuse, NY: Syracuse University Press.

Harik, J.P. (2006) *Hezbollah: The Changing Face of Terrorism*, 2nd edn. London: I.B. Tauris.

Human Rights Watch (2006) 'Fatal Strikes: Israel's Indiscriminate Attacks Against Civilians in Lebanon', *Human Rights Watch*, 18(3).

Human Rights Watch (2007) 'Report on Civilian Casualties in Lebanon during the 2006 War', *Human Rights Watch*, 19(5). doi: 10.1525/jps.2008.37.2.193.

Jaber, H. (1997) *Hezbollah: Born with a Vengeance*. New York, NY, United States: Columbia University Press.

Jenks, C. (2009) 'Notice Otherwise Given: Will In Absentia Trials at the Special Tribunal for Lebanon Violate Human Rights?' *ExpressO*.

Karouny, M. (2010) *Hariri tribunal to accuse Hezbollah members: Nasrallah*. Available at: http://uk.reuters.com/article/2010/07/22/us-lebanon-hezbollah-idUSTRE66L5 GK20100722 (Accessed: 18 August 2016). Reuters.

Kerr, M. (2012) 'Before the Revolution'. In: Knudsen, A. and Kerr, M. (eds), *Lebanon: After the Cedar Revolution*. London: Hurst and Co., pp. 23–38.

Knudsen, A. (2007) 'The Law, the Loss and the Lives of Palestinian Refugees in Lebanon', *CMI Working Paper*, 1.

Knudsen, A. (2012) 'Special Tribunal for Lebanon: Homage to Hariri?' In: Knudsen, A. and Kerr, M. (eds), *After the Cedar Revolution*. London: Hurst and Co.

Knudsen, A. and Kerr, M. (2012) 'Introduction: The Cedar Revolution and Beyond'. In: Knudsen, A. and Kerr, M. (eds), *Lebanon: After the Cedar Revolution*. London: Hurst and Co., pp. 3–23.

Michalski, M. and Gow, J. (2007) *War, image and Legitimacy: Viewing Contemporary Conflict*. London: Routledge.

Milanovic, M. (2007) 'An Odd Couple: Domestic Crimes and International Responsibility in the Special Tribunal for Lebanon'. *Journal of International Criminal Justice*, 5(5), pp. 1139–1152. doi: 10.1093/jicj/mqm074.

Morley, J. (2005) *The Branding of Lebanon's 'revolution'*. Available at: www.washingtonpost.com/wp-dyn/articles/A1911-2005Mar2.html (Accessed: 18 August 2016).

Muir, J. (2010a) *Deep divisions haunt Lebanese politics*. Available at: www.bbc.co.uk/news/world-middle-east-11392034 (Accessed: 18 August 2016).

Muir, J. (2010b) *Lebanon tense as fingers point over Hariri killing*. Available at: www.bbc.co.uk/news/world-middle-east-11837816 (Accessed: 18 August 2016).

Mégret, F. (2008) 'A Special Tribunal for Lebanon: The UN Security Council and the Emancipation of International Criminal Justice', *Leiden Journal of International Law*, 21(02). doi: 10.1017/s0922156508005062.

Nasrallah, H. (2005) 'You will today decide the fate of your nation and country'. Speech given on 8 March 2005.

Neumann, J. (2011) *Hariri assassination still clouds Lebanese politics*. Available at: http://m.voanews.com/a/173296.html (Accessed: 18 August 2016).

Noe, N. (ed.), (2007) *Voice of Hezbollah: The Statements of Sayed Hassan Nasrallah*. London: Verso.

Norton, A.R. (1999) *Hizballah of Lebanon: Extremist Ideals v. Mundane Politics*. New York: Council on Foreign Relations.

Norton, Augustus R. (2007) *Hezbollah: A Short History*. Princeton: Princeton University Press.

Norton, Augustus Richard (2007) 'The Role of Hezbollah in Lebanese Domestic Politics'. *The International Spectator*, 42(4), pp. 475–491. doi: 10.1080/03932720701722852.

Noueihed, L. (2005) *Anti-Syrian politician killed in Lebanon*. Available at: www. washingtonpost.com/wp-dyn/content/article/2005/06/21/AR2005062100390.html (Accessed: 17 August 2016).

Pons, N. (2010) 'Some Remarks on In Absentia Proceedings before the Special Tribunal for Lebanon in Case of a State's Failure or Refusal to Hand Over the Accused'. *Journal of International Criminal Justice*, 8(5), pp. 1307–1321. doi: 10.1093/jicj/mqq068.

Prosecutor v. Ibrahim Al Amin and Akhbar Beirut S.A.L [2016] Contempt Judge STL Judgment. 06/T/CJ/F0262/PRV/20160715/R007725-R007795/EN/af.

Qassem, N. (2005) *Hizbullah: The Story from Within*. London: Saqi Books.

Raad, N. (2005) *Opposition demands 'intifada for independence'*. Available at: www. dailystar.com.lb/News/Politics/Feb/19/Opposition-demands-intifada-for-independence. ashx#axzz2UDfhafhB (Accessed: 18 August 2016).

Ranstorp, M. (1997) *Hizb'allah in Lebanon: The Politics of the Western Hostage Crisis*. New York, NY, United States: St Martin's Press.

Reuters Editorial (2010a) *Hariri says was wrong to accuse Syria over killing*. Available at: www.reuters.com/article/2010/09/06/us-lebanon-hariri-idUSTRE68510420100906 (Accessed: 17 August 2016).

Reuters Editorial (2010b) *Hariri tribunal to accuse Hezbollah members: Nasrallah*. Available at: http://uk.reuters.com/article/2010/07/22/us-lebanon-hezbollah-idUSTRE66L5GK 20100722 (Accessed: 17 August 2016).

Reuters and Ladki, N. (2008) *Hezbollah says Beirut government declares war*. Available at: www.reuters.com/article/homepageCrisis/idUSL08466882._CH_.2400 (Accessed: 18 August 2016).

Sakr, E. (2010) *Nasrallah: We will not allow arrest of fighters*. Available at: www.dailystar.com.lb/News/Politics/Nov/12/Nasrallah-We-will-not-allow-arrest-of-fighters. ashx#ixzz2ZwxjM5uL (Accessed: 18 August 2016). *Daily Star*.

Scharf, M.P. (2011) 'Special Tribunal for Lebanon Issues Landmark Ruling on Definition of Terrorism and Modes of Participation', *ASIL Insights*, 15(6).

Security Council (2000) *'Security Council Endorses Secretary-General's Conclusion on Israeli Withdrawal From Lebanon as of 16 June'*. Press release SC/6878.

Seeberg, P. (2007) 'Fragmented loyalties: Nation and Democracy in Lebanon after the Cedar Revolution'. *Centre for Contemporary Middle East Studies, University of Southern Denmark: Working Paper Series*, 8.

Sharro, K. (2010) *The Forensic Alternative to the Truth: Thoughts on the Nasrallah Speech and the Difficulty of Writing History in Lebanon'*. Available at: www.karlremarks.com/2010/08/forensic-alternative-to-truth-thoughts.html (Accessed: 18 August 2016). Karl ReMarks.

Sharro, K. (2011) *'The Indictment': A Thriller lacking in action. The STL Predicament*. Available at: www.karlremarks.com/2011/06/indictment-thriller-lacking-in-action.html (Accessed: 18 August 2016). Karl ReMarks.

Smith, R. (2005) *The Utility of Force: The Art of War in the Modern World*. London: Penguin.

Order Directing the Lebanese Judicial Authority Seized with the Case Concerning the Attack Perpetrated against Mr Elias El-Murr on 12 July 2005 to Defer to the Special Tribunal for Lebanon [2011] STL. STL-11-02/D/PTJ.

Order on the Prosecutor's Motion for Variation of the Order for Non-disclosure of the Indictment [2011a] STL STL-11-01/I/PTJ/F0026/20110728/R091381-R091384/EN/pvk.

STL (2011b) *Timeline Jamil El Sayed: Press Release of the Special Tribunal for Lebanon*.

STL (no date) *About the Ayyash et al. Trial.* Available at: www.stl-tsl.org/en/the-cases/about-the-trial (Accessed: 16 August 2016).

Terrorism, Conspiracy, Homicide, Perpetration, Cumulative Charging [2011] STL Interlocutory Decision on the Applicable Law. STL-11-01/I.

The Economist (2015) *Hizbullah's learning curve: Deadly experience.* Available at: www.economist.com/news/middle-east-and-africa/21661826-costly-valuable-lessons-guerrilla-army-once-fought (Accessed: 16 August 2016).

The Economist (2016) *Hizbullah's military commander is killed.* Available at: www.economist.com/news/middle-east-and-africa/21698768-israel-usual-suspectbut-may-not-have-been-responsible-time-hizbullahs (Accessed: 16 August 2016).

'The Victory of May', speech by Hassan Nasrallah (2009) ShiaTV, 25 May at 7 minutes.

UNHCR Inter-Agency Information Sharing Portal (2016) *UNHCR Syria regional refugee response.* Available at: http://data.unhcr.org/syrianrefugees/country.php?id=122 (Accessed: 16 August 2016).

Ventura, M.J. (2011) 'Terrorism According to the STL's Interlocutory Decision on the applicable Law: A Defining Moment or a Moment of Defining?' *Journal of International Criminal Justice*, 9(5), pp. 1021–1042. doi: 10.1093/jicj/mqr046.

Victoroff, J. (2006) *Tangled Roots: Social and Psychological Factors in the Genesis of Terrorism.* Edited by J. Victoroff. Washington DC: IOS Press.

Von Glahn, G. (1992) *Law among Nations: An Introduction to Public International Law.* New York: Macmillan.

Waldmann, P. (2006) *The Radical Community: A Comparative Analysis of the Social Background of ETA, IRA, and Hezbollah.* Amsterdam: IOS.

Weber, M. (1964) *The Theory of Social and Economic Organization.* New York: Free Press.

Worth, R.F. (2014) *Hezbollah makes its case on Hariri killing.* Available at: www.nytimes.com/2010/07/25/world/middleeast/25lebanon.html?_r=0 (Accessed: 18 August 2016). *New York Times.*

Yun, J. (2010) 'Special Tribunal for Lebanon: A Tribunal of an International Character Devoid of International Law'. *Santa Clara Journal of International Law*, 7(2), pp. 181–196.

6 The International Criminal Court and the self-referral of the situation in Northern Mali

Until it was plunged into turmoil by the January 2012 reawakening of a Tuareg rebellion in the northern part of the country and a military coup in Bamako in March 2012, Mali was often acclaimed as an example of a relatively successful African democracy. But despite a democratic political system, a rich culture and relatively tolerant nature, Mali had been dealing with severe hardships – limited natural resources, droughts and endemic corruption – for generations. Most destabilising were the recurring armed rebellions by Tuareg in the north. In early 2012, the *Mouvement National pour la Libération de l'Azawad* (MNLA), an organisation consisting of veterans of previous Tuareg rebellions, launched attacks on government targets to take control of Mali's three northern regions. The MNLA was initially successful against the Malian Army, further aided by the state of chaos in which the central government was left following the military coup in Bamako, and the organisation declared the independence of Azawad as a Tuareg homeland in April 2012.

The Northern Mali uprising was not sparked by Islamic fundamentalism initially – its origins can be found in age-old irredentist sentiments of disenfranchisement, marginalisation and continued impoverishment of the northern Tuareg – yet the violence in Northern Mali did provide Islamic militants with unprecedented opportunities to become major actors. Both foreign and homegrown radical Islamist factions were quick to fill the void, in terms of ungoverned space, created by the Tuareg rebellion and subsequent collapse of government control. By June 2012, Islamists had taken over control of most of Northern Mali. These developments transformed the historically balanced relations between state and religion in Mali, based on secularism and moderation. This posed a threat not only to Mali and neighbouring states, Niger in particular, but also to stability in the wider region and to international peace and security.

The evidence of war crimes committed by various parties in the conflict that soon started to appear meant that the situation at first glance seemed to be a clear-cut case for the ICC. Especially as Mali had been one of the first states to sign and ratify the Rome Statute and, in July 2012, the government of Mali, requested the Chief Prosecutor of the ICC to investigate the most serious crimes committed in the northern part of its territory after January 2012. However, by that time, the ICC was reaching the limits of its capacity and was already under heavy fire, from the African Union (AU) and many others, for its focus on Africa. The last thing the Court needed was another investigation in Africa. Moreover, self-referrals by States Parties – while in theory facilitating easier procedures and the collection of evidence – were increasingly watched with suspicion as they threatened to create the image of a 'court of convenience'; a court at the convenience of states to neutralise their non- or quasi-state opponents by means of international justice.[1] Nevertheless, the Prosecutor of the ICC, in January 2013, announced that the Court would open an investigation into the situation in Northern Mali.

The present chapter will argue that the self-referral of Mali indeed demonstrates that the government trusted that it would benefit from the involvement of the ICC, and that it sought international criminal procedures to boost its legitimacy while simultaneously delegitimising the various QSEs that also vied for control over territory and statehood functions in Mali. The first part of this chapter will provide a background of the statehood issues that arose in the run-up to the referral of the situation in Northern Mali, the underlying grievances, the QSEs that emerged to challenge the government's power and the crimes committed in the conflict that ensued. The second part will focus on the politics of self-referral of situations to the ICC, and how, by prosecuting the most serious international crimes, 'the ICC provides a vocabulary with which opponents can label the enemy as a violator of universal norms, and, thereby, as the enemy of humanity itself'.[2] It will describe the potential pitfalls of self-referral cases for the ICC and, indeed, for states that refer situations in their own territory. The third part of the chapter will discuss the acceptance of the self-referral by the Prosecutor of the ICC and the significance of the self-referral of Mali, in particular. Finally, the (potential) impact of the ICC investigation on the legitimacy of the MNLA and its statehood project will be assessed and the change in narratives under pressure of international criminal justice and the ICC referral will be discussed.

The International Criminal Court: a decisive blow for impunity?

To understand the impact of the ICC, it is useful to look at the Court's set-up and jurisdiction as well as its justifications, history and functioning. Plans for a permanent mechanism of international criminal justice had first emerged at the end of World War I, but had not resulted in the establishment of such a tribunal within the League of Nations framework. In 1948, the UN General Assembly recognised the need to establish an international criminal court and invited the ILC 'to study the desirability and possibility of establishing an international judicial organ for the trial of persons charged with genocide or other crimes of similar gravity'.[3] The ILC drafted statutes in 1951 and 1953, but during the Cold War, the process of drafting was postponed, at times reconsidered, and postponed again. In 1989, the General Assembly, after a request by Trinidad and Tobago to prevent drug trafficking and transnational organised crime, asked the

ILC to start work on a permanent court once more. However, confronted with the horrors of the breakup of Yugoslavia and the subsequent establishment of the ICTY, the draft statute that the committee finished in 1994 was designed to hold individuals accountable for war crimes, crimes against humanity and genocide. The General Assembly then established the Preparatory Committee on the Establishment of an International Criminal Court that completed drafting the text of a statute in April 1998.[4] It was at the United Nations Diplomatic Conference of Plenipotentiaries on the Establishment of an International Criminal Court, held in Rome, that the Statute was finalised and, on 17 July 1998, 120 states adopted the Rome Statute, thereby forming the legal basis for the establishment of the first permanent international criminal court.[5]

After the 60th state ratified the Rome Statute, in April 2002, UN Secretary-General Kofi Annan announced: 'Impunity has been dealt a decisive blow'.[6] Three months later, the Statute came into force, creating the ICC, with the aim 'to put an end to impunity for the perpetrators of [the most serious crimes of concern to the international community as a whole] and thus to contribute to the prevention of such crimes'.[7] The mandate the ICC was given might not always be sufficient to live up to those high ambitions – it certainly can be doubted whether it can deal impunity a decisive blow – yet, despite its shortcomings, it is the ICC that represents the future of international criminal justice.

A permanent international criminal court, it could be argued, poses a more immediate threat to perpetrators of the most horrible atrocities than the uncertain prospect that an *ad hoc* tribunal might be created *ex post facto*. Quick prosecutions are more likely before a permanent court than in a situation in which the UN Security Council, if its five permanent members can reach an agreement, have the possibility of establishing an *ad hoc* tribunal under Chapter VII. Although the establishment of a hybrid court is often politically a more likely scenario than an *ad hoc* tribunal, the threat of prosecution by a permanent court is more immediate.[8] Hybrid tribunals will play an important role but, if international criminal justice is to have a noticeable structural effect, it will be through a permanent court that has the means and know-how to start an investigation at short notice, that is widely perceived to be independent, and whose decisions carry sufficient weight.

Unlike the ICTY, ICTR and STL, which were established by the UN Security Council under Chapter VII, the ICC is a treaty-based court.[9] Its establishment by statute means that, despite the close cooperation with the UN, the ICC is an independent international organisation with international legal personality.[10] Although its seat is in The Hague, proceedings can take place anywhere. The independence of the court means that it depends on cooperation, and that its funding comes from the states party to the Rome Statute, the UN and voluntary contributions.[11]

The jurisdiction of the ICC

Besides the level of cooperation of member states and the UN, and the enforcement mechanisms the Court has at its disposal, the impact of the ICC depends on the jurisdiction of the Court and the admissibility of cases. The jurisdiction *ratione materiae*, the subject-matter jurisdiction the Rome Statute provides the ICC with, is limited to the 'most serious crimes of concern to the international community as a whole'.[12] In Article 5, these are listed as encompassing war crimes, crimes against humanity, genocide and the crime of aggression. While the first three crimes are defined in Articles 6, 7 and 8, the ICC will remain unable to exercise jurisdiction over the crime of aggression until the crime is defined and the conditions under which the Court shall exercise jurisdiction with respect to this crime are set out.[13] Although amendments to the Statute to this effect were accepted at the Review Conference in Kampala in 2010, jurisdiction of the ICC over the crime of aggression will only come into force after 1 January 2017.[14]

The jurisdiction *ratione temporis* of the ICC is fairly straightforward; it has jurisdiction over crimes committed after the entry into force of the Rome Statute, on 1 July 2002 or after its entry into force in a State that became party to the Statute at a later date, unless a declaration has been lodged with the registrar, accepting the exercise of jurisdiction by the Court with respect to the crime in question.[15] The Court may exercise its jurisdiction when a crime described in Article 5 of the Statute appears to have been committed in a situation that: (1) was referred to the Prosecutor by a State Party; or (2) after a referral by the Security Council; or (3) when the Prosecutor initiated an investigation *proprio motu*.[16]

The jurisdiction of the ICC in part depends on the States Parties to the Rome Statute. The Statute came into force in July 2002 after 60 states had ratified the treaty. As of August 2016, it is in force in 124 states and has 139 state signatories.[17] Although the treaty is in force in most of Africa, almost the whole of Europe and all of South America, it is not ratified by three of the five permanent members of the Security Council – the United States, Russia and China.[18] This has a direct impact on the jurisdiction that the ICC can exercise, but it also sends a message – that ending impunity for the most horrible crimes is not their primary concern.

The admissibility of cases

One of the most significant characteristics of the ICC is that the Rome Statute foresaw a system complementary to national criminal jurisdictions.[19] It limits the cases admissible to the Court to those situations in which a state that has jurisdiction has not investigated a situation or 'is unwilling or unable genuinely to carry out the investigation or prosecution'. Article 17 of the Statute stipulates that cases are inadmissible when the case 'is not of sufficient gravity to justify further action by the Court'.[20] However, unwillingness on behalf of the state to prosecute is presumed when proceedings were undertaken, or the decision was taken not to prosecute after an investigation into a case, with the purpose of shielding a person from the ICC using its jurisdiction.[21] Inability to prosecute a case is determined when a 'substantial collapse or unavailability of its national judicial system' renders the state unable to obtain the accused, testimonies or evidence, or otherwise be unable to carry out its proceedings.[22] Before an investigation is opened, *proprio motu*, or based on a state referral, the Prosecutor will notify the state which then has a month to open an investigation under its national jurisdiction, after which the Prosecutor can either defer the case to the state, or request the Pre-Trial Chamber to authorise the investigation.[23] The *ne bis in ibid.* principle of Article 20 prevents other courts from prosecuting individuals for conduct they have been convicted of, or acquitted of, by the Court.[24] Vice versa, the ICC will not prosecute a person for the same conduct that has led to a conviction or acquittal by a national court, unless that conviction or acquittal was meant to shield the person from the jurisdiction of the ICC, or proceedings were not conducted independently and impartially.[25]

Without a police force of its own, the ICC can only enforce its decisions through the cooperation of states. Under the Rome Statute, all States Parties are obligated to take necessary measures to enforce the ICC's indictments and otherwise support its work.[26] In theory, this enforcement mechanism enables the Court to use the resources of States Parties to make sure its decisions are executed, but where a State Party fails to comply with a request to cooperate by the Court, the only steps the ICC can take is that it may refer the matter to the Assembly of States Parties or, where the Security Council referred the matter to the Court, to the Security Council.[27]

The ICC in numbers

Since the Court came into being on 1 July 2002, it opened investigations into ten situations, nine of which were in Africa: the situations in Uganda, the Democratic Republic of the Congo (DRC), the Central African Republic (CAR) I and II and Mali were referred to the Court by the concerned States Parties themselves; the situations in Darfur, Sudan and Libya were referred by the UN Security Council; and investigations in Kenya, Côte d'Ivoire and Georgia commenced after the Pre-Trial Chamber authorised the Prosecutor to open an investigation *proprio motu*.[28] By mid-2016, the ICC had publicly indicted 39 individuals, however only 6 of those were in ICC custody while 13 were at large.[29] Thomas Lubanga Dyilo, Germain Katanga and Jean-Pierre Bemba were convicted, and Cui Ngudjolo was acquitted. In 13 cases the proceedings concluded without a conviction because the suspect died or because the charges were dismissed, withdrawn or the case was inadmissible.

Among the individuals publicly indicted by the ICC, two were serving heads of state – Omar al-Bashir of Sudan and Uhuru Kenyatta of Kenya – although the latter was indicted before he became president. Laurent Gbagbo formerly was president of Côte d'Ivoire, and former 'Brotherly Leader and Guide of the Revolution' Muammar Gaddafi was de facto head of state of Libya, although his capturers killed him rather than transferring him to The Hague. In the situations in the DRC, CAR, Uganda and Mali, cases were brought against individuals who had no official connection to state authorities, predominantly leaders, or former leaders, of QSEs. Conversely, in the cases of Côte d'Ivoire and Libya, the accused committed the crimes they were accused of during the spiral of legitimacy loss that resulted in their ousting. Kenyatta and William Ruto won elections in Kenya while procedures before the ICC against them were ongoing, and became president and deputy president of Kenya. The proceedings against them finished with 'charges withdrawn before trial' and 'terminated with no prejudice to re-prosecution' respectively. Omar al-Bashir continued to be president of Sudan, and Joseph Kony has been evading arrest for the better part of a decade. Although in summer 2016 there was uncertainty whether Saif al-Islam Gaddafi remained imprisoned in the Libyan town of Zintan, there is no prospect of him being transferred to The Hague.[30]

Based on these statistics, it may be hard to see the successes that indicate significant ICC impact, more so in light of the continuing crimes taking place in many of the conflicts under investigation by the ICC, and the fact that many more unimaginable atrocities were committed in situations across the world that were not under official investigation by the Prosecutor. As Judge Sang-Hyun Song noted, looking at statistics is by no means an adequate way of determining the impact of the ICC,[31] yet the list of cases reveals some of the ICC's shortcomings: first, the absence of ICC investigations into some of the most atrocious conflicts makes it painfully obvious how the limited jurisdiction of the ICC affects the impact the Court can have; second, the number of outstanding arrest warrants, and the time that has passed since they were issued, illustrates that the ICC can not always depend on states to enforce its decisions; third, the numbers show that all but one of the official investigations opened by 2016 were into situations in Africa, that all cases opened were in Africa, and that all individuals publicly indicted by the ICC so far are African.

The ICC and Africa

Although the Office of the Prosecutor (OTP) opened several preliminary investigations outside Africa, by mid-2016, these had only led to an official investigation into Georgia.[32] The focus on Africa led to much criticism, and hampers its performance. Yet the problem lies in the absence of possibilities to open investigations outside Africa rather than in the opening of investigations into situations in Africa. Numerous African countries experienced civil war over the last decade and a half, in which horrendous crimes were committed. It was because their legal systems were often not capable of putting the leaders most responsible for those crimes on trial and mainly because the Treaty was ratified in large parts of Africa that the ICC could step in. Moreover, the governments of Uganda, DRC, CAR and Mali self-referred situations to the ICC, either because they believed that the ICC would be better equipped to prosecute crimes committed in their territory, or because they thought they would benefit from a self-referral. Côte d'Ivoire accepted the jurisdiction of the Court and asked the Prosecutor to open an investigation; a self-referral in all but name. The other investigation that the Prosecutor started, *proprio motu*, in Kenya, was not an example of the ICC forcing its jurisdiction on an African country either, as its leaders later claimed it was. When the Prosecutor submitted a request to the Pre-Trial Chamber in late

2009, there was widespread support for an ICC investigation among the Kenyan population.[33] More important, the OTP took action on the recommendation of the 'Commission of Inquiry into the Post-Election Violence' – a Kenyan investigation commission, led by Kenyan judge Philip Waki – which concluded that the government failed to make good on its own promise to set up a special tribunal to prosecute those responsible for the worst crimes.[34] Only the situations in Darfur and Libya ended up with the ICC as a result of outside interference, in both cases by the Security Council that referred the situations.

More relevant than whether the criticism about the African focus of the Court was always warranted, is that it affected the legitimacy of the Court in constituencies across the continent. The narrative that the ICC is a 'prosecutorial tool of Northern Hemispheric states to help subordinate Africa under the rule of international law' fits in with pre-existing ideas in many African constituencies.[35] Branding the ICC a neocolonialist tool of the West, a rhetoric favoured by Omar al-Bashir since he was indicted for crimes against humanity and war crimes in March 2009 and genocide in July 2010, does not seem to fall on deaf ears in Sudan and in many other African countries.[36] Moreover, the indictment of al-Bashir created a rift between the Court and the AU.[37] The stance of the AU does not help in giving the Court a strong base: in 2009, the AU Assembly requested that the Security Council use its powers under Article 16 of the Statute to defer the proceedings against al-Bashir, and decided that the AU Member States 'shall not cooperate pursuant to the provisions of Article 98 of the Rome Statute of the ICC relating to immunities, for the arrest and surrender of President Omar El Bashir of The Sudan'.[38] The backtracking of the Kenyan government and the election of two ICC suspects to the highest offices further encouraged the Sudanese government and other African opponents of the ICC in their campaign against the Court. By the time Gambian lawyer Fatou Bensouda took over as Chief Prosecutor in June 2012, African governments were very hesitant to work with the Court.[39] In October 2013, the AU, at a meeting in Addis Ababa, even discussed the possibility of the withdrawal of all 34 African States Parties from the Court *en masse*.[40] The attempts to sabotage the ICC, by then led by Kenyan President Kenyatta and supported by Al Bashir, played on a sentiment that was widely felt on the continent.[41] Kenyatta castigated the ICC as a tool of the West and called it 'a toy of declining imperial powers' that violates the sovereignty of African states and conducts a radical witch-hunt on the continent.[42]

At the same time another sound could be heard on the continent and a coalition of human rights groups called on Africa's leaders to stay in the ICC. Desmond Tutu recalled that most cases were referred to the court by African governments themselves. He reminded those who 'play both the race and colonial cards' that the ICC is 'very clearly an African court' as five of the Court's 18 judges are African, including its vice president, Sanji Mmasenono Monageng of Botswana, and the Chief Prosecutor, Fatou Bensouda is from Gambia.[43] According to Tutu: 'Those leaders seeking to skirt the court are effectively looking for a license to kill, maim and oppress their own people without consequence'.[44] The October 2013 proposal to withdraw from the ICC failed to get support because the continent's heavyweights, Nigeria and South Africa, objected, but the AU did request the Court to defer the prosecution of sitting heads of state and decided to support immunity for Kenyatta and al-Bashir.[45] This kind of opposition to the Court contributed to sustaining a situation in which al-Bashir could travel around the continent and Kony could hide. The cases against Kenyatta and Ruto could even be weakened by witnesses pressured into withdrawing their testimonies to such an extent that the OTP had to terminate their prosecution (at least for now), in 2015 and 2016 respectively, due of a lack of evidence.

By looking at the statistics, it becomes clear that the Court is struggling to get its decisions enforced and suspects into custody. The willingness of a state to assist the Court will often depend upon that state's political motivations, rather than legal obligations.[46] The lack of enforcement mechanisms is therefore a handicap left to the Court by the Rome Statute, but the lack of political clout that is employed to compel states to cooperate may prove to be even more of a handicap. In a special UN Security Council meeting on peace and justice in October 2012, several states brought forward the misalignment between the expectations of the court and the means it has, in terms of the funding and assistance it gets, and in enforcement.[47] The Security Council also takes little action towards enforcement of ICC arrest warrants, even in the cases it referred to the Prosecutor. Under the guise of protecting their sovereignty, but usually due to a conflict with other political interests, governments have proven to be 'fickle or outright obstructive' in fulfilling their obligations to arrest individuals and hand them over to the ICC.[48] However, with the right incentives, the political balance can be tipped towards cooperation with courts, as illustrated by the arrest and transfer of Charles Taylor to the SCSL after political pressure on Nigeria.

Cooperation with the UN Security Council

That, in large parts of the world, the most atrocious crimes can still be committed without the Prosecutor of the ICC being able to open an investigation, is a direct result of the treaty basis of the Court. In an ideal situation, the Rome Treaty would be ratified by all states. However, despite the fact that the jurisdiction of the ICC is limited to the territory, or nationals, of State Parties, or to when the UN Security Council can reach agreement on a referral, its jurisdiction is still more far-reaching than any mechanism of international criminal justice that preceded it. The unanimous adoption of UN Security Council Resolution 1970 of 26 February 2011, referring the situation in Libya to the ICC demonstrates that, despite the US 'Hague Invasion Act', the fact that Russia did not accede to the Treaty and that China did not sign it, there was a certain acceptance of the Court's role and importance, even among these permanent members of the Security Council.[49] Moreover, the Libya referral shows that it was possible for the Council to come to an agreement to request the Prosecutor to open an ICC investigation, even if the changes in the political environment since 2011 seem to make such agreement increasingly unlikely.[50]

The inconsistency of the Council in using its prerogative to refer is problematic. So far, it has only referred two situations to the Prosecutor of the ICC.[51] In the wake of the Libya referral, and while the Syrian Civil War was going on, Costa Rica, Jordan, Liechtenstein, Singapore and Switzerland – the so-called Small Five – proposed rules of procedure for the Council to follow to enhance 'the systematic use of all mechanisms available under international law to ensure accountability for the most serious crimes'.[52] They did so in a wider bid to urge the Council members to 'refrain from using their veto power to block collective Council action to prevent and halt genocide, crimes against humanity and war crimes'.[53] However, they had to retract their draft General Assembly Resolution, despite the continuing situations in which, according to international human rights organisations and UN agencies, 'unimaginable atrocities that deeply shock the conscience of humanity' were committed, but over which the Court could not exercise jurisdiction based on Article 12 of the Statute.[54]

The most obvious, albeit by no means the only, example of such a situation is the civil war in Syria and Iraq, in which serious and numerous violations of humanitarian law were reported by both human rights organisations and the UN Human Rights Council.[55] However, NATO's wide interpretation of UN Security Council Resolution 1973, installing a no-fly zone over Libya in March 2011, and the subsequent military intervention in Libya, made Chinese, and especially Russian, cooperation in the Security Council less likely.[56] It seemed that this, combined with other Russian interests in Syria, contributed to the disagreement between Russia and other permanent Council members France, the United Kingdom and the United States, on coming to a Chapter VII resolution regarding the war in Syria.

The inability of the Security Council to reach agreement to refer situations to the ICC, and its inconsistency in doing so, might lead to the perception that the ICC can be used as a political tool. It might even reverse some of the positive effects that were attributed to the treaty-based foundation of the Court. Despite the obvious downside of limiting the Court's jurisdiction, the fact that the ICC is treaty-based also has advantages in terms of independence from political involvement. The selection of situations investigated, and cases brought forward, lies not just with a political body, the Security Council, or with states, but also with the Prosecutor. The Court has a certain degree of independence from the Council, and the five permanent members, in that it can act without its approval where and when it has jurisdiction. However, while Article 15 allows the Prosecutor to use his or her own initiative, without any form of control by a political body, Article 16 allows the Security Council to intervene and stop a prosecution, albeit temporarily.[57] So, while the ICC is not entirely free of external political control in the selection of situations, 'it nevertheless represents a considerable development in this respect even when measured against the ad hoc tribunals for the former Yugoslavia and Rwanda'.[58] Antonio Cassese argued that the advantages of this independence, in terms of the legitimacy of the Court, should not be underestimated.[59]

Complementarity

The shortcomings of the Court that become apparent when looking at the number of successfully prosecuted cases before it, by no means paint a complete picture of the ICC. The numbers do not do justice to the impact the Court has, and can have, on the legitimacy and conduct of both states and QSEs. The limits of the Court's jurisdiction, as marked by the Rome Statute, are not necessarily the best indicator of how the ICC functions either. That the ICC prosecutes individuals and not states, QSEs or other organisations, does not mean that the Court has no impact on these entities. The crimes over which the Court has jurisdiction must be committed as part of a 'plan or policy', or a 'widespread or systematic attack', and are, therefore, only feasible when committed in an organisational framework, usually that of a state or QSE. The OTP has made clear that the 'gravity threshold', in practice also means that the Prosecutor will focus on those individuals who bear the greatest responsibility for crimes within the jurisdiction of the Court.[60] Moreover, Chief Prosecutor Moreno-Ocampo, from the outset focused the ICC's efforts on the 'big fish'.[61] When leaders are accused, or prosecuted, the formal individualisation of criminal responsibility hardly ever means that the legitimacy of the entities in whose name they ordered, or who committed these crimes, is not affected.

When the Rome Statute was drafted, it remained to be seen how the ICC would be able to operate within the limits of its mandate, and how its interaction with states, QSEs and the UN Security Council would develop. It was not clear how important elements, such as the referral mechanism of Article 14 and the system of complementarity, would function and both turned out to function differently than expected.[62] The system of complementarity was incorporated as a means to make an agreement possible between those who wanted to establish a court with something as closely resembling universal jurisdiction as possible and those who wanted to defend state sovereignty.[63] Complementarity was a compromise, as ICC primacy over national courts was never a viable option if the ICC were to be widely accepted among states. Yet, it was expected that complementarity would lead to lengthy battles with states over jurisdiction and cooperation. In 1998, Louise Arbour, then Chief Prosecutor of the ICTY and ICTR, even called complementarity 'an absolute recipe for disaster'.[64]

Yet, the Statute not only made the ICC a 'court of last resort', it also reaffirmed the duties and rights of national governments to prosecute crimes under international law.[65] Although it might limit the Court's power in some situations, complementarity presents a way in which the ICC can increase its potential positive impact on both domestic and international criminal justice.[66] It has even been claimed that the greater impact of the ICC, with respect to prevention, will be in its interaction with domestic systems. According to Freeland, 'it is this development of national laws that may represent the most important criteria by which the effectiveness of the system of international criminal justice should be measured'.[67] Upon becoming Chief Prosecutor, Luis Moreno-Ocampo stated that:

As a consequence of complementarity, the number of cases that reach the Court should not be a measure of its efficiency. On the contrary the absence of trials before this Court, as a consequence of the regular functioning of national institutions, would be a major success.[68]

Moreover, the Court has such limited means that it lacks the ability to investigate all potential situations; empowering domestic jurisdictions is a more cost-effective way of spreading international justice. The conviction of former Chadian military ruler, Hissene Habre, by a special court in Senegal was seen as a success for complementarity. Moreover, talk of an African Union Hybrid War Crimes Court in South Sudan and the CAR passing a law in April 2015 to establish a Special Criminal Court made up of national and international judges to prosecute war crimes and crimes against humanity can be seen as a sign that complementarity has an effect.[69]

Self-referrals: an unexpected basis for jurisdiction

Article 14 of the Rome Statute, which deals with the referral of a situation by a State Party, used by states to refer situations in their *own* territory, unexpectedly became the most important basis of jurisdiction of the Court. In 1998, Louise Arbour could not 'think of a single state that will voluntarily defer to the jurisdiction of the ICC if one of their nationals is implicated'.[70] So far, half the situations investigated by the Court are 'self-referrals', demonstrating a mutuality of interests between the Court and States Parties.[71] This mutuality of interests is a result of the unprecedented capacity of QSEs to commit large-scale atrocities and the failure of interstate human rights mechanisms.[72] Payam Akhavan notes that, in contemporary conflict, 'states are sometimes the victims rather than the villains'.[73] Although QSEs do have an increased ability to carry out violent acts, it is equally true that states want to be seen as the victim rather than as the villain, especially because, in what Lawrence Freedman called 'compared victimology', the ICC can play a significant role.[74]

Instead of counting on states to protect human rights, it was expected that it would be the *proprio motu* powers of the Prosecutor and Security Council referrals that would primarily lead to investigations being opened,[75] not least because the assumption was that the ICC would be primarily acting against states.[76] However, Uganda referred the situation concerning the Lord's Resistance Army (LRA) to the ICC in December 2003.[77] In reaction to a notification by the Prosecutor that he might use his *proprio motu* powers to open an investigation into crimes committed on its territory, the government of the DRC also asked the Prosecutor to open an investigation in 2004.[78] The government of the CAR followed with a self-referral in 2005, and Mali in 2012.[79] Instead of an interstate mechanism, Article 14 became a self-referral mechanism.[80] Côte d'Ivoire accepted the court's jurisdiction and asked the Prosecutor to initiate an investigation, resulting in a new type of 'self-referral in all but name' for states that have not ratified the Rome Statute.[81]

The ICC as a tool to delegitimise QSEs

There can be several reasons for a self-referral. One is that, in a deeply divided nation, 'prosecutions in The Hague are more likely to be perceived as fair trials, whereas national proceedings may be portrayed with suspicion and as biased, or politically motivated'.[82] Another possible advantage of self-referral is that trials before national courts of political leaders can deteriorate the security situation.[83] In the twenty-first century, the vast majority of mass atrocities are committed in internal conflicts that involve states and QSEs fighting over statehood in which both can commit horrible crimes.[84] But self-referral by states does not only serve the purposes of justice that the state cannot provide; the government that refers a situation will calculate whether or not it will benefit from the referral.[85] The outcome of this calculation may be that by referring a situation on its territory the government can 'criminalize domestic opponents and itself gain international legitimacy'.[86]

In cases where the ICC prosecutes those fighting to change the status quo, the state has the potential to 're-brand political actors as criminals'.[87] When the accused are members of a QSE in conflict with the state, 'their stigmatization and isolation inadvertently serves the interests of a State that has referred the situation to preserve its sovereignty'.[88] The negative impact on the legitimacy of these QSEs can be substantial. At the same time, a narrative of support for international justice is received well in the international community, especially the West, and strengthens the government's legitimacy in these external constituencies. As Sarah Nouwen and Wouter Werner described, the Court has the ability to brand some 'as enemies of mankind, *hostes humani generis*', while it elevates those who assist or cooperate with the Court to 'the stage of virtue [...] enforcing universally valid norms and fighting humanity's enemies for humanity's sake'.[89] Moreover, 'prosecution may convince other international actors to support the government in its fight against these "enemies of mankind"'.[90]

In theory, governments could miscalculate the impact of a self-referral. Governments can only refer situations, not specific cases, and cannot limit the Court's jurisdiction to members of one particular group.[91] In self-referral situations, the Prosecutor could open a case both against members of the government, or other state entities, and the leaders of QSEs. Yet, in the situations that have come within the Court's jurisdiction, pursuant to self-referrals, the DRC, Uganda, CAR and Mali, so far no one has been charged for acts committed in an official state capacity. For the ICC, these first self-referrals came at the right moment. The opening of an investigation into the situation in Uganda 'was an attempt to engage an otherwise aloof international community by transforming the prosecution of LRA leaders into a litmus test for the much celebrated promise of global justice'.[92] Although self-referrals potentially clash with the intended purpose of the complementarity principle, so far the Court has not ruled that such a conflict exists. On the contrary, besides unwillingness motivated by the desire to obstruct the course of justice, the Trial Chamber came up with a second form of 'unwillingness' in the Katanga case. 'This second form of "unwillingness", which is not expressly provided for in Article 17 of the Statute, aims to see the person brought to justice, but not before national courts'.[93] Exactly how much freedom states have to choose whether to exercise jurisdiction, or relinquish it to the ICC, is not entirely clear. A volatile security situation or, in a divided nation, the 'perceived impartiality and fairness of the ICC', may warrant a self-referral, and even the high costs of a complex trial are sometimes considered to represent reasonable grounds for relinquishing jurisdiction.[94] The latter reason for referral would transform the ICC from a 'court of last resort' to a 'court of convenience'.[95]

The MNLA and the conflict in Northern Mali

Mali is the second-largest country in West Africa and the border – or buffer – between West Africa and the Maghreb. This made the area not only the historic gateway of trade which brought with it Islam from the Arab world, but today these ancient trade routes are used by international criminal groups for smuggling and made the area vulnerable to the influx of weapons and radical Islamists. Mali has one of the youngest populations in the world and is made up of multiple ethnicities. Growing populations and competition for limited resources increasingly led to conflicts between sedentary groups from the south and nomadic, or semi-nomadic, groups from the north. Though ethnically diverse, Mali is religiously homogeneous; an estimated 90 per cent of Malians follow (Sunni) Islam, although traditional religious practices remain common in many rural communities.[96] After Mali gained independence from France in 1960, African Socialist Modibo Keïta continued to promote the French principle of *laïcité* to neutralise Islamic clerics.[97] Moussa Traoré – who overthrew Keïta in 1968 – kept the secular Malian constitution during his 22-year-long rule, although in practice Islamic Sufi orders and various Muslim groups were engaged by the military regime of the devout General Traoré.[98] The same delicate balancing act between official secularism and deference to Islam continued under Presidents Alpha Oumar Konaré (1992–2002) and Amadou Toumani Touré (2002–2012).[99] The democratisation process Mali went through from 1992 onwards meant that more Islamic organisations were formed and radical voices and practices (mostly Wahhabi) started to become more visible, however the Malian constitution continued to forbid religion-based political parties.[100] While Muslim leaders continued to gain political influence during those years, Mali maintained a secular legal and institutional framework.[101]

Poverty and disenfranchisement lead to political instability in the north

Mali has often been cited as an illustration of the possibilities of a democratic political system in Africa. It became known for its rich and diverse culture, and was a favourite with Western tourists, but while Mali was acclaimed for its 'remarkable ability to remain open and tolerant', it did so despite severe long-standing strains and hardships.[102] The goodwill of the donor community might have contributed to promising economic growth, but the country kept its place among the bottom ranks of the Human Development Index.[103] Mali has been plagued by recurring droughts, very limited natural resources, a notoriously fractious political class and has a poor record of fighting corruption.[104] However, the most destabilising factor Mali faced were the recurring armed rebellions in the north.

The Tuareg of Northern Mali fought the central government for generations; they opposed the French and, unsuccessfully, fought the colonial power for their own state. After Malian independence, they continued to fight the Bamako government which focused on the sub-Saharan part of the country, south of the Niger, where the majority of Malians live.[105] The Tuareg felt neglected and disenfranchised by the state and a regional famine sparked a crisis and a Tuareg rebellion, in Northern Mali and Niger, in the early 1990s. In 1995, a peace agreement promised the northern regions more resources and aid from the government.[106] It was to the credit of Mali's 'traditions of accommodation, that the Tuareg crisis [...] was dealt with by a set of solutions that not only brought the Tuareg into national decision-making circles but also gave them a measure of hitherto unreachable autonomy'.[107] However, resources remained limited and attempts to absorb rebels into the Malian Army and reintegration of combatants in civilian life failed.[108] In late 2007, the rekindled insurgency of Tuareg in Niger that demanded a share in the uranium wealth, spread into Mali. Despite several ceasefires and an 'uneasy peace', brokered by Libya and Algeria, attacks on the army and hostage taking continued as did the political and socio-economic grievances of the Tuareg.[109] In 2011, the demise of the Gaddafi regime in Libya had a catalyst effect on the crisis in Northern Mali. Tuareg who had been incorporated into Gaddafi's foreign legions returned to Mali, bringing with them heavy and sophisticated arms that changed the balance of power between the Tuareg and the Malian military.

The MNLA, Ansar Dine and AQIM

The *Mouvement National pour la Libération de l'Azawad* (MNLA), brought together several leaders and factions of the 1990s rebellion, reactivated old claims for autonomy as a response to grievances of neglect and disenfranchisement by the Malian state, and launched attacks on garrisons of the Malian Army in Northern Mali, in January 2012.[110] The MNLA was led by Bilal Ag Acherif and Mohamed Ag Najim; both were veterans of previous Tuareg rebellions and Ag Najim had served as a colonel in the Libyan Army.[111] The MNLA declared its official purpose to be to recover 'the specific rights confiscated from the people of Azawad' and aimed to fight for the independence of Azawad as a Tuareg homeland in Northern Mali, but as a secular Tuareg nationalist movement it claimed no religious ideology.[112] The MNLA was better organised and armed than the Tuareg during previous rebellions and, by mid-March 2012, the rebels claimed control of several localities in the northeast of Mali.[113] A critical aspect of this development was the lax attitude of Malian president Amadou Toumani Touré who, contrary to his Nigerien counterpart, had failed to demand the disarmament of returning armed Tuareg fighters and multiplied gestures of appeasement that emboldened them and convinced them that the Malian state had no will to resist their bid for independence.

Soon after the start of fighting in early 2012, several Islamist factions joined the MNLA in fighting government forces. Among them was Ansar Dine ('defenders of the faith'), founded by another leader of the 1990s rebellion, Iyad Ag Ghaly, after he lost the leadership of the secular MNLA.[114] Ag Ghaly supposedly converted to Salafism while serving as a diplomat in Saudi Arabia before being expelled for his alleged ties to al-Qa'ida.[115] Although the organisation branded itself as a Tuareg jihadist Salafist movement aiming to impose Sharia law across Mali, it remained unclear whether radical Islamism was really at the heart of its goals, instead of access to ungoverned territory for the purpose of smuggling, hostage taking and hiding. The group was added to the US list of Foreign Terrorist Organizations in early 2013.

Regarding other organisations that joined the rebellion, there was less doubt about their motivations. Al-Qa'ida in the Islamic Maghreb (AQIM) had its roots in the Algerian Civil War of the early 1990s. It truly emerged in early 2007, after the Algerian Salafist Group for Preaching and Combat (GSPC) allied itself to Osama Bin Laden's international franchise.[116] The organisation counted fighters from across West Africa among its ranks but was led by Algerians.[117] Financed primarily by ransoms, AQIM has between 2007 and 2013 kidnapped and held more than 50 Western hostages, earning well over $100m in payments, according to estimations by *Al Jazeera*.[118] The declared goal of AQIM was to spread Sharia law as well as to liberate Malians from the French colonial legacy.[119] AQIM splinter group MOJWA had the wider objective of spreading jihad to West Africa, rather than confining itself to the Sahel and Maghreb regions like AQIM.[120]

The March 2012 coup d'état in Bamako

As the MNLA and Islamist groups quickly gained territory, in March 2012, the conflict in the north reached the Malian capital. Out of discontent with the government's weak response to the rebellion, a group of officers staged a coup d'état against President Amadou Toumani Touré.[121] The officers took over the presidential palace, state television and military barracks on March 21 and, the following day, announced they had formed the National Committee for the Restoration of Democracy and State (CNRDR).[122] The coup led to widespread international condemnation and the suspension of Mali from the AU.[123] Moreover, the chaos provided an opportunity for the various rebel factions to progress further southward.[124] A week after the coup, the northeastern city of Kidal fell into the hands of the MNLA, supported by Ansar Dine and AQIM. A day later, the MNLA took control over Gao, a decisive victory, as it was the location of the regional army headquarters.[125] On 1 April, the MNLA seized Timbuktu, the last large city in the north still under government control and not only a symbol for Mali's cultural, musical and intellectual heritage, but also a UNESCO World Heritage Site.[126]

The independent state of Azawad

On 6 April 2012, the Secretary-General of the MNLA, Bilal Ag Acherif, signed the declaration of independence of Azawad in Gao.[127] The declaration – in the name of the people of Azawad 'through the voice of the National Movement for the Liberation of Azawad' and recalling the UN Charter, Mali's colonial history and previous rebellions – claimed independence based on 'the accumulation of more than 50 years of bad governance', endangering the people of Azawad.[128] The statement stressed that the new state would recognise international borders and that the MNLA was committed to work towards establishing the 'conditions for a durable peace', and to a state based on a democratic constitution.[129] The Executive Committee of the MNLA invited the entire international community to recognise the independent State of Azawad without delay.[130] This, of course, did not happen. The Commission of the African Union immediately rejected the announcement, calling it 'null and of no value whatsoever'; ECOWAS declared that it would 'take all necessary measures, including the use of force, to ensure the territorial integrity of the country'; and the EU, the United States, France and neighbouring countries, all expressed support for the territorial integrity of Mali.[131]

The MNLA proved that in order to be a successful QSE, conquering territory, being able to deploy violence and drafting declarations of independence is not enough. A successful QSE also has to be able to fulfil functions usually connected to statehood, better and more effectively than the original state or other QSEs. The reality was that by the time the state of Azawad was declared to be independent the statehood project of the MNLA was already dead in the water, not primarily because of the complete lack of support for an independent Azawad from regional powers and the international community, but because by then the MNLA had lost, or was in the process of losing, control over most rudimentary statehood functions, such as providing justice, in the territory it claimed in its unilateral declaration, to Islamist factions.

In the first half of 2012, while making a quick advance southwards and with the Malian Army unable to stop them, the Tuareg nationalists of the MNLA and Islamist groups had operated in unison. But, as the QSEs of Northern Mali progressed against the government forces, the statehood objectives of the MNLA and the goals of Islamist movements proved to differ too widely: Ansar Dine claimed to seek an Islamic state, under Sharia law, on the whole territory of Mali; AQIM fought for a caliphate, covering the whole Maghreb; and MOJWA aimed for Islamic rule in entire West Africa. Apart from their official objectives, it was doubtful whether all Islamist organisations really aimed for a stable Islamic state or state-like environment, as they benefited from an environment in which they could exercise some quasi-state functions while continuing their criminal activities. Meanwhile, the MNLA fought for a viable, independent Azawad State in Northern Mali.[132] By April 2012, the adage 'the enemy of my enemy is my friend' no longer applied to the relationship between the MNLA and the Islamic movements, and as a result of the insistence of the Islamists on providing justice by implementing Sharia law, the movements started to fight each other:[133] Ansar Dine drove the MNLA out of Timbuktu; MOJWA fighters took control over Goa in late June 2012, after a battle with the MNLA; and by mid-July MOJWA and Ansar Dine had wrested all major cities in Northern Mali from the MNLA.[134] Both organisations claimed to govern territory, and although providing justice is one of the tasks of a government, Ansar Dine and MOJWA did not provide many other services than their brutal version of justice, imposing a strict interpretation of Sharia law on the local population.[135] Claiming they were idolatrous and un-Islamic, Ansar Dine vowed to destroy every mausoleum in Timbuktu and, in June, started to destroy the fourteenth-century mausoleums on the site of the Djinguereber Mosque, a UNESCO World Heritage Site.[136] In Timbuktu, a man accused of drinking alcohol was reported to have been whipped; in Aguelhoc, a town controlled by Ansar Dine, Islamists stoned to death a couple accused of adultery, in late July; and only days later, members of MOJWA cut off a man's hand as a punishment for theft in Ansongo.[137]

The self-referral of the situation in Northern Mali to the ICC

What started as a rebellion in Northern Mali turned into a perfect storm of crises, with each having a profound effect on the others. The crisis in Northern Mali not only led to a coup in Bamako, but also to attacks on Tuareg, Berbers and Arabs in the south, who were easily recognisable by their lighter skin.[138] The crisis further deteriorated the humanitarian situation across Mali as water scarcity, poor rural infrastructure and volatile prices gave rise to food insecurity.[139] According to the Food and Agriculture Organization, by August 2012, 4.6 million people were in need of assistance, and the combination of violence and food insecurity led to 500,000 displaced Malians, including over 250,000 registered refugees, in neighbouring Niger, Burkina Faso and Mauritania.[140]

It was against that background that, on 13 July 2012, the government of Mali self-referred 'the situation in Mali since January 2012' to the Prosecutor of the ICC, requesting an investigation to determine whether one, or more, persons should be charged for crimes committed in the conflict.[141] The request followed a recommendation to refer the situation to the ICC by ECOWAS' Contact Group on Mali, showing that the referral had the support of the West African region.[142] In the referral letter, the government of Mali alleged that in the northern region of the country gross human rights violations and war crimes had been committed, including summary executions of soldiers, rape of women and young girls, killing of civilians, the recruitment of child soldiers, torture, pillaging, enforced disappearances and the destruction of property (including government buildings, humanitarian installations, religious establishments and gravesites).[143] Moreover, Mali claimed that it would be unable to prosecute, or try, the perpetrators of these crimes.

Mali was the fifth African country formally to request the ICC to investigate crimes in its territory and the fourth to self-refer a situation to the Court, although it was the first State Party to do so in over seven years. ICC Chief Prosecutor Fatou Bensouda ordered a preliminary examination of the report of killings, abductions, rapes and conscription of children, and stressed that the deliberate destruction of the shrines of Muslim saints in the city of Timbuktu may constitute a war crime under Article 8 of the Rome Statute.[144] Immediately after the referral, many questioned whether the ICC could use another African investigation.[145] Although the AU never specifically criticised the ICC for investigating self-referred situations, and it was argued that, as self-referrals are inherently cooperative, and require the state and the ICC to cooperate, Mali's self-referral could, ultimately, even have a positive effect on the perception of the ICC as being biased against Africa.[146] But, by 2012, the Court was reaching the limit of the number of cases it could handle – constrained by funding and staff – and besides, another investigation in Africa would provide new ammunition to those opposing the ICC by claiming it was a Western tool to oppress Africans. Moreover, there were the arguments against the policy of accepting self-referrals of situations to the ICC, mainly born out of the fear that the ICC would become a 'court of convenience' for states to brand their opponents war criminals.

Accepting jurisdiction: the ICC as a court of convenience for State Parties

The self-referral of Mali shows that the ICC was still expected to have an impact on the legitimacy of QSEs. Nouwen and Werner pointed out that, ironically, the more successful the ICC 'portrays itself as neutral, universal, and above politics, the more attractive it will become as an instrument for the labelling and neutralization of enemies of a particular political group'.[147] The ICC apparently retained some of that ability, and thereby its appeal to the Malian government. It did so amid a storm of criticism. In terms of international support for the ICC, especially African, a lot changed following the self-referrals of Uganda and the DRC. The enthusiasm of the Ugandan government waned when the ICC also proved unable to arrest the LRA leadership and dismissed plans for a local court to prosecute them. The DRC did not always cooperate with the Court, as it had promised when it asked for an investigation. Moreover, the motivation for the self-referrals by the governments of Uganda, the DRC and the CAR, as well as the request of Côte d'Ivoire for the ICC to exercise jurisdiction, should be treated with some scepticism.[148] Rather than yearning for real justice for all parties in the conflict, or wanting to end impunity for international crimes, the governments that referred situations aimed to incapacitate their adversaries by means of the ICC. The referral of Mali should also be seen in that light. Referring the situation was a calculated decision to use the ICC as a weapon for reaching political goals, to defeat the QSEs that had taken over state functions and to restore the government's control over the northern part of the country.[149] This is especially relevant because the transitional government that had taken over power in Bamako had to deal with a legitimacy crisis itself, both internally and in the international community.

By the time the Malian government in Bamako self-referred the situation in Northern Mali there were considerable arguments against the opening of such an investigation by the Prosecutor. First, the Court had, and would continue to have, many African cases under investigation. As a result, it had to deal with criticism of its focus on Africa, and sometimes met outright hostility on that subject. Second, self-referral might give the impression that the Court is biased in favour of the government. The image of Chief Prosecutor Moreno-Ocampo shaking hands with Yoweri Museveni, the President of Uganda, during a joint declaration announcing the opening of the investigation into the situation in Northern Uganda, was only the most visible example of how the former Chief Prosecutor sent the wrong messages. Later declarations, by the OTP, that all parties to the conflict would be investigated could not prevent the idea taking hold among many Ugandans 'that the ICC is an instrument of the government', and that the Court initially had to deal with hostility among the northern population and local civil society organisations.[150] Third, as conflicts were ongoing, QSEs might become state entities, or make peace with state entities, or their leaders might become part of the government, and the states that were happy to see their former enemies branded as war criminals might end cooperation, as these relationships shifted.[151] These situations put the Court at risk of becoming part of political disputes. Finally, there was discussion on the legal limits of self-referral in cases where the state was technically not unable, nor unwilling, to prosecute domestically.

It might be questioned whether the Malian judiciary was really unable, or unwilling, to prosecute those who allegedly committed grave crimes, It was, however, unable to arrest them. After the officers, who initially had taken power, resisted foreign military intervention, it seems that the transitional government hoped that an ICC investigation would 'instigate international pressure and perhaps even a military intervention to restore the government's authority'.[152] The weak position of the Malian government seems to have played a role in that, as Ottilia Maunganidze and Antoinette Louw commented,

> The self-referral could thus be characterised as an attempt by the interim government – which is weak and in search of support and legitimacy both locally and abroad – to put down the rebellion in the north, and eliminate opposition from those who might seek to destabilise a new government.[153]

Yet there is every reason to believe that 'most serious crimes of concern to the international community as a whole' were committed in Mali.[154] The motivation of the Malian government for self-referral and the ambition of the Court to strengthen its legitimacy by opening cases outside of Africa, did not reduce the gravity of these crimes. Moreover, in Mali, the ICC was given an opportunity to demonstrate that it could act expeditiously and demonstrate that it had the potential to deter crimes by acting in real time, not only through post-conflict investigation and prosecution.[155]

The investigation into alleged crimes committed in Mali since January 2012

On 16 January 2013, Chief Prosecutor Bensouda formally opened an investigation into alleged crimes committed in Mali since January 2012. The Prosecutor stated that 'at each stage during the conflict, different armed groups have caused havoc and human suffering through a range of alleged acts of extreme violence' and 'determined that some of these deeds of brutality and destruction may constitute war crimes as defined by the Rome Statute'.[156] The Prosecutor further vowed that the OTP would 'ensure a thorough and impartial investigation and will bring justice to Malian victims by investigating who are the most responsible for these alleged crimes'.[157] That same day, the ICC's first report on the situation in Mali was published in which the Prosecutor set out why the ICC had jurisdiction, why the case was admissible and why pursuing prosecution was in the interests of justice.[158]

The ICC report listed a number of war crimes allegedly committed by individuals in the name of various entities fighting in the conflict. The most serious included the attack on a military camp in Aguelhoc by the MNLA and/or 'other unspecified "armed groups"', on 24 January 2012, in which, according to several sources, up to 153 Malian soldiers were detained and later tortured and executed.[159] The report further mentioned the stoning to death of an unmarried couple and the public execution of a member of the MNLA, although more information about these cases was required.[160] Besides these allegations of unlawful killings, there were indications that a wide array of other war crimes had been committed in the conflict. Based on reports by Human Rights Watch, the OTP had reason to believe that at least eight amputations imposed by armed groups and 100 lashes that an unmarried couple received amounted to mutilation and torture.[161] Moreover, OTP received information that many sentences and executions without due process – a war crime – had been imposed, with many of those punishments carried out in public.[162] Furthermore, the FIDH recorded more than 50 cases of rape after the takeover of Northern Mali, and Amnesty International collected statements that indicated that children had been recruited and used as combatants in Northern Mali, but did not name specific entities that allegedly did so.[163]

The deliberate damaging of shrines and mausoleums might constitute another 'serious violation of the laws and customs applicable in armed conflicts', under Article 8(2)(c)(iv) of the Rome Statute.[164] The report described attacks by members of Ansar Dine, AQIM and possibly also MOJWA between 4 May and 10 July 2012 against at least nine mausoleums, two mosques and two historical monuments in Timbuktu listed as World Heritage Sites by UNESCO.[165] It was this part of the investigation that led to the first and, up to mid-2016, only case opened in the situation of Mali.

However, the report of the OTP was not limited to allegations that members of QSEs committed war crimes but included possible war crimes committed by Malian government soldiers and specified three such incidents that were under investigation. The OTP had reason to believe that war crimes were committed by the Malian Army in the shooting of 16 unarmed Muslim preachers at an army checkpoint.[166] It continued to investigate the detention and execution of at least four Tuareg members of the Malian security services.[167] The killing of three unarmed individuals accused of being MNLA spies also remained under investigation.[168] This was a strong indication that the OTP had learned from its own mistakes in previous self-referral investigations and that it had set out to make good on the promise that it would investigate alleged crimes committed by all parties to the conflict and suppressed allegations of bias in favour of the government that referred the situation.

The impact of the ICC investigation on the conflict in Mali

The Malian government self-referred the situation in July 2012 and the Prosecutor opened the official investigation in January 2013. After that, for almost three years, it was conspicuously quiet around the ICC investigation into Mali. This may have been because the OTP had more ongoing investigations in hand than its resources allowed it to deal with. It may not have issued indictments publicly because it was unable to investigate sufficiently to build a case and locate suspects, or maybe it awaited the outcomes of the French intervention and the deployment of the MINUSMA Mission and the peace negotiations that were ongoing.[169] Yet, on 18 September 2015, the Court issued an arrest warrant for Ahmad al-Mahdi, an alleged member of Ansar Dine, for the war crime of intentionally directing attacks against buildings dedicated to religion, specifically the mausoleums and mosques located in Timbuktu. On 26 September 2015, Ahmad al-Mahdi was sent from Niger, where he was detained, to The Hague to stand trial from 22 August 2016 onwards. The opening of the case against Ahmad al-Mahdi was significant for being the first time a person had been charged with the destruction of cultural sites as a war crime and his being the first Islamic extremist to be prosecuted at the ICC.

Despite the delay before a case was opened and the fact that so far only one case has been opened, it was at the beginning of the ICC involvement when the Malian government decided to self-refer, and when the ICC opened the investigation that the effect of international criminal justice narratives in the conflict could be clearly distinguished. It was the self-referral, in July 2012, that showed a perceived mutuality of interests between the Malian government and the Court, despite the increasingly strong counter narratives against the ICC by the AU and many of its members. Possibly the strongest indication, so far, that international criminal justice, in the form of the ICC, can have an impact on the capacity of QSEs in Mali to create and maintain legitimacy is the belief of the Malian government that it can do so. Whether Malian state institutions could be bolstered significantly, or enough, to restore their authority and legitimacy in Northern Mali, and what the long-term effect of the ICC investigation on the various QSEs opposing the state's authority in Northern Mali would be, remained unclear at the end of 2013. Yet, there were some early signs that the decision of the government to involve the ICC in this conflict would pay off for the government, despite the efforts of the Prosecutor to avoid the mistakes made in earlier self-referral situations that allowed the Court to be used a court of convenience. The preliminary investigation, as well as the later official investigation into war crimes by the Prosecutor of the ICC, meant that war crimes narratives and international criminal justice narratives became part of the discourse of both the Malian government and the MNLA.

The self-referral in July 2012 and the opening of the official investigation in January 2013 both came at pivotal moments in the conflict. The first occurred as the MNLA was losing hold of positions in Northern Mali, and the chances of realising its statehood goals started to disappear, mainly at the hands of its former allies. The opening of the official investigation by the OTP came as international support for the Malian government started to be translated into actions rather than words, and the French Army commenced Operation Serval, in support of Malian government forces. For Western governments, besides the UN Security Council resolutions, an ICC investigation into war crimes probably made it easier to sell to their home constituencies the idea of sending troops to Mali. When the government of Mali asked for foreign military help to retake the north, initially, more governments signed up to provide troops than were needed.

The allegations of war crimes committed by its members already impacted on the capacity of the MNLA to create legitimacy for its institutions, actions and its Azawad statehood project, despite the preliminary report of the OTP being cautiously worded and also including crimes allegedly committed by the Malian armed forces. Soon after the self-referral, the Malian government succeeded in getting international assistance against the QSEs it was fighting. It would go too far to attribute international support to the ICC investigation into war crimes committed by the MNLA alone, but a narrative of preventing war crimes and crimes against humanity added legitimacy to this support. Because of the threat the Malian crisis posed to the wider region, Mali became a priority for surrounding countries and for ECOWAS. But the fear that the MNLA's former allies – Ansar Dine, MOJWA and AQIM – would maintain a stronghold in Northern Mali, creating a safe haven for fundamentalists to plot terrorist actions similar to areas of Afghanistan, Yemen and Somalia, made Mali a problem for the West too.[170] While the Malian military initially rejected ECOWAS proposals to deploy AU troops, eventually the government asked for an international intervention in September 2012.[171] On 12 October 2012, the UN Security Council unanimously adopted Security Council Resolution 2071, proposed by France, which determined that the situation in Mali constituted a threat to international peace and security under Chapter VII of the Charter.[172] It called on ECOWAS and the AU for 'detailed and actionable recommendations' for military intervention.[173] The text of the Resolution also clearly supported the government and blamed its quasi-state adversaries for committing crimes:

Condemning strongly the abuses of human rights committed in the north of Mali by armed rebels, terrorist and other extremist groups, including violence against its civilians, notably women and children, killings, hostage-taking, pillaging, theft, destruction of cultural and religious sites and recruit-ment of child soldiers, stressing that some of such acts may amount to crimes under the Rome Statute and that their perpetrators must be held accountable and noting that the Transitional authorities of Mali referred the situation in the north of Mali since January 2012 to the International Crimi-nal Court on 18 July 2012.[174]

However, the Resolution also called upon 'Malian rebel groups to cut off all ties to terrorist organizations'.[175] This showed that a distinction was made between Tuareg QSEs fighting for an Azawad homeland and Islamist groups.

The conflict in Northern Mali severely disturbed the delicate balance of reli-gion and state in the whole of Mali and the predominantly moderate Muslims of Northern Mali suffered, not only from the violence of the conflict, but also from the Sharia law enforced by the (often foreign) factions the MNLA had associated with earlier. The organisation had to face allegations of war crimes committed by its members and was linked to those committed by members of the Islamist factions it was now fighting against. The MNLA was forced to step up its efforts to provide a legitimating narrative to constituencies in the international com-munity. It found itself in a spiral of legitimacy crisis. Although the aim of an Azawad homeland provided a strong base for legitimacy, among its Tuareg core constituencies a lack of performance became painfully clear when the MNLA lost control of the main northern cities. At the same time, the strict enforcement of Sharia law by its former associates weakened popular support at home, while allegations of war crimes further diminished the already weak bases of legiti-macy that secessionists usually have in international constituencies.

In an attempt to overcome this legitimacy crisis, and forced by the self-referral by the government, the MNLA had to change its narratives to regain the legitimacy it had lost among the northern home constituencies, but also to create, at least, some belief in the justness of its causes and actions among various international constituencies. In the weeks after the OTP started its pre-liminary investigation, the MNLA claimed to have been 'misunderstood by the international community', and its spokesperson said that it did not feel threatened by the ICC.[176] The MNLA spokesperson in Europe, Mossa Ag Attaher, actively sought support from the international community for the Azawad State. In an interview, Ag Attaher denied an agreement with Ansar Dine, claiming that the MNLA had 'no pact with the devil' and that the situ-ation was misunderstood as a result of the Western media's 'simple explana-tions of a very complex reality', and not taking the time or effort to understand Azawad's problems in depth.[177] Emphasising that the MNLA was now fighting the Islamists, Ag Attaher claimed that the MNLA had backed out of every form of cooperation when it realised that the main objective of Ansar Dine was to impose Sharia law.[178] But he also warned that the Western world now had a choice between letting the situation in Mali 'explode in their face', which would threaten the entire region, or they would 'take the MNLA by the hand, a movement that shows all interest to fight terrorists and that knows the terrain; we are the only ones fighting against them'.[179]

On 12 October 2012, the (Dutch) lawyers of the MNLA wrote to the President of the UN Security Council stating that:

> [T]he MNLA is deeply concerned that innocent civilians may have been subjected to attacks and protected monuments may have been destroyed in the course of the current armed conflict in Mali. Furthermore, the MNLA is determined to take all necessary and reasonable measures to ensure that its members continue to respect the relevant laws and customs of war.[180]

The MNLA also submitted an 'Action Plan: Respecting the Laws of War', in which it expressed the desire for an investigation 'into mass human rights abuses committed in Mali since the Rome Statute came into force in July 2002' (as opposed to the present investigation that follows the referral by the Malian government and only investigates events that took place after 1 January 2012).[181] The MNLA expressed its willingness to cooperate with the ICC, in its preliminary examination into alleged crimes committed in Mali, and announced that it would engage with, and submit deeds of commitment to, Geneva Call, an organisation with the aim of persuading non-state actors 'towards compliance with the norms of international humanitarian law and human rights law'.[182] Furthermore the 'Action Plan' affirmed that the MNLA was determined to ensure that its members respected international humanitarian law and that it would investigate any credible allegation of mass human rights abuses committed by MNLA troops and take the appropriate action.[183] The rhetoric of the MNLA seems to suggest that international criminal justice, in the form of the ICC, had an impact. Or, at least, it suggests that the MNLA thought that international justice had some part in the legitimacy crisis it was facing and that counter narratives with international law at its centre were needed, or would contribute, to overcome this crisis.

On the other hand, rhetoric was all they had at that point; other bases for legitimacy were under severe strain and the MNLA could neither claim military success nor success in providing government and stability in the north. The MNLA had already been forced out of all the major northern cities by Ansar Dine and MOJWA, and had retreated to rural areas, making the chances of its statehood project succeeding increasingly small. Furthermore, on the same day that the MNLA expressed to the UN Security Council its commitment to international law, the Council adopted Resolution 2071, further diminishing the chances of a successful Azawad State. Although the Resolution, in itself, did not authorise the use of force yet, it foresaw the deployment of ECOWAS troops in Mali.[184] Security Council Resolution 2085, adopted unanimously on 20 December 2012, authorised the deployment of the African-led International Support Mission to Mali (AFISMA), organised by ECOWAS. Following the Resolution, and after the Malian government requested military intervention from France, as the Islamists were advancing south, France launched Operation Serval on 11 January 2013.

Only a few days after the Prosecutor announced the beginning of an official investigation into the situation in Mali, French and Chadian troops overran Islamist strongholds in the north. The MNLA offered support to the French troops and entered Kidal, when the French had ousted Islamists from their last stronghold. The French, in turn, refused to disarm MNLA members, and kept the Malian Army away from Kidal to avoid clashes with the MNLA.[185] France made it clear that it was fighting Islamist factions and wisely demanded that the Malian government sort out its statehood issues with the MNLA at peace talks taking place in Burkina Faso.

On 13 February 2013, the MNLA published a declaration in which it called for the immediate opening of negotiations with the Malian government 'to establish the conditions for exercise of authority, administration and development of Azawad'.[186] Some interpreted the MNLA statement that it would not 'undermine the internationally recognised borders of Mali while recalling clearly the existence of Azawad as a whole' as renouncing its declaration of independence, something that was later denied by the MNLA.[187] But, what is especially relevant, was that the MNLA continued to use the narrative of international criminal justice by denying responsibility for what it called the 'unfortunate Aguelhoc events in January 2012', and also by expressing support for the ICC and requesting investigations into crimes it alleged to be committed by Malian state institutions.[188]

Despite the talks between Bamako and the MNLA in Burkina Faso, war crimes, crimes against humanity and international justice continued to be part of the discourse of both parties in the conflict. While talking about peace they continued to accuse each other of war crimes, summary executions and ethnic violence, a narrative that had to be seen as mainly aimed at outside constituencies.[189] The MNLA wanted to send a message that, without an Azawad State, the safety of the Tuareg people could not be guaranteed, hoping for international support for its causes. At the same time, the Malian government aimed for international interference to restore its authority in its entire territory, instead of only ousting the Islamist factions and leaving the Tuareg that were fighting for statehood to be dealt with. The most relevant international actors, however – France, ECOWAS, the AU and the UN Security Council – had so far wisely made a distinction between the statehood issues of the MNLA and those of Islamists aiming for Caliphates and Sharia law. In June 2013, negotiations led to the MNLA signing a peace deal with the Malian government in preparation for the election that followed a month later.[190] Both the loss of legitimacy internally, in their constituencies that were opposed to the Islamic norms forced upon them by the MNLA's former allies, and the international condemnation might have played a role in the MNLA making peace with the government.

Intervention in Mali, by ECOWAS, France, the AU and later the UN, had the characteristics of classic anti-insurgency missions. However, as a contingent effect of international criminal justice, these foreign interventions can be packaged as stabilisation missions. Security Council Resolution 2100 of 25 April 2013, establishing the United Nations Multidimensional Integrated Stabilization

Mission in Mali (MINUSMA) included in its mandate: 'To monitor, help investigate and report to the Council on any abuses or violations of human rights or violations of international humanitarian law', and to

> support, [...] to bring to justice those responsible for war crimes and crimes against humanity in Mali, taking into account the referral by the transitional authorities of Mali of the situation in their country since January 2012 to the International Criminal Court.[191]

It is clear that the opening of an investigation changed the dynamic, and as a contingent effect made military intervention possible, or at least easier to justify.

At the end of 2013 the MNLA pulled out of the peace agreement after the army repressed protests in Kidal and a new agreement was signed in February 2015 in Algiers. This agreement stipulated that the MNLA would also give up drug smuggling and cooperation with Islamic groups in return for promises by the government. Yet, the implementation of the peace agreement, as in the 1990s, proved problematic and according to MNLA Vice President Mohamoudou Djeri Maiga, 'people on the ground haven't enjoyed the gains'.[192] The reauthorisation for MINUSMA included an increase in personnel and an extended aggressive mandate to target armed groups, and the French Operation Serval was replaced by Operation Barkhane. Yet terrorist attacks in central Mali and Bamako, and continued armed clashes in the north between the MNLA, the various Islamist groups and the French Army, the UN mission and the Malian Army, kept Northern Mali unstable enough for smuggling, drug running and hostage taking to continue.

The self-referral of Mali shows that, despite heavy criticism of the ICC from within Africa, and while the Court often lacked support in words and deeds from the UN Security Council, the Malian government expected ICC involvement to have a delegitimising effect on its QSE adversaries. Mali was not the first state government that used narratives of war crimes or crimes against humanity to boost its legitimacy, while simultaneously delegitimising its opponents, nor was it the first government to attempt to use international criminal procedures to boost these kinds of narratives. Mali believed that the ICC would be able to provide a narrative of international criminal justice, by which it could brand one party as the violator of universal norms, an enemy of humanity, while cooperation with the Court would convey messages of defending those norms and of being a friend of the international community. However, this meant that the Court faced the possibility of becoming a 'court of convenience', a tool employed by states in an attempt to delegitimise their quasi-state adversaries, and the Court acted more wisely than it did in earlier self-referral cases and also opened an investigation into alleged crimes committed by Malian government forces. The military intervention by France, although prompted by concerns for ungoverned territory in Northern Mali that would serve as a safe haven for terrorists, was easier to justify after international criminal justice narratives entered the equation. Together with the accusations of war crimes it had to face, international involvement further diminished the chances of the MNLA reaching its objective of an independent Azawad State. The ICC forced the MNLA to distance itself further from Ansar Dine, AQIM and MOJWA, organisations it had worked with, and that were also deemed responsible for horrible crimes. The opening of an investigation by the OTP also forced the MNLA to vow commitment to the norms of international criminal law, and to work together with the ICC investigation, in an attempt to overcome a crisis of legitimacy, especially in Western constituencies.

Notes

1 S. Nouwen and W. Werner, ' The Law and Politics of Self Referrals', in: A. Smeulers (ed.), (2010) *Collective Violence and International Criminal Justice: an Interdisciplinary Approach*, Antwerp: Intersentia, pp. 255–271, p. 259.
2 S. Nouwen and W. Werner, 'Doing Justice to the Political: The International Criminal Court in Uganda and Sudan', *The European Journal of International Law*, Vol. 21, No. 4, 2011, pp. 941–965, p. 962.
3 UN General Assembly Resolution 260, 9 December 1948.
4 Rome Statute of the ICC, 'Overview'.
5 Rome Statute of the ICC, Rome, 17 July 1998, entry into force 1 July 2002 in accordance with Article 126, Registration 1 July 2002, No. 38544, United Nations Treaty Series, vol. 2187, p. 3.
6 Press Release, Office of the Secretary-General, Transcript of Press Conference with President Carlo Ciampi of Italy and Secretary-General Kofi Annan in Rome and New York by Videoconference, UN Doc. SG/SM/8194 (11 April 2002) (following ratification of the Rome Statute of the ICC in Rome, Italy).
7 Rome Statute of the ICC, Rome, 17 July 1998, entry into force 1 July 2002 (hereinafter 'Rome Statute'), Preamble §§ 4, 5, and 11.
8 Hybrid (or internationalised) courts combine both international and national features; they apply elements of both systems in their procedural and applicable law, and consist of international and local registrars, prosecutors and judges.
9 For a discussion on the ICTY as a measure to 'restore and maintain' rather than 'restore', 'maintain', or 'restore or maintain' international peace and security, see: M. Futamura and J. Gow, 'The Strategic Purpose of the ICTY and International Peace and Security', in: J. Gow, R. Kerr and Z. Pajić, (2013) *Prosecuting War Crimes*, London: Routledge, pp. 15–28, p. 17.
10 Rome Statute, Article 4 (1).
11 Ibid., Articles 3, 115 and 116.
12 Ibid., Article 5.
13 Ibid., Article 5 (2).
14 Amendments on the crime of aggression to the Rome Statute of the ICC, Kampala, 11 June 2010, Resolution RC/Res.6 of the Review Conference of the Rome Statute.
15 Rome Statute, Article 11 *j*° Article 12 (3).
16 Ibid., Article 13.
17 Rome Statute, United Nations Treaty Series, vol. 2187, p. 3.
18 As per August 2016.
19 Rome Statute, Preamble § 10, Articles 1 and 17.
20 Rome Statute, Article 17 (1) (d). For more on the 'gravity threshold' see: S. SaCouto and K. Cleary, 'The Gravity Threshold of the International Criminal Court', *American University International Law Review*, vol. 23, no. 5, 2007, pp. 807–854, and K.J. Heller, 'Situational Gravity Under The Rome Statute'. In: C. Stahn and L. van den Herik (eds), *Future Directions in International Criminal Justice*, 2007, Cambridge: Cambridge University Press.

21 Rome Statute, Article 17 (2) (a).
22 Ibid., Article 17 (3).
23 Ibid., Article 18.
24 Ibid., Article 20 (2).
25 Ibid., Article 20 (3) (a), and (b).
26 Ibid., Article 86.
27 Ibid., Article 87 (7).
28 As per August 2016.
29 International Criminal Court (2016) Available at: https://www.icc-cpi.int/Pages/ Home.aspx (Accessed: 8 August 2016).
30 Reuters (2016) *Gaddafi's son Saif still in prison in western Libya, military source says.* Available at: http://uk.reuters.com/article/uk-libya-gaddafi-idUKKCN0ZN2CZ ?il=0 (Accessed: 8 August 2016).
31 S-H. Song, 'From Punishment to Prevention: Reflections on the Future of International Criminal Justice'. Speech by Judge President of the International Criminal Court, *Wallace Wurth Memorial Lecture*, University of New South Wales, Sydney, Australia 14 February 2012.
32 *Situation in Georgia*, Decision on the Prosecutor's request for authorization of an investigation, Pre-Trial Chamber I, January 2016, ICC-01/15-12, 27.
33 1300 people were killed and more than 300,000 forced from their homes in an outbreak of violence incited by prominent politicians in the aftermath of the December 2007 elections. The Commission of Inquiry into the Post-Election Violence, chaired by Kenyan judge Philip Waki, in 2009, handed over a list of people it deemed most responsible for the violence to the UN with the request to hand it to the ICC, as there had been no effort to conduct a successful investigation into the events and it had little faith that the culprits would be brought to justice within the corrupt Kenyan justice system. This feeling was widely shared among the Kenyan population and initially led to wide popular support for the ICC investigation. X. Rice, 'Annan hands ICC list of perpetrators of post-election violence in Kenya', *The Guardian*, 9 July 2009.
34 *Situation in The Republic of Kenya*, Decision Pursuant to Article 15 of the Rome Statute on the Authorization of an Investigation into the Situation in the Republic of Kenya, Pre-Trial Chamber II, 31 March 2010 ICC-01/09.
35 H.J. Richardson, 'African Grievances and the International Criminal Court: Issues of African Equity under International Criminal Law', in: V.O. Nmehielle (ed.), *Africa and the Future of International Criminal Justice*, The Hague: Eleven, 2012, pp. 81–123, p. 82.
36 *The Prosecutor v. Omar Hassan Ahmad Al Bashir ('Omar Al Bashir')*, Warrant of Arrest for Omar Hassan Ahmad Al Bashir, Pre-Trial Chamber I, 4 March 2009, ICC-02/05-01/09. *The Prosecutor v. Omar Hassan Ahmad Al Bashir ('Omar Al Bashir')*, Second Warrant of Arrest for Omar Hassan Ahmad Al Bashir, Pre-Trial Chamber I, 12 July 2010, ICC-02/05-01/09.
37 'African Union in rift with court', *BBC News*, 3 July 2009.
38 Decision on the Application by the ICC Prosecutor for the Indictment of the President of the Republic of the Sudan, Assembly/AU/Dec.221(XII), February 1–3, 2009. Decision on the Meeting of African States Parties to the Rome Statute of the ICC, Assembly/AU/Dec.245(XIII) Rev.1 July 1–3, 2009.
39 F. Chothia, 'Africa's Fatou Bensouda is new ICC chief prosecutor', *BBC Africa*, 12 December 2011. 'ICC case against Kenyan leader suffers blow', *Al Jazeera*, 18 July 2013.
40 'Will Africa pull out of the ICC?' *BBC News*, 11 October 2013.
41 K. Lindijer, 'Afrikaanse Unie eist immuniteit voor zittende leiders bij Strafhof', *NRC Handelsblad*, 14 October 2013, p. 12.

42 K. Manson, 'ICC rules Kenyatta can miss part of trial', *Financial Times*, 18 October 2013.

43 D. Tutu, 'In Africa, Seeking a License to Kill', *New York Times*, 10 October 2013.

44 Tutu, 'In Africa, Seeking a License to Kill'.

45 'African Union urges ICC to defer Uhuru Kenyatta case', *BBC News*, 12 October 2013.

46 Alexander, 'The International Criminal Court and the Prevention of Atrocities', p. 11.

47 UN Security Council, Sixty-seventh year, 6849th meeting, 17 October 2012, S/PV.6849.

48 R. Dicker and E. Evenson, 'ICC Suspects Can Hide – and That Is the Problem', *Human Rights Watch*, 24 January 2013.

49 UN Security Council Resolution 1970, 26 February 2011, § 4.

50 Almost six years earlier, on 31 March 2005, UN Security Council Resolution 1593 referring the situation in Darfur, Sudan to the ICC was adopted with four abstentions, including the United States and China.

51 The situation in Darfur, Sudan by UN Security Council Resolution 1593 of 31 March 2005 and the situation in Libya by UN Security Council Resolution 1970 of 26 February 2011.

52 United Nations General Assembly, Sixty-sixth session, 3 May 2012, revised draft resolution, *Enhancing the accountability, transparency and effectiveness of the Security Council*, A/66/L.42/Rev.1, § 17.

53 Ibid., § 20.

54 Rome Statute, Preamble §2.

55 Report of the Independent International Commission of Inquiry on the Syrian Arab Republic, Human Rights Council, Twenty-third session, 4 June 2013, A/HRC/23/58. For an oversight of reports on Syria by Human Rights Watch see: www.hrw.org/middle-eastn-africa/syria (accessed 12 August 2013).

56 UN Security Council Resolution 1973, 17 March 2011.

57 Rome Statute Articles 15 and 16. W.A. Schabas, 'Victor's Justice: Selecting "Situations" at the International Criminal Court', *The John Marshall Law Review*, vol. 43, 2009–2010, pp. 535–552, p. 540.

58 Schabas, 'Victor's Justice', p. 541.

59 A. Cassese, 'The Legitimacy of International Criminal Tribunals and the Current Prospects of International Criminal Justice', *Leiden Journal of International Law*, vol. 25, no. 2, June 2012, pp. 491–501, p. 495.

60 SaCouto and Cleary, 'The Gravity Threshold of the International Criminal Court', p. 810.

61 Alexander, 'The International Criminal Court and the Prevention of Atrocities', p. 14.

62 Seils, Paul (2016) *Handbook on Complementarity: An Introduction to the Role of National Courts and the ICC in Prosecuting International Crimes*, The Hague: ICTJ.

63 B.N. Schiff, *Building the International Criminal Court*, Cambridge: Cambridge University Press, 2008, p. 73.

64 J.J. Llewellyn, and S. Raponi, 'The Protection of Human Rights through International Criminal Law: A Conversation with Madame Justice Louise Arbour, Chief Prosecutor for the International Criminal Tribunals for the Former Yugoslavia and Rwanda', *University of Toronto Faculty of Law Review*, vol. 57, no. 1, 1999, pp. 83–99, p. 97.

65 Rome Statute, Preamble. S. Freeland, 'The "Effectiveness" of International Criminal Justice', *ALTA Law Research Series*, no. 16, 2008, pp. 1–9, p. 5.

66 K.A. Marshall 'Prevention and Complementarity in the International Criminal Court: A Positive Approach', *Human Rights Brief*, vol. 17, no. 2, 2010, pp. 21–26, p. 21.

67 Freeland, 'The "Effectiveness" of International Criminal Justice', pp. 5–6.

68 L. Moreno-Ocampo, *Statement made at the ceremony for the solemn undertaking of the Chief Prosecutor of the ICC*, The Peace Palace, The Hague, 16 June 2003.

69 Nichols, M. (2016), 'U.S., Britain back South Sudan war crimes court', *Reuters*. Available at:www.swissinfo.ch/eng/u-s-britain-back-south-sudan-war-crimes-court-/42217362 (Accessed: 7 August 2016). Human Rights Watch (2015) Central African Republic: Progress on special court. Available at: https://www.hrw.org/news/2015/12/23/central-african-republic-progress-special-court (Accessed: 7 August 2016).
70 Llewellyn and Raponi, 'A Conversation with Madame Justice Louise Arbour', p. 96. S. Nouwen and W. Werner, 'The Law and Politics of Self Referrals', in: A. Smeulers (ed.), (2010) *Collective Violence and International Criminal Justice: an Interdisciplinary Approach*, Antwerp: Intersentia, pp. 255–271, p. 255.
71 P. Akhavan 'Self-Referrals Before the International Criminal Court: Are States the Villains or the Victims of Atrocities?' *Criminal Law Forum*, vol. 21 (2001) pp. 103–120, p. 103.
72 Ibid., p. 103.
73 Ibid., p. 103.
74 L. Freedman, 'Victims and Victors: Reflections on the Kosovo War', *Review of International Studies*, vol. 26, no. 3, 2000, pp. 335–358, at p. 357.
75 Akhavan, 'Self-Referrals Before the International Criminal Court', p. 105. P. Akhavan, 'Enforcement of the Genocide Convention', *Harvard Human Rights Journal*, vol. 8, no. 1, 1995, pp. 229–258, p. 237.
76 Akhavan, 'Self-Referrals Before the International Criminal Court', p. 105.
77 Press Release, President of Uganda refers situation concerning the LRA to the ICC, ICC-20040129-44.
78 Press Release, ICC – Prosecutor receives referral of the situation in the Democratic Republic of Congo, ICC-OTP-20040419-50.
79 Press Release, ICC – Prosecutor receives referral concerning Central African Republic, ICC-OTP-20050107-86. Malick Coulibaly, Ministry of Justice of Mali a Madame la Procureure pres la Cour Penale Internationale, 'Renvoi de la situation au Mali', Bamako 13 July 2012.
80 Akhavan, 'Self-Referrals Before the International Criminal Court', p. 105. According to Schabas the *travaux préparatoires* do not suggest that the possibility of self-referrals was considered. W.A. Schabas, 'First Prosecutions at the International Criminal Court', *Human Rights Law Journal*, vol. 27, no. 1, 2006, pp. 25–40, p. 27. M.H. Arsanjani and W.M. Reisman, 'The Law-in-Action of the International Criminal Court', *American Journal of International Law*, vol. 99, no. 2, 2005, pp. 385–403. *The Prosecutor v. Germain Katanga and Mathieu Ngudjolo Chui*, Reasons for the Oral Decision on the Motion Challenging the Admissibility of the Case (Article 19 of the Statute), Trial Chamber II, 16 June 2009, ICC-01/04-01/07, §§ 77–80.
81 Situation in the Republic of Côte d'Ivoire, Decision Pursuant to Article 15 of the Rome Statute on the Authorisation of an Investigation into the Situation in the Republic of Côte d'Ivoire, Pre-Trial Chamber III, 3 October 2011, ICC-02/11-14. R. Currie, 'Côte d'Ivoire and the ICC: A New Kind of "Self-Referral"?' *International and Transnational Criminal Law Update*, Chapter 4, 20 May 2011.
82 Akhavan, 'Self-Referrals Before the International Criminal Court', pp. 110–111.
83 Ibid., p. 111. The trial of Charles Taylor for instance took place in The Hague amid fears of a new outburst of violence in the region if Taylor would be tried in Sierra Leone.
84 Ibid., p. 114.
85 Nouwen and Werner, 'The Law and Politics of Self Referrals', p. 269.
86 Ibid.
87 Ibid.
88 Akhavan, 'Self-Referrals Before the International Criminal Court', p. 115.
89 Nouwen and Werner, 'Doing Justice to the Political', p. 962.
90 Nouwen and Werner, 'The Law and Politics of Self Referrals', p. 269.

91 W.W. Burke-White, 'Complementarity in Practice: The International Criminal Court as Part of a System of Multi-Level Global Governance in the Democratic Republic of Congo', *Leiden Journal of International Law*, vol. 18, no. 3, 2005, pp. 557–590.
92 P. Akhavan, 'Developments at the International Criminal Court: The Lord's Resistance Army Case: Uganda's Submission of the First State Referral to the International Criminal Court', *AJIL vol.* (2005) p. 404.
93 *The Prosecutor v. Germain Katanga and Mathieu Ngudjolo Chui*, Reasons for the Oral Decision on the Motion Challenging the Admissibility of the Case (Article 19 of the Statute), Trial Chamber II, 16 June 2009, ICC 01/04-01/07, §77.
94 Akhavan, 'Self-Referrals Before the International Criminal Court', pp. 110–111.
95 Nouwen and Werner, 'The Law and Politics of Self Referrals', p. 259.
96 International Religious Freedom Report 2010: Niger, Bureau of Democracy, Human Rights, and Labor, 17 November 2010.
97 D. Schulz, *Sharia and National Law in Mali*. In: J.M. Otto (ed.), *Sharia Incorporated: A Comparative Overview of the Legal Systems of Twelve Muslim Countries in Past and Present*, Leiden: Leiden University Press, 2010, p. 537.
98 Ibid.
99 V. Le Vine, *Mali: Accommodation or Coexistence?* in: W.F.S. Miles (ed.), *Political Islam in West Africa*, Boulder, CO: Lynn Rienner, 2010, pp. 85–91.
100 Ibid. pp. 87–88.
101 Schulz, *Sharia and National Law in Mali*, p. 542.
102 B. N'Diaye, 'Youth Vulnerability and Exclusion (YOVEX) in West Africa: Mali Country Report', CSDG Papers, No. 25, April 2009, p. 11.
103 Ibid. (Since the adoption of democracy, its gross domestic product grew by 4.1 per cent between 1990 and 2000, and nearly 6 per cent between 2000 and 2005. Nevertheless, in 2006 Mali ranked 175th out of 177 countries on the UN Development Programme Human Development Index.)
104 N'Diaye, 'Youth Vulnerability and Exclusion (YOVEX) in West Africa', p. 11.
105 F. Jacobs, 'All Hail Azawad', New York Times Opinionator, 10 April 2012.
106 N'Diaye, 'Youth Vulnerability and Exclusion (YOVEX) in West Africa', p. 10.
107 Le Vine, *Mali: Accommodation or Coexistence?* p. 90.
108 'Mali: Avoiding Escalation', Crisis Group Africa Report, No. 189, 18 July 2012, p. 3.
109 A. Morgan, 'The Causes of the Uprising in Northern Mali', *Think Africa Press*, 6 February 2012.
110 'Tuareg rebels attack fifth town in Mali', *Al Jazeera English*, 26 January 2012.
111 'Rébellion du MNLA au Mali: Ag Najem, ou la soif de vengeance', *Jeune Afrique*, 27 January 2012.
112 M. Rondot, 'The ICC's Investigation into Alleged War Crimes in Mali', American Non-Governmental Organizations Coalition for the International Criminal Court, Columbia University Institute for the Study of Human Rights. G.B. Nama, 'Rebelles Touaregs: "Pourquoi nous reprenons les armes"', *Courrier International*, no. 1113, 1 March 2012.
113 Morgan, 'The Causes of the Uprising in Northern Mali'.
114 Iyad Ag Ghaly, previously led the Azawad Popular Movement (MPA), a moderate Tuareg faction that opted for peace, in 1992, and was disbanded in 1996. M. Rondot, 'The ICC's Investigation into Alleged War Crimes in Mali'; 'War crimes in North Mali', AMDH-FIDH, p. 9.
115 'War crimes in North Mali', AMDH-FIDH, p. 9. Morgan, 'The Causes of the Uprising in Northern Mali'. 'Mali and al-Qaeda: Can the jihadists be stopped?' *The Economist*, 10 November 2012. Rondot, 'The ICC's Investigation into Alleged War Crimes in Mali'. S. Metcalf, 'Iyad Ag Ghaly – Mali's Islamist leader', *BBC Monitoring*, 17 July 2012.
116 Rondot, 'The ICC's Investigation into Alleged War Crimes in Mali'.
117 'War crimes in North Mali' (AMDH-FIDH).

118 'Making sense of Mali's armed groups', *Al Jazeera*, 17 January 2013.
119 'Mali crisis: Key players', *BBC News*, 12 March 2013.
120 'Sahel: MUJAO à la conquête des "jeunes de l'Afrique noire"', *Alakhbar Mauritanian Independent News Agency*, 28 April 2012.
121 'Mali court meets to choose interim president', *Al Jazeera*, 9 April 2012.
122 Ibid.
123 ECOWAS Press Release, No. 084/2012, 28 March 2012, Abidjan – Cote d' Ivoire.
124 Daniel, Serge, Mali junta denounces 'rights violations' by rebels, *AFP*, 4 April 2012.
125 'War crimes in North Mali', AMDH-FIDH, p. 8.
126 Ibid.
127 Déclaration d'indépendance de l'Azawad, Gao, 6 April 2012, Bilal Ag Acherif. 'Tuaregs claim "independence" from Mali', *Al Jazeera*, 6 April 2012.
128 Déclaration d'indépendance de l'Azawad.
129 Ibid.
130 Ibid.
131 AUC NEWS, The Newsletter of the African Union, April 2012, p. 1. 'ECOWAS Commission Declaration Following the Declaration of Independence of Northern Mali by the MNLA', Abuja, 6 April 2012, H.E. Kadré Désiré Ouédraogo, President of the Commission.
132 'Malian rebels and Islamic fighters merge', *Al Jazeera*, 27 May 2012.
133 Tuareg to Ansar Dine: Yes to Islam but no to sharia, Middle East Online, 2 June 2012.
134 A. Nossiter, 'Jihadists' Fierce Justice Drives Thousands to Flee Mali', *New York Times*, 18 July 2012.
135 M. Affa'a-Mindzie, 'The Malian "Twin Crisis": More Collaboration Needed from Unlikely Partners', Global Observatory, 22 August 2012.
136 'Islamists vow to smash every mausoleum in Timbuktu', *BBC News*, 1 July 2012.
137 'Mali "thief's" hand amputated by Islamists in Ansongo', *BBC News*, 9 August 2012. 'Mali unwed couple stoned to death by Islamists', *BBC News*, 30 July 2012.
138 Morgan, 'The Causes of the Uprising in Northern Mali'.
139 The United Nations Office for the Coordination of Humanitarian Affairs has declared that 80 per cent of Mali's humanitarian needs are located in the south. Affa'a-Mindzie, 'The Malian "Twin Crisis"'.
140 Affa'a-Mindzie, 'The Malian "Twin Crisis"'.
141 ICC Prosecutor Fatou Bensouda on the Malian State referral of the situation in Mali since January 2012. Press Release: 18.07.2012, ICC-OTP-20120718-PR829.
142 The ECOWAS Contact Group on Mali was composed of Benin, Burkina Faso, Côte d'Ivoire, Liberia, Niger, Nigeria and Togo. O.A Maunganidze and A. Louw, 'Mali: Implications of Another African Case As Mali Self-Refers to the ICC', *Institute for Security Studies Analysis*, 24 July 2012.
143 M. Coulibaly, Le Ministre de la Justice, Garde des Seaux Republique du Mali, *Lettre a Madame la Procureure pres la Cour Penale Internationale, 'Renvoi de la situation au Mali'*, Bamako, 13 July 2012. Maunganidze and Louw, 'Mali: Implications of Another African Case As Mali Self-Refers to the ICC'.
144 ICC Prosecutor Fatou Bensouda on the Malian State referral of the situation in Mali since January 2012, Press Release: 18.07.2012, ICC-OTP-20120718-PR829.
145 W.A. Schabas, 'Mali Referral Poses Challenge for International Criminal Court', *PhD Studies in Human Rights*, 19 July 2012. M. Kersten, 'The ICC in Mali: Just Another ICC Intervention in Africa?' *Justice in Conflict*, 19 July 2012. ICC Watch Press Release, 17 January 2013.
146 M. Kersten, 'The ICC in Mali: Just Another ICC Intervention in Africa?' *Justice in Conflict*, 19 July 2012. ICC Watch Press Release, 17 January 2013.
147 Nouwen and Werner, 'Doing Justice to the Political', p. 963.

148 Maunganidze and Louw, 'Mali: Implications of Another African Case As Mali Self-Refers to the ICC'.
149 Kersten, 'The ICC in Mali'.
150 P. Wegner, 'Arguing for a Department for Impact Assessment within the ICC', *Justice in Conflict*, 2 September 2011.
151 Nouwen and Werner, 'Doing Justice to the Political', p. 963.
152 Kersten, 'The ICC in Mali'.
153 Maunganidze and Louw, 'Mali: Implications of Another African Case As Mali Self-Refers to the ICC'.
154 Rome Statute Article 5.
155 K.R. Striffolino, '3 Things You Should Know about Mali and the International Criminal Court', *Amnesty International*, 17 January 2013.
156 ICC Watch Press Release, 17 January 2013.
157 Ibid.
158 'Situation in Mali', Article 53(1) Report, 16 January 2013, §§ 5–7.
159 'War crimes in North Mali', AMDH-FIDH, p. 5, p. 13. 'Situation in Mali', Article 53(1) Report, 16 January 2013, §90–93. Unlawful killings constitute a war crime under Article (8)(2)(c)(i), if the person or persons killed were either *hors de combat*, or were civilians, medical personnel or religious personnel taking no active part in the hostilities.
160 'Situation in Mali', Article 53(1) Report, 16 January 2013, §§ 94–95.
161 Ibid., §§ 101–102. Human Rights Watch, 'Mali: War Crimes by Northern Rebels', 30 April 2012. Human Rights Watch, 'Mali: Islamist Armed Groups Spread Fear in North', 25 September 2012.
162 'Situation in Mali', Article 53(1) Report, 16 January 2013, §§ 103–108.
163 Rape is a war crime pursuant to Article 8(2)(e)(vi) and using, conscripting and enlisting children pursuant to Article 8(2)(e)(vii) of the Rome Statute. FIDH, 'War crimes in North Mali', p. 14. HRW, 'Mali: War Crimes by Northern Rebels', 30 April 2012. AI, 'Mali: Five Months of Crisis, Armed Rebellion and Military Coup', May 2012, p. 15. 'Situation in Mali', Article 53(1) Report, 16 January 2013, §§ 117–121.
164 Article 8(2)(c)(iv) Intentionally directing attacks against buildings dedicated to religion, education, art, science or charitable purposes, historic monuments, hospitals and places where the sick and wounded are collected, provided they are not military objectives.
165 'Situation in Mali', Article 53(1) Report, 16 January 2013, §§ 110–113.
166 'Mali army kills 16 at Segou checkpoint in Diabali', *BBC News*, 9 September 2012. 'Situation in Mali', Article 53(1) Report, 16 January 2013, § 97.
167 Human Rights Watch, 'Mali: War Crimes by Northern Rebels'. 'Situation in Mali', Article 53(1) Report, 16 January 2013, § 96.
168 FIDH/AMDH, 'Crimes de guerre au Nord-Mali', 11 July 2012, p. 21.
169 Kersten, M. (2015) Whither ICC justice in Mali? Available at: https://justicehub.org/article/courtside-justice-whither-icc-justice-mali (Accessed: 7 August 2016).
170 'Mali and al-Qaeda: Can the jihadists be stopped?' *The Economist*, 10 November 2012. 'Terror in the Sahara: Getting the UN's intervention plan right is more important than implementing it fast', *The Economist*, 10 November 2012.
171 Affa'a-Mindzie, 'The Malian "Twin Crisis" '.
172 UN Security Council Resolution 2071, 12 October 2012.
173 Ibid.
174 Ibid.
175 Ibid.
176 S. Houttuin, 'Mali: MNLA's Struggle for Azawad Continues', *Radio Netherlands Worldwide*, 20 July 2012.
177 Ibid.
178 Ibid.

179 Ibid.
180 'Action Plan: Respecting the Laws of War', submitted by the *Mouvement National de Libération de l'Azawad* to the United Nations Security Council, 12 October 2012.
181 'Action Plan: Respecting the Laws of War', submitted by the *Mouvement National de Libération de l'Azawad* to the United Nations Security Council, 12 October 2012.
182 Geneva Call, About Us. www.genevacall.org/about/about.htm (accessed 20 October 2013).
183 'Action Plan: Respecting the Laws of War', submitted by the *Mouvement National de Libération de l'Azawad* to the United Nations Security Council, 12 October 2012.
184 UN Security Council Resolution 2071, 12 October 2012. 'ECOWAS agrees to Mali intervention force', *Al Jazeera*, 11 November 2012.
185 'Mali army clashes with separatist MNLA rebels', *BBC News*, 5 June 2013.
186 Communiqué N° 52/Déclaration du MNLA, Kidal, 11 February 2013, Le Secrétaire Général, Président du Conseil Transitaire de l'Etat de l'Azawad (CTEA), Bilal Ag Acherif.
187 Ibid.
188 Ibid.
189 'Tuareg rebels ask ICC to probe Mali army "crimes" ', *AFP*, 5 March 2013.
190 A. Hirsch, 'Mali signs controversial ceasefire deal with Tuareg separatist insurgents', *Guardian*, 19 June 2013.
191 UN Security Council Resolution 2100 of 25 April 2013.
192 Anara, S.A. (2016) 'Mali's peace pact under strain, deepening jihadi threat', *Reuters*. Available at: http://af.reuters.com/article/topNews/idAFKCN0ZV2AE (Accessed: 9 August 2016).

Bibliography

Affa'a-Mindzie, M. (2012) 'The Malian "Twin Crisis": More Collaboration Needed from Unlikely Partners'. *Global Observatory*.

AFP (2013) *Tuareg rebels ask ICC to probe Mali army 'crimes'*. Available at: http://english.ahram.org.eg/NewsContent/2/9/66189/World/International/Tuareg-rebels-ask-ICC-to-probe-Mali-army-crimes.aspx (Accessed: 18 August 2016).

African Union (2009) *Decision on the Application by the International Criminal Court (ICC) Prosecutor for the Indictment of the President of the Republic of the Sudan, Assembly/AU/Dec.221(XII), February 1–3, 2009*.

African Union Commission (2012) *AUC News: The Newsletter of the African Union*. Available at: www.au.int (Accessed: 18 August 2016).

Akhavan, P. (1995) 'Enforcement of the Genocide Convention'. *Harvard Human Rights Journal*, 8(1), pp. 229–258.

Akhavan, P. (2005) 'The Lord's Resistance Army Case: Uganda's Submission of the First State Referral to the International Criminal Court'. *American Journal of International Law*, 99(2), p. 403. doi: 10.2307/1562505.

Akhavan, P. (2010) 'Self-referrals before the international criminal court: Are states the villains or the victims of atrocities?' *Criminal Law Forum*, 21(1), pp. 103–120. doi: 10.1007/s10609-010-9112-2.

Al Jazeera (2012) *Tuareg rebels attack fifth town in Mali*. Available at: www.aljazeera.com/news/africa/2012/01/201212614823523986.html (Accessed: 18 August 2016).

Al Jazeera (2013a) *ICC case against Kenyan leader suffers blow*. Available at: http://m.aljazeera.com/story/2013718163424230569 (Accessed: 18 August 2016).

Al Jazeera (2013b) *Making sense of Mali's armed groups*. Available at: www.aljazeera.com/indepth/features/2013/01/20131139522812326.html (Accessed: 18 August 2016).

Al Jazeera (2016a) *ECOWAS agrees to Mali intervention force.* Available at: www.aljazeera. com/news/africa/2012/11/20121111192710305682.html (Accessed: 18 August 2016).

Al Jazeera (2016b) *Mali court meets to choose interim president.* Available at: www. aljazeera.com/news/africa/2012/04/20124914524561479.html (Accessed: 18 August 2016).

Al Jazeera (2016c) *Malian rebels and Islamic fighters merge.* Available at: www.aljazeera. com/news/africa/2012/05/201252623916484555.html (Accessed: 18 August 2016).

Al Jazeera (2016d) *Tuaregs claim 'independence' from Mali.* Available at: www.aljazeera. com/news/africa/2012/04/20124644412359539.html (Accessed: 18 August 2016).

Anara, S.A. (2016) *Mali's peace pact under strain, deepening jihadi threat.* Available at: http://af.reuters.com/article/topNews/idAFKCN0ZV2AE (Accessed: 18 August 2016).

Annan, K. (2002) *Press Release, Office of the Secretary-General, Transcript of Press Conference with President Carlo Ciampi of Italy and Secretary-General Kofi Annan in Rome and New York by Videoconference.* U.N. Doc. SG/SM/8194.

Arsanjani, M.H. and Reisman, W.M. (2005) 'The Law-in-Action of the International Criminal Court', *American Journal of International Law*, 99(2), p. 385. doi: 10.2307/1562504.

BBC (2009) *African union in rift with court.* Available at: http://news.bbc.co.uk/1/hi/8133925.stm (Accessed: 18 August 2016).

BBC (2012a) *Islamists vow to smash every mausoleum in Timbuktu.* Available at: www. bbc.co.uk/news/world-africa-18665522 (Accessed: 18 August 2016).

BBC (2012b) *Mali 'thief's' hand amputated by Islamists in Ansongo.* Available at: www. bbc.co.uk/news/world-africa-19195985 (Accessed: 18 August 2016).

BBC (2012c) *Mali army kills 16 at Segou checkpoint in Diabali.* Available at: www.bbc. co.uk/news/world-africa-19538018 (Accessed: 18 August 2016).

BBC (2012d) *Mali unwed couple stoned to death by Islamists.* Available at: www.bbc. co.uk/news/world-africa-19053442 (Accessed: 18 August 2016).

BBC (2013a) *African Union urges ICC to defer Uhuru Kenyatta case.* Available at: www. bbc.co.uk/news/world-africa-24506006 (Accessed: 18 August 2016).

BBC (2013b) *Mali army clashes with separatist MNLA rebels.* Available at: www.bbc. co.uk/news/world-africa-22791147 (Accessed: 18 August 2016).

BBC (2013c) *Mali crisis: Key players.* Available at: www.bbc.co.uk/news/world-africa-17582909 (Accessed: 18 August 2016).

BBC (2013d) *Will Africa pull out of the ICC?* Available at: www.bbc.co.uk/news/world-africa-24452288 (Accessed: 18 August 2016).

Burke-White, W.W. (2005) 'Complementarity in Practice: The International Criminal Court as Part of a System of Multi-Level Global Governance in the Democratic Republic of Congo', *Leiden Journal of International Law*, 18(03), p. 557. doi: 10.1017/s0922156505002876.

Cassese, A. (2012) 'The Legitimacy of International Criminal Tribunals and the Current Prospects of International Criminal Justice'. *Leiden Journal of International Law*, 25(02), pp. 491–501, doi: 10.1017/s0922156512000167.

Chothia, F. (2011) *Africa's Fatou Bensouda is new ICC chief prosecutor.* Available at: www.bbc.co.uk/news/world-africa-16029121 (Accessed: 18 August 2016).

Coulibaly, M. (2012) *M. Coulibaly, Le Ministre de la Justice, Garde des Seaux Republique du Mali, Lettre a Madame la Procureure pres la Cour Penale Internationale, 'Renvoi de la situation au Mali'.* Bamako.

Currie, R. (2011) 'Côte d'Ivoire and the ICC: A New Kind of "Self-Referral"?' *International and Transnational Criminal Law Update.*

Daniel, S. (2012) *Mali junta denounces 'rights violations' by rebels.* Available at: www. google.com/hostednews/afp/article/ALeqM5grilySJ5EdrgURoNp1mt3AIJhTgg?docId =CNG.915a5505555757d7df5029b5b99451cc.261 (Accessed: 18 August 2016).

Decision on the Meeting of African States Parties to the Rome Statute of the International Criminal Court (ICC) (2009) *Assembly/AU/Dec.245(XIII) Rev.1 July 1–3, 2009.*

ECOWAS (2012a) *ECOWAS Commission Declaration Following the Declaration of Independence of Northern Mali by the MNLA, 6 April 2012*, Abuja: H.E. Kadré Désiré Ouédraogo President of the Commission.

ECOWAS (2012b) *ECOWAS Press Release, no. 084/2012, 28 March 2012, Abidjan – Cote d' Ivoire.* Available at: http://news.ecowas.int/presseshow.php?nb=084&lang=en&annee= 2012 (Accessed: 18 August 2016).

FIDH (2016) *War crimes in North Mali.* Available at: www.fidh.org/en/africa/Mali,305/ War-Crimes-in-North-Mali-12660 (Accessed: 18 August 2016).

Freedman, L. (2000) 'Victims and Victors: Reflections on the Kosovo War'. *Review of International Studies*, 26(3), pp. 335–358, doi: 10.1017/s0260210500003351.

Futamura, M. and Gow, J. (2013) 'The Strategic Purpose of the ICTY and International Peace and Security'. In: Gow, J., Kerr, R., and Pajić, Z. (eds), *Prosecuting War Crimes.* London: Routledge, pp. 15–28.

Geneva Call (2013) *Mission.* Available at: www.genevacall.org/about/about.htm (Accessed: 18 August 2016).

Geneva Convention relative to the Protection of Civilian Persons in Time of War, Geneva, 12 August 1949 (1949).

Heller, K.J. (2007) 'Situational Gravity Under The Rome Statute'. In: Stahn, C. and van den Herik, L. (eds), *Future Directions in International Criminal Justice.* Cambridge: Cambridge University Press.

Hirsch, A. (2013) *Mali signs controversial ceasefire deal with Tuareg separatist insurgents.* Available at: www.theguardian.com/world/2013/jun/19/mali-peace-deal-tuareg-insurgents-aid (Accessed: 18 August 2016).

Houttuin, S. (2012) *Mali: MNLA's Struggle for Azawad Continues.* Available at: http:// allafrica.com/stories/201207201404.html?viewall=1 (Accessed: 18 August 2016).

Human Rights Council (2013) *Report of the Independent International Commission of Inquiry on the Syrian Arab Republic, Human Rights Council, Twenty-third session, 4 June 2013, A/HRC/23/58.*

Human Rights Watch (2012a) *Mali: Islamist Armed Groups Spread Fear in North.*

Human Rights Watch (2012b) *Mali: War Crimes by Northern Rebels.*

Human Rights Watch (2015) *Central African Republic: Progress on special court.* Available at: https://www.hrw.org/news/2015/12/23/central-african-republic-progress-special-court (Accessed: 18 August 2016).

Human Rights Watch, Dicker, R. and Evenson, E. (2013) *ICC Suspects Can Hide – and That Is the Problem.*

ICC Press Office (2012) *ICC Prosecutor Fatou Bensouda on the Malian State referral of the situation in Mali since January 2012. Press Release: 18.07.2012, ICC-OTP-20120718-PR829.*

International Crisis Group (2012) 'Mali: Avoiding Escalation'. *Crisis Group Africa Report*, 189.

Kersten, M. (2012) *The ICC in Mali: Just another ICC intervention in Africa?* Available at: http://justiceinconflict.org/2012/07/19/the-icc-in-mali-just-another-icc-intervention-in-africa/ (Accessed: 18 August 2016).

Kersten, M. (2015) *Whither ICC justice in Mali?* Available at: https://justicehub.org/ article/courtside-justice-whither-icc-justice-mali (Accessed: 18 August 2016).

Le Vine, V. (2010) 'Mali: Accommodation or Coexistence?' In: Miles, W.F.S. (ed.), *Political Islam in West Africa*. Boulder, CO: Lynn Rienner, pp. 85–91.

Lindijer, K. (2013) 'Afrikaanse Unie eist immuniteit voor zittende leiders bij Strafhof', *NRC Handelsblad*, 14 October.

Llewellyn, J.J. and Raponi, S. (1999) 'The Protection of Human Rights through International Criminal Law: A Conversation with Madame Justice Louise Arbour, Chief Prosecutor for the International Criminal Tribunals for the Former Yugoslavia and Rwanda'. *University of Toronto Faculty of Law Review*, 57(1), pp. 83–99.

Manson, K. (2013) 'ICC rules Kenyatta can miss part of trial'. *Financial Times*, 18 October.

Marshall, K.A. (2010) 'Prevention and Complementarity in the International Criminal Court: A Positive Approach'. *Human Rights Brief*, 17(2), pp. 21–26.

Maunganidze, O.A. and Louw, A. (2012) 'Mali: Implications of Another African Case As Mali Self-Refers to the ICC'. *Institute for Security Studies Analysis*.

Middle East Online (2012) *Tuareg to Ansar Dine: Yes to Islam but no to sharia.* Available at: www.middle-east-online.com/english/?id=52613 (Accessed: 18 August 2016).

MNLA (2012) *Action Plan: Respecting the Laws of War, submitted by the Mouvement National de Libération de l'Azawad to the United Nations Security Council, 12 October 2012.*

MNLA (2013) *Communiqué N° 52/Déclaration du MNLA*. Kidal: Le Secrétaire Général, Président du Conseil Transitoire de l'Etat de l'Azawad (CTEA), Bilal Ag Acherif.

Moreno-Ocampo, L. (2003) *Statement made at the ceremony for the solemn undertaking of the Chief Prosecutor of the ICC*. The Peace Palace, The Hague. 16 June.

Morgan, A. (2012) *The Causes of the Uprising in Northern Mali.* Available at: www.andymorganwrites.com/bko2kdl/ (Accessed: 18 August 2016). First published in Think Africa Press.

Nama, G.B. (2012) *Rebelles touaregs: 'Pourquoi nous reprenons les armes…'.* Available at: www.courrierinternational.com/article/2012/03/01/rebelles-touaregs-pourquoi-nous-reprenons-les-armes (Accessed: 18 August 2016).

N'Diaye, B. (2009) 'Youth Vulnerability and Exclusion (YOVEX) in West Africa: Mali Country Report', *CSDG Papers*, 25.

Nichols, M. (2016) *U.S., Britain back South Sudan war crimes court'.* Available at: www.swissinfo.ch/eng/u-s-britain-back-south-sudan-war-crimes-court-/42217362 (Accessed: 18 August 2016). Reuters.

Nossiter, A. (2012) *Jihadists' fierce justice drives thousands to flee Mali.* Available at: www.nytimes.com/2012/07/18/world/africa/jidhadists-fierce-justice-drives-thousands-to-flee-mali.html (Accessed: 18 August 2016).

Nouwen, S.M.H. and Werner, W.G. (2010) 'Doing Justice to the Political: The International Criminal Court in Uganda and Sudan'. *European Journal of International Law*, 21(4), pp. 941–965. doi: 10.1093/ejil/chq064.

Nouwen, S. and Werner, W. (2010) 'The Law and Politics of Self Referrals'. In: Smeulers, A. (ed.), *Collective Violence and International Criminal Justice: an Interdisciplinary Approach*. Antwerp: Intersentia, pp. 255–271.

Ouazani, C. (2012) *Rébellion du MNLA au Mali: Ag Najem, ou la soif de vengeance.* Available at: www.jeuneafrique.com/Article/JA2663p010-012.xml1/ (Accessed: 18 August 2016).

Reuters (2016) *Gaddafi's son Saif still in prison in western Libya, military source says.* Available at: http://uk.reuters.com/article/uk-libya-gaddafi-idUKKCN0ZN2CZ?il=0 (Accessed: 18 August 2016).

Review Conference of the Rome Statute (2010) *Amendments on the crime of aggression to the Rome Statute of the International Criminal Court, Kampala, 11 June 2010, Resolution RC/Res.6 of the Review Conference of the Rome Statute.*

Rice, X. (2009) *Annan hands ICC list of perpetrators of post-election violence in Kenya.* Available at: https://www.theguardian.com/world/2009/jul/09/international-criminal-court-kofi-annan (Accessed: 18 August 2016).

Richardson, H.J. (2012) 'African Grievances and the International Criminal Court: Issues of African Equity under International Criminal Law'. In: Nmehielle, V.O. (ed.), *Africa and the Future of International Criminal Justice.* The Hague: Eleven, pp. 81–123.

Rome Treaty (1998) *Rome Statute of the International Criminal Court, Rome, 17 July 1998, entry into force 1 July 2002 in accordance with Article 126, Registration 1 July 2002, No. 38544, United Nations Treaty Series, vol. 2187.*

Rondot, M. (2013) 'The ICC's Investigation into Alleged War Crimes in Mali', *American Non-Governmental Organizations Coalition for the International Criminal Court.*

SaCouto, S. and Cleary, K. (2007) 'The Gravity Threshold of the International Criminal Court'. *American University International Law Review,* 23(5), pp. 807–854.

Schabas, W.A. (2006) 'First Prosecutions at the International Criminal Court'. *Human Rights Law Journal,* 27(1), pp. 25–40.

Schabas, W.A. (2010) 'Victor's Justice: Selecting "Situations" at the International Criminal Court'. *The John Marshall Law Review,* 43, pp. 535–552.

Schabas, W.A. (2012) 'Mali Referral Poses Challenge for International Criminal Court'. *PhD Studies in Human Rights.*

Schiff, B.N. (2008) *Building the International Criminal Court.* Cambridge: Cambridge University Press.

Schulz, D. (2010) 'Sharia and National Law in Mali'. In: Otto, J.M. (ed.), *Sharia Incorporated: A Comparative Overview of the Legal Systems of Twelve Muslim Countries in Past and Present,* Leiden: Leiden University Press.

Seils, P. (2016) *Handbook on Complementarity: An Introduction to the Role of National Courts and the ICC in Prosecuting International Crimes.* The Hague: ICTJ.

Situation in Georgia [2016] Pre-Trial Chamber I, Decision on the Prosecutor's request for authorization of an investigation ICC-01/15-12, 27.

Song, S.H. (2012) *From Punishment to Prevention: Reflections on the Future of International Criminal Justice'. Speech by the President of the International Criminal Court, Wallace Wurth Memorial Lecture.* University of New South Wales, Sydney. 14 February.

Striffolino, K.R. (2013) '3 Things You Should Know about Mali and the International Criminal Court'. *Amnesty International.*

The Economist (2012a) *Can the jihadists be stopped?* Available at: www.economist.com/news/middle-east-and-africa/21566011-hectic-diplomacy-and-preparations-un-backed-war-against-branch-al-qaeda (Accessed: 18 August 2016).

The Economist (2012b) *Terror in the Sahara.* Available at: www.economist.com/news/leaders/21565959-getting-uns-intervention-plan-right-more-important-implementing-it-fast-terror (Accessed: 18 August 2016).

Tutu, D. (2013) *In Africa, seeking a license to kill.* Available at: www.nytimes.com/2013/10/11/opinion/in-africa-seeking-a-license-to-kill.html?_r=0 (Accessed: 18 August 2016).

Wegner, P. (2011) *Arguing for a department for impact assessment within the ICC.* Available at: http://justiceinconflict.org/2011/09/02/arguing-for-a-department-for-impact-assessment-within-the-icc/ (Accessed: 18 August 2016).

7 Conclusion

Over the course of the last decades, international criminal justice has gone from a distant memory of the IMTs in Nuremberg and Tokyo to being firmly established as a functioning system of international judicial mechanisms to prosecute those individuals most responsible for the most heinous crimes. However, the enormous development of international criminal tribunals has also given rise to high expectations regarding the outcome of the proceedings before them. Yet despite these high hopes, the money and means invested and the extensive research into the effectiveness of international criminal justice, it remains unclear how far prosecuting individuals for violations of humanitarian law has had an effect in line with the various objectives and justifications attributed to international criminal tribunals.

As suggested in the introduction, the direct answer to the question of *what the impact is of international criminal justice on the capacity of quasi-state entities to maintain and create legitimacy for their actions and institutions*, is that international criminal justice can present critical challenges that affect the legitimacy of QSEs, directly or indirectly, thereby affecting their prospects of success. As international judicial attention to QSEs and their conflicts spread, it is evident that legal procedures against individuals had critical impact on the legitimacy of the QSEs in the conflicts in which those individuals were involved. At the same time, these judicial procedures also affected their opponents' ability to create and maintain legitimacy – one way or another. The shifting of legitimacy, and the changes in narratives aimed at creating legitimacy which I have explored in this study, reveal the impact of international criminal justice. As I have argued, by assessing the influence of international criminal justice on the capacity of QSEs to create and maintain legitimacy – an essential requirement for their success – it is possible to distinguish the discrete impact of international tribunals on the outcome of conflicts and the political and social conditions for QSE success. I have shown this in relation to three QSEs (the KLA, Hezbollah and the MNLA) in three different conflicts (Kosovo, Lebanon and Mali) which were a focus of interest for three different types of international judicial body (the ICTY, the STL and the ICC).

This conclusion will draw together the concepts of critical legitimacy and QSEs with international justice. First, it considers the entanglement of international criminal justice and international politics. Then, the impact of international criminal justice on the legitimacy of QSEs in the three examples discussed in depth in this book will be briefly reassessed. Beyond this, I shall offer reflection on what can be learned from looking at these concepts in conjunction with each other and, before this, on QSEs and legitimacy as success. Finally, I conclude that although legitimacy is hard to gauge, this can in part be negotiated by looking at critical legitimacy crises resulting from international criminal justice, revealing the impact these judicial proceedings have. Looking at narratives may enable us to establish a causal link between legitimacy crises and international criminal justice. Evidently, trials do not only impact on the individual prosecuted, but also on the entities and societies they represent. Although it is more appropriate to assess effects than effectiveness, some outcomes of international criminal justice are immeasurable altogether, and one has to realise that international proceedings can have many contingent effects. One should keep in mind that international criminal justice narratives are effective because the acts committed are abhorred, and that the more horrible the crimes the greater the outrage and the deeper the accompanying impact the narratives of justice for the victims have on legitimacy. This study made clear that timing is everything in relation to the potential effect of international criminal justice, and that impact will depend on the legitimacy of the tribunal itself. Importantly, genocide, war crimes and crimes against humanity entered the narratives of all conflicts and of entities claiming legitimacy in them; their use has changed the political reality of contemporary conflict. While they do not depend entirely on the existence of a court that has the ability to apply, and develop, international criminal law, they are very greatly enhanced by the existence of such a body, the discourse that surrounds it, the documentation, testimony and judgements it produces and the spurs to narrative it makes possible.

Quasi-state entities

QSEs became one of the main types of actor in contemporary armed conflict. The rise of QSEs, in armed conflict, was not only fully revealed by the same changing circumstances in international politics that made international criminal justice a possibility, but also, at the same time, their role and the atrocities they committed in armed conflict created an environment that called for international mechanisms to prosecute those responsible for these crimes. The collapse of the bipolar structure, in which both blocs supported proxies revealed a multitude of dormant, or suppressed, internal conflicts. In the 1990s, the main threat to international stability no longer came from states waging war against each other, but from conflicts fought within states. These intrastate conflicts also fully revealed new dominant paradigms in warfare; wars were no longer fought for a decisive military victory, but were fought for what Rupert Smith calls 'the will of the people' and 'amongst the people' and, usually, at least one of the belligerents was a QSE. These entities usually revolved around a shared ethnicity, religion or culture, or were based on a common language or history; they came in many forms and went by many monikers, but they all challenged the legitimacy of an existing state. What QSEs have in common is that the goals they seek to attain all have to do with statehood. They not only aspire to change the state, but often carry out functions usually associated with statehood.

In these statehood conflicts, the unprecedented capacity of QSEs to commit large-scale atrocities meant that war crimes, crimes against humanity, and even genocide were by no means uncommon. To attain their (statehood) goals, QSEs sometimes committed the most horrendous atrocities, as did their state adversaries, in order to maintain the status quo. Sometimes, violations of humanitarian law were part of the strategy of one or more parties to a conflict or even inherent in the aims of one of the belligerents, as could be seen in the Kosovo case, for instance, when changing the ethnic make-up of a territory was the goal in itself.

The war in Yugoslavia and the genocide in Rwanda gave rise to the outrage and condemnation that contributed to the establishment of the first international courts, especially because in these conflicts QSEs and state entities employed a strategy of war crimes, or attempted to change the ethnical make-up of a territory. But, although the rise of international criminal justice had to be seen in the light of the changing interpretation of sovereignty and the practical consequences attached to that principle, the international community remained firmly dominated by states; a community that proved vigilant in upholding the privileges that come with state sovereignty. As statehood remained the holy grail, contemporary conflicts were essentially statehood conflicts. These conflicts were about changing the borders of an existing state, its ethnic make-up or its system. These entities developed quasi-state institutions or fulfilled statehood functions to a greater or lesser degree. They had the capacity and willingness to employ organised, restrained coercive violence. They operated in a state-centred environment. In many ways they behaved like states, but they lacked the status of sovereign statehood. I have argued, therefore, a more appropriate term to describe this type of actor, or entity, would be 'quasi-state entity' or QSE.

Although, at any one time, what these entities are might overlap with being a rebel army, a nationalist movement or de facto state, and while these entities, and the conflicts they fight in, evolve, many of the labels attached to them might change, there is a constant in what these entities are, QSEs, a concept importantly and conceptually distinct from, for instance, nationalist movements, de facto states and rebels or insurgents. The use of the term 'quasi-state entity' is useful for understanding that the nature of these entities, and the nature of the conflicts in which they are involved, make creating and maintaining legitimacy for their actions and institutions a prerequisite for their success. It emphasises what these conflicts are about, but also that these entities lack the privileges that come with full sovereign statehood. QSEs are not part of the international political process that establishes Courts: they have no say in international organisations, they are not parties to the Rome Statute and cannot refer situations to the ICC – but they might be covered by the ICC; their members are subject to international proceedings, but they remain on the sidelines of, at least, one of the political dimensions that border on international criminal justice. Because QSEs lack a solid basis of legitimacy in the international community of states, QSEs are arguably more affected by changing discourse and by legitimacy crises brought about by international criminal justice. For instance, as the case of shifting legitimacy in Kosovo and the position of the KLA vis-à-vis Milošević and the Serbian state, showed, the impact of international criminal justice on the capacity of states to create and maintain legitimacy for their aims and institutions is significant. Moreover, these changes in legitimacy can be seen by the same method: detecting critical legitimacy moments, or legitimacy crises, and narratives changing under the pressure of international criminal justice.

Legitimacy as success

Legitimacy is a useful concept with which to gauge impact. It is useful, despite the difficulties in establishing its existence, its complexity as a concept, its constantly changing nature and the fact that it differs among various relevant constituencies. First and foremost, this is because in contemporary 'statehood' conflict, the ability to create and maintain legitimacy is a prerequisite for success for both states and QSEs alike. Even the party that is able to deploy superior military means in order to alter the boundaries, or system, of an existing state, or maintain the status quo, needs legitimacy. Both QSEs and state entities need to establish and maintain legitimacy for their actions and institutions within their core constituencies – among the people they claim to represent, those who fight for them and among the political elite of the group with which they identify themselves. But they also need the ability to create and maintain legitimacy in other relevant constituencies – among the secondary Clausewitzian trinity of people, military and political elite of other local constituencies and regional allies; they need to influence their opponents' triangle, and they need a certain level of legitimacy among members of various constituencies in the international community. However, here it is demonstrated that legitimacy is not a constant quality that an entity has, or its institutions have. On the contrary, it depends on many different internal and external factors and can be gained, or lost, almost overnight. Moreover, the ability of entities to engage in the constant process of legitimation in multiple constituencies simultaneously is, therefore, extremely hard to gauge. At best, legitimacy is tangible in its absence and, by observing the (in)ability to overcome legitimacy crises, its existence and its workings can be detected. It is in the critical test of legitimacy, the moment the possibilities and means to regain legitimacy are retracted at the same time as these means are needed the most, that legitimacy can best be noticed. Here it is argued that, although both the effects of international criminal justice and the outcomes of legitimisation are independently very hard to gauge, it is possible to detect both the intended and unintended effects of international criminal justice on QSEs by analysing legitimacy crises – the point where international criminal justice and legitimacy come together.

Politics, justice, politics

Reflecting on international criminal justice, critical legitimacy moments caused by international criminal justice and the capacity of QSEs to create and maintain legitimacy, several observations can be made. First, international criminal law could only come into existence because of the unique circumstances, in the early 1990s, which simultaneously called for the prosecution of those responsible for violations of international criminal law and created an international political environment that made establishing international criminal courts and tribunals feasible. The huge steps that were taken in the field of international criminal justice should therefore be viewed in the wider political and diplomatic environment in which it could flourish. Not only was the establishment of international criminal tribunals a political decision, but international criminal justice also remained a set of legal tools, wedged between the political considerations in the establishment of courts (or referrals of the UN Security Council to the ICC) on one side, and the political outcomes of prosecuting individuals for violations of humanitarian law on the other. That the ICC had a structural shortage of people and means was the outcome of political processes, as was the inability of the Security Council to refer situations that called for international judicial intervention to the Court (the prime example of this would be Syria). For states to become party to the Rome Statute, or to cooperate with the ICC in investigations and the apprehending of suspects, were all political decisions. International relations and politics are intrinsically intertwined with international law and criminal procedures. They are part of a complex process, constantly both influencing and depending on each other, and should all be taken into consideration when assessing the impact of international criminal justice. Conversely, the (potential) impact of international criminal justice should be considered when assessing the situations in which violations of humanitarian law are committed.

Although intrinsically interwoven with one another, international criminal justice and politics moved completely out of tune with each other. While, according to Harold Wilson, 'a week is a long time in politics', in international criminal justice 20 years is a fairly short period of time. The difference in pace was not only problematic for maintaining attention for something that was so surrounded by (international) politics, it also further complicated the already difficult process of assessing the impact of international criminal justice as a whole. Despite the fact that international criminal law was nothing new, in itself, international criminal justice in its current incarnation was a relatively recent phenomenon. Consequently, the number of completed cases that could provide empirical evidence for the impact of international criminal proceedings on QSEs was limited. Criminal procedures at international tribunals are very time consuming, expensive and, consequently, only a limited number of cases that merit prosecution end up in an international court. This further limits the number of cases that could provide empirical evidence for this book. Although conflicts over statehood tend to drag on for a long time, and reaching a final status often takes decades, the discrepancy between the pace of legal procedures and the pace of (international) politics means that conflicts in which the violations of humanitarian law were committed are often over by the time prosecution begins. The ICTR, for instance, was established in November 1994 and announced its first indictments in December 1995, while the genocide in Rwanda, generally, was considered to have ended in July 1994. Moreover, criminal procedures tended to take a long time to come to an end, even more so when suspects remained at large. The trials of Radovan Karadžić and Ratko Mladić at the ICTY began in 2011 and 2012, respectively, while the last alleged war crimes they were accused of were committed in 1995. In some cases, not only did the conflicts end by the time the violations of humanitarian law were addressed in a court, but the entities to which the individuals facing prosecution were connected no longer existed. The Khmer Rouge, for instance, was dissolved in 1996, while international criminal procedures against its senior members only started ten years later, in 2006, more than 30 years after the beginning of its campaign of gross human rights violations. With regard to the ICC, in particular, one may therefore argue that it was too early in its existence to be able to see a systematic and constant impact on the ability to create and maintain legitimacy in various constituencies of those entities whose members were suspected, or convicted, by the Court. However, with the establishment of the ICC – and its readily available expertise and investigating capacity – the threat of prosecution for violations of humanitarian law drew closer; its establishment took away the need for the Security Council to establish a court before there was even a possibility of commencing prosecutions of war crimes. Moreover, establishment of the ICC took the decision to prosecute out of the realm of international politics and made it a legal decision. Yet the case of Mali demonstrated that, even when the Court sprang into action relatively quickly, no cases were opened, while the belligerents moved on and alternated peace talks with fighting the next conflict.

To have an effect and to maintain and create legitimacy for their own institutions and verdicts, courts need to come to final verdicts. However, it is not only convictions that have an impact on legitimacy. This work assessed three examples where the impact of international criminal justice could be seen through changing narratives and legitimacy crises. However, in two of the examples, it so did at an early stage, and in the third the main suspect died before he could be convicted. The Milošević indictment and its impact on the legitimacy of the KLA and its Kosovo statehood project was examined because the war in Kosovo occurred while the ICTY was up and running. Nevertheless, that did not mean that the approach used in the present book could not be developed and tested in relation to the war in Bosnia. Moreover, the indictment of Ramush Haradinaj also had an impact on the Kosovo statehood project, albeit in a very different way than the indictment of Milošević had six years earlier. Additionally, given the way Haradinaj handled his indictment, further exploration of the Haradinaj case would likely shed more light on the workings of international criminal justice narratives and the complicated process of legitimation.

The situation in Mali was especially relevant to seeing how the ICC functioned, as the circumstances in which it operated changed significantly between opening its first investigations and later developments under Chief Prosecutor Fatou Bensouda. In the case of the ICC investigation into the Northern Mali conflict, no indictments were published (at the time of writing) and, although the STL had indicted five individuals, it had yet to start proceedings in the absence of the accused. Notwithstanding the fact that the full impact of these procedures on the legitimacy of both state and QSEs, whose members were accused, will be revealed as these cases progress and as the political situations, in which these crimes were committed, progress, they already proved pivotal in changing legitimacy. The threat of prosecution influenced the actions and statements of QSEs. Indictments and arrest warrants limited the freedom to travel of those indicted. Investigations sent a clear message to all relevant constituencies. Because the ability to commit crimes against humanity, or war crimes, depended upon an individual's power and position within a state, or QSE, prosecution, sentencing and imprisonment were not always necessary to have a delegitimising effect on the individual, or entity, to the point that he/it was no longer as ready to commit such crimes.

Even statements by actors other than prosecutors and judges can have an impact on legitimacy: the UN Security Council, most obviously, when it asks for an investigation into possible war crimes, but accusations made by NGOs, states or influential individuals can also have an impact on legitimacy in certain constituencies. Implied and explicit messages that influenced the success of parties seeking legitimacy were sent, in every possible way, by statements and by actions, not only by the actors seeking legitimacy but also those of other actors and international organisations like the ICC, the UN or NGOs. Moreover, the international community was susceptible to normative judgements about violations of international humanitarian law made by international organisations, and especially by courts, even when they did not involve convictions but merely accusations. Once charged with crimes against humanity or genocide, it became unlikely that an individual leader and the entity they represented would regain legitimacy in the international community.

The impact of international criminal tribunals on quasi-state entities

At the height of the war in Kosovo and the NATO bombing campaign against Serbia, the new-found ability of the Prosecutor at the ICTY to collect evidence of crimes committed in Kosovo led to the indictment by the ICTY of Milošević and four other senior Serbian leaders for war crimes and crimes against humanity. Only days later, Milošević gave in to the demands of NATO, ensuring a victory for the Alliance and putting Kosovo under UN authority, but the resistance of Western politicians and NATO diplomats to (publishing) the indictment demonstrates that the outcomes of ICTY involvement were wholly unexpected. Nevertheless, the indictment turned out to be a turning point in the conflict and also in future statehood issues surrounding Kosovo. It transformed the position of the KLA from a QSE without the ability to enforce its statehood objectives militarily and lacking the legitimacy it needed to be successful (especially in the various constituencies in the international community), into a victorious combatant on a path to statehood whose legitimacy was supported by those who, a year earlier, had defended Serbia's territorial integrity.

The indictment of Milošević was a pivotal moment in the chain of events that led to the de facto independence of Kosovo in that it inverted the bases of legitimacy and revolutionised the environments of support. For Milošević it created a critical legitimacy moment that forced him to make choices under the pressure of international criminal justice. It catalysed a spiralling legitimacy crisis in various constituencies in the international community in which, up until then, there had been at least some legitimacy for maintaining the territorial integrity of Serbia. This forced Milošević to salvage what was left of his power in Serbia and give in to NATO demands. Not least, this was because the indictment against Milošević *cum suis* added to the legitimacy of NATO bombardment. The indictment added weight to the human rights narratives used by NATO – aimed at creating legitimacy for its actions in its 19 home constituencies; a level of legitimacy beyond that in the wider international community – and, contrary to Serbia's expectations, managed to maintain that legitimacy when the air campaign lasted much longer than expected. It helped in finding a narrative to justify the severe means NATO used to reach its aim of ending, and preventing further, ethnic cleansing. Investigations by the ICTY prosecutor and evidence of humanitarian disaster and ethnic cleansing presented in the indictment could not be discarded as NATO, or Kosovar, propaganda. At the same time, Serbia lost what Freedman called the 'game of comparative victimology'. The indictment made victims of human rights violations of those the KLA represented, and turned the KLA into a force fighting an enemy of the international community. It changed beliefs in various constituencies, especially the West, about the legitimacy of Serbian leadership and, conversely, increased beliefs in the justice of a Kosovar statehood project. The indictment, plus narratives that included international criminal justice, transformed the legitimacy of the KLA and, thereby, the chances of success for its statehood project.

Although narratives of international criminal justice were ubiquitous in Lebanese politics and public debate, since the establishment of the STL in 2007 identifying the impact of the Court on the legitimacy of Hezbollah and other Lebanese actors remains complicated. First, this is because the STL was the odd one out among international criminal tribunals. The STL was established to prosecute the murder of Rafik Hariri, a crime that had an effect on international peace and security according to the Security Council. This very limited jurisdiction was reflected in its objectives as described in the Statute of the STL. Although it was also implied that one of the aims of the Tribunal was to contribute to ending impunity for political assassinations in Lebanon, this was not part of its explicit justification, nor was the STL's design and jurisdiction capable of ending impunity for political violence in Lebanon. The limited jurisdiction of the STL could be seen in the narrative that the STL offers, which was more easily met by a counter narrative, and generated less outrage than narratives of war crimes, crimes against humanity and genocide. Moreover, the rather technical indictments against members of Hezbollah did not make for a powerful delegitimising narrative compared to the images of streams of refugees and mass graves the ICTY investigations provided. The timing of the establishment of the tribunal further cast doubt on the political motivation for its foundation; arguably, the STL was established to challenge further the legitimacy of Syria in Lebanon and to get the most out of the Hariri assassination (for the Sunni and Western powers). When it turned out that it would not be Syrian intelligence operatives who would be indicted, but that it would be members of Hezbollah, the opponents of Hezbollah at times refrained from using international criminal justice narratives out of fear the situation in Lebanon would escalate into civil war. More important was the time that leaks allowed Hezbollah to develop counter narratives, meaning that the impact of the indictments themselves was more limited than might have been the case otherwise. The ability to overcome legitimacy crises demonstrated by Hezbollah is such that it provides a model for success in contemporary armed conflict. Its strong bases in Shia constituencies, further strengthened by a growing Sunni–Shia rift in Lebanese politics, meant that, in that constituency, the impact of the STL on Hezbollah's legitimacy was limited. The narrative Hezbollah offered about who killed Hariri, and about what the STL was, had more appeal to its core constituents than the narratives its opponents offered, even when those were backed up by the findings of the prosecutor of the STL. Nevertheless, the shifting beliefs of what Hezbollah is, and what it ought to be, can clearly be seen in various constituencies. Moreover, although other factors in Lebanese politics simultaneously shifted beliefs about the legitimacy of Hezbollah in various constituencies inside and outside Lebanon, the influence of the establishment of the STL, its investigation and the indictments published by the Tribunal on these changes in legitimacy in Lebanon could be clearly noticed. This impact could be seen in the critical legitimacy moments that forced Hezbollah to make choices, from the establishment of the Tribunal onwards. In particular, being implicated in the case by the STL made it increasingly difficult for Hezbollah to balance its legitimating narratives and actions in a way that appealed to the various constituencies it needed to influence. The message Hezbollah had been trying to get across was aimed simultaneously at maintaining legitimacy in its core Shia constituencies while creating and maintaining a certain level of legitimacy in other Lebanese, regional and even international constituencies. The rumours of an indictment and, later, the indictment itself forced Hezbollah to choose between showing loyalty to its fighters by attacking the Tribunal, and preventing distrust in non-Shia constituencies by distancing themselves from its members facing indictment. As in the previous serious legitimacy crisis Hezbollah had to overcome, it focused on its core constituency, thereby rekindling its image as an Iranian/Syrian tool among non-Shia, in the region and beyond, and lost the capacity to project the image of a resistance against Israel that – in the eyes of many Lebanese and in the region – it needed to legitimise its arms. In this instance, the mere promise of possible international criminal prosecution seemed to have influenced the capability to create and maintain the legitimacy, and conduct, of this QSE. This is not to say that the STL cannot have a stronger effect on the ability of Hezbollah to maintain legitimacy in the future, especially if the STL reached a verdict, and thereby provided a more convincing narrative about the events and culpability surrounding Hariri's assassination and connected cases.

The self-referral letter of 13 July 2012 to the Prosecutor of the ICC in which the government of Mali alleges that gross human rights violations and war crimes have been committed in the country since 1 January 2012, especially in its northern regions, demonstrates in the first place that the government of Mali believed the ICC was to have an effect on legitimacy. Despite increasing and intensifying criticism on the functioning of the ICC from within Africa, and while the Court often lacked support in word and deed from the UN Security Council, the Malian government expected involvement of the ICC to have an effect and that it would benefit from its involvement. Mali was not the first state government that attempted to use international criminal procedures to boost its legitimacy, or to delegitimise the institutions and actions of QSE opponents. They seek to benefit from the ability of the ICC to provide a narrative of international criminal justice by which it could brand one party as the violator of universal norms an 'enemy of humanity', while cooperation with the Court conveys a message of defending those norms and of being a friend of the international community. This ability of the ICC to shift legitimacy, especially in the various relevant constituencies in the Western world, led to the self-referral by states of situations to the ICC but also put the Court at risk of becoming a 'court of convenience', a tool employed by states to delegitimise their quasi-state adversaries. In the case of Mali, the impact of the self-referral and the opening of an investigation by the ICC can be seen to have shifted legitimacy. But the Court acted more wisely than it did in earlier self-referral cases and prevented itself from being used by the state to keep the MNLA from reaching its statehood goals. Significant in this was that the ICC opened an investigation into acts committed by the MNLA, and also into whether acts, allegedly committed by Malian Army troops, constituted war crimes. Nevertheless, the use of international criminal justice narratives probably made it easier for Western countries, especially France, to justify intervening in Mali. The states that compose the international community had a natural reflex towards protecting the territorial integrity of Mali against any statehood project of the Tuareg, and it did so in the case of the unilaterally declared Azawad State by the MNLA. However, the main concerns of the international community and motivations for international intervention had to do more with the prospect of a failed state's providing a safe harbour for Islamist organisations like AQIM, Ansar Dine and MOJWA. The opening of an ICC investigation created a critical legitimacy moment in that it forced the MNLA to further distance itself from the Islamist factions with which it had cooperated. More important, the crimes allegedly committed in Mali led to expressions of concern among members of the international community and expressions of outrage from international NGOs and humanitarian organisations. While being implicated in those crimes, the MNLA had to express commitment to the norms of international criminal law and the ICC investigation in an attempt to prevent, or halt, a legitimacy crisis. The self-referral, and thereby introduction of international crimes and justice to the discourse, was intended as a tool to create legitimacy for the government while delegitimising its opponents. The changing narratives of the MNLA, in an attempt to end up on the right side of the ICC, showed that its involvement created withdrawal of legitimacy. Together with the international military involvement and strife between the MNLA and its former allies, the ICC investigation prevented the MNLA from attaining some, or all, of its statehood objectives, or at least it further diminished the chances of a successful Azawad State. Despite talks between the MNLA and the Malian government, and despite both the Malian Army and the MNLA being subject to ICC investigation, both parties continued to use narratives accusing each other of war crimes and crimes against humanity in attempts to gain legitimacy for their aims, actions and institutions.

The analysis of critical legitimacy moments to gauge the impact of international criminal justice

When assessing the impact of international criminal justice, one has to take into account that changing abilities of actors in contemporary conflict, the rise of international criminal tribunals and the changes in international relations and politics are intrinsically interwoven. It has to be taken into consideration that sovereignty is the alpha and omega of the international order, and that the ability to create and maintain legitimacy in various constituencies simultaneously is both the beginning and the end of success for states and QSEs alike in reaching their statehood objectives. Yet, even then, the effects of international criminal procedures on the outcomes of statehood clashes remain complicated to gauge.

First, legitimacy in its positive form is extremely difficult to distinguish, it is at most seen when and where it is questioned. Therefore, in order to learn something about legitimacy, its workings and how and when it is lost and gained, one has to interpret the signs of legitimacy crisis. But, even before that critical moment is reached – when an entity is fighting for survival – the indicators of crisis management can already be detected. The effect that international criminal justice can have on the capacity of entities successfully to claim legitimacy is significant. The changing discourse is a function of the impact of international criminal justice. For instance, the use of an international criminal justice narrative by those implicated by international criminal proceedings can be identified, or conversely, use by the opponents of those accused might be identified. To gauge how, and how far, international criminal justice influences legitimacy, one can assess the changing discourses that reveal critical legitimacy moments. By analysing whether international criminal justice creates critical legitimacy moments in certain constituencies, and then by assessing the ability of state entities and QSEs to overcome such crises resulting from international criminal justice, one can detect the impact these proceedings have.

Second, once it has been identified that an entity has to deal with a legitimacy crisis in a certain constituency, at a certain time, a causal link between the 'critical legitimacy moment' and international criminal justice should be established. This may encounter some of the same difficulties as gauging legitimacy itself did. However, in legitimacy crises the counter narratives provided by opponents and aimed at delegitimisation are telling; so are the questions asked in the constituency in which legitimacy is lost. In line with the dictum, 'that which is not in question is legitimate', when concerns are raised about the legitimacy of an entity or its actions, looking at the questions asked about legitimacy helps explain why legitimacy is failing. Moreover, evidence of a causal link can often be found in the narratives provided by the entity that has to overcome a legitimacy crisis. For instance, the impact of international criminal proceedings can be seen when a QSE attempts to delegitimise a court, or starts denying war crimes or accuses opponents of committing crimes under international law.

International criminal courts and tribunals, the threat of international legal proceedings or even the statements of third parties that an individual should be prosecuted, send messages to the same constituencies that QSEs have to influence in order to be successful. 'International criminal justice narratives' can have an interruptive effect on the narratives of QSEs, but where their antagonists in 'statehood clashes' have to face international criminal justice, QSEs may benefit from incorporating international criminal justice in their own messages from the narratives of third parties, and from the actions of courts; international criminal justice can bolster their legitimacy. Using an international criminal justice narrative provides the opportunity to brand opponents as enemies of mankind, while presenting the entity itself a as a good citizen of the international community, even when entities do not possess full citizenship of that community. Legitimacy is not a zero-sum game, but when one narrative loses its attractiveness in a certain group the entity offering the opposing narrative will typically gain legitimacy.

Third, international criminal tribunals prosecute individuals and not states, QSEs or other organisations, yet the crimes they are accused of are usually part of an organised activity. They are committed as part of a 'plan or policy' or a 'widespread or systematic attack' and are, at least in practice, only feasible when committed in an organisational framework, usually that of a state or QSE. Sometimes, these crimes are even an integral part of the strategy of an entity. In theory, international criminal justice may remain silent on the culpability of the QSE and state, or it may not always become immediately evident how connected the accused is to an entity. However, in reality, it is less relevant what evidence exists of a connection between an individual and an entity; if in a certain constituency it is believed there is a connection, it will influence the legitimacy of that entity. Moreover, during a trial it usually becomes clear what the organisational and command structure is, especially when the accused uses the 'superior orders' defence or is convicted for taking part in a joint criminal enterprise. Even when there is a chance for an entity to distance itself from the accused individual(s), QSEs are not always willing to do so, as the example of Hezbollah and its members indicted by the STL illustrates.

Fourth, this book looked at effects, rather than effectiveness. This does not mean that the effects that are observed do not work towards the aims of international criminal justice. It is difficult, however, to set a benchmark for success. Is it the absence of all crimes under international law? Or is it when perpetrators of these crimes are caught? This also illustrates that it is difficult to determine a hierarchy between various goals of, and justifications for, international criminal justice. The effectiveness of international criminal justice depends, in the first place, on what one considers to be the aims and justifications of international criminal tribunals. Different stakeholders hold different opinions on these justifications. However, whether one considers post-conflict state building, retribution, ending impunity or general and special prevention of future atrocities to be the principal aim of international justice, the effectiveness of any legal proceeding, or court, remains hard to measure. Moreover, some things are impossible to measure altogether, such as whether a sense of justice has been sufficiently restored, for instance, or the effectiveness of retribution.

By looking at the effects, rather that the effectiveness, of international criminal justice, the contingency of international criminal justice intervention also becomes apparent. For instance, by analysing the indictment by the ICTY of Milošević, or the self-referrals to the ICC, it became clear that many of the consequences of opening investigations, publishing indictments and starting prosecutions were unexpected. However, while some consequences, although unintended, may work towards the objectives used to justify international criminal justice in the widest sense, other consequences do not. The contingent effect of international criminal justice can, for instance, include making outside military intervention more feasible, but it can also unexpectedly strengthen legitimacy of a certain entity in a certain constituency. Studying the effects of previous international criminal justice interventions might provide more insight to provide for possible contingencies in the future.

Fifth, the narratives of international criminal justice depend on the narratives of the crimes they investigate and the atrocities for which they prosecute the perpetrators. It was no coincidence that the Yugoslav War led both to the first international criminal tribunal and marked the beginning of an era in which television was ubiquitous in war. The impact of the moving images of atrocities was instrumental in the outrage and the calls for the punishment of the perpetrators, especially among Western audiences, that contributed to the foundation of the first international courts. Moving images of the consequences of crimes against humanity also have more effect on the legitimacy of the individuals that committed them, and the entities in whose name they are committed, than when these crimes were less visible. The spread of internet use made (moving) images of war and its horrible consequences even more readily available to an even wider public than 20 years ago, and in the competition to get legitimating narratives accepted, images and, especially, moving images, play a central role. International criminal justice narratives are effective because the acts are abhorred by the members of the relevant constituencies. The more horrible the crimes and the greater the outrage, the deeper the impact the narratives calling for justice have on legitimacy.

Sixth, the timing of the moment international criminal justice narratives enter the discourse is pivotal in the effect international criminal justice has, and this is not only the case in terms of the vulnerability of those affected by them. Milošević, for instance, was already dealing with a spiral of legitimacy loss in many relevant constituencies when he was confronted by the indictment. It is also important in terms of whether an indictment comes as a surprise, and whether the QSE, or state, whose operatives are indicted had time to provide counter narratives. A prime example of the latter would be Hezbollah having time to prepare for the indictment of its members by the STL. But also, the longer the gap between a crime, or crimes, taking place and an indictment being published, a trial taking place or a verdict being rendered, the less the impact is likely to be in terms of legitimacy.

Seventh, the impact of the actions and statements of an international tribunal and the threat international criminal justice poses will, in part, depend on the legitimacy that a court has in a certain constituency, and in how far norms of international criminal law are internalised within that constituency. In Western constituencies, international criminal law is often an integral part of the existing norm set and, therefore, it can be expected that international criminal justice will have a stronger impact on the beliefs held in these constituencies. This is one of the reasons that the impact of the ICC is somewhat negated within home constituencies of the perpetrators, for instance. Yet, more important, it also makes the narratives against the ICC, which are increasingly heard in Africa, so relevant, as well as the limited support the ICC receives from the Security Council and the fact that three of its five permanent members did not ratify the Rome Statute.

The mandate the ICC was given might not always be sufficient to live up to the high ambitions with which it is burdened − to punish crimes that are unforgivable − and to the possibly even higher hopes that are vested in it, namely to end impunity that, without intervention, could go on endlessly. Yet, the potential impact of the ICC on the legitimacy of QSEs can come about in different ways. An investigation, indictment or conviction of a member of a QSE can potentially impact on the capacity of that QSE to create and maintain legitimacy, in certain constituencies. Or, conversely, when the capacity to claim legitimacy of a state entity in certain constituencies is affected by international criminal justice, it will be easier for its QSE adversaries to successfully create legitimating narratives for their actions and institutions to these constituencies. This is illustrated by the belief of State Parties to the ICC that such an impact exists. Although unexpected, the most common basis for jurisdiction of the Court turned out not to be the *proprio motu* powers of the Prosecutor, referrals of situations on the territory of another State Party, nor a referral by the Security Council, but self-referral. Four of the eight situations officially investigated by the ICC were due to a self-referral of a State Party to the Rome Statute. Safely presuming that state governments only self-refer situations if they are confident they will gain something from it, this is an indication that the ICC investigation has either a positive impact on their legitimacy in certain constituencies, or a negative one on the capacity of their quasi-state adversaries to create and maintain legitimacy. This is so despite the fact that, at the same time, when 'one of their own' (e.g. President of Sudan, Omar al-Bashir) is involved, many African states rather stay away from a narrative of war crimes and crimes against humanity. Nevertheless, the lack of support from the Security Council, the intense criticism from African leaders and limited means with which to open cases in situations where the most horrendous crimes are committed on a massive scale, all endanger the capabilities of the ICC.

Finally, 'The Hague' has entered the jargon of international politics and the vocabulary of both international human rights organisations and local activists around the world as a call for international criminal justice, whenever the norms of international criminal law are believed to have been violated. What changed is that genocide, war crimes and crimes against humanity entered the narratives of entities claiming legitimacy. This 'war crimes' discourse is used to claim legitimacy and to counter legitimacy. International criminal justice changed the political reality of contemporary conflict. It is a factor to be reckoned with. The ICC, despite its shortcomings, limited cases and all the obstacles that have been put in its way, is a prerequisite for this. Without a permanent international criminal court, narratives of international criminal justice would all but disappear.

Index